"This is a book of enormous erudition. I am stunned by Richler's courage and insight. He dares to take on the pathology orchestrated by the military apologists in our political, academic and media establishment; debunking it, dismembering it, eviscerating it. Rarely does someone of letters take on such a subject and convey the argument with such force and clarity. There's no question that the apologists will have exquisite apoplexy, but surely that's the ultimate tribute. The rest of us will exult in his embrace of the values of peace and decency, in a Canada that once was and might yet be again."
        —Stephen Lewis, former Canadian Ambassador to the UN

"Well-written and passionate, this is a fine polemic about important issues. You don't have to agree with everything Noah Richler says—I don't—but you must take him seriously."
        —Margaret MacMillan, author of *Paris 1919*

"Noah Richler has written an important book of great clarity, insight and courage. Like George Grant's classic *Lament for a Nation*, it ranges from politics to philosophy, from literature to the mass media, in support of an intelligent, passionate and highly articulate argument: *What We Talk About When We Talk About War* deserves to be read and discussed in every political office, classroom, book club and legion hall in the country."
        —Ron Graham, author of *The Last Act*

"Since May 2nd, 2011, Canadians have watched their country swerve from the middle lane to the far right. A country once proud of its role as a peace-making moderate, is being reconstructed as a Canada defined by war, violence and death. The change is brutal and deeply divisive. Noah Richler has taken the trouble to tell us why Canadians should worry."
        —Desmond Morton, author of *Who Speaks for Canada?*

"In a way that is utterly free of jingoism, *What We Talk About When We Talk About War* demonstrates that the rabid outpourings of the mid-war years in Afghanistan have been blown away in a gust of Arctic air. A tonic to the spirit, Richler's book explores the rootedness of Canadian values and connects them to the experience of life in an enormous and damn lucky country."
        —James Laxer, author of *Tecumseh and Brock*

"Noah Richler's important book reminds us why it is essential that we question the motives of military missions bathed in slogans. *What We Talk About When We Talk About War* provides a thorough analysis of our country's myths of combat and of peace and, separating rhetoric from truth, incisively exposes the key players bent on convincing us of the merits of a 'just' war."
—Amy Millan, author of *Masters of the Burial*

"A timely and thought-provoking examination of how we, as a nation, have allowed our perception of ourselves to be changed from peacekeepers to warriors, how the real-life experiences of the monstrous brutality of World War I have become the nation-building myth of today, and how our preference for 'peace, order and good government' has graduated to a willingness to die for the sake of a greater cause. Richler urges us not to ignore these major, unexamined changes in the Canadian narrative lest we are redefined into a people we have never wished to be."
—Anna Porter, author of *The Ghosts of Europe*

"The questions Noah Richler's *What We Talk About When We Talk About War* poses resonate deeply, and while I may not agree with some of his conclusions, Richler offers a compelling perspective and unearths a treasure chest of sources, references and incidents that will richly enhance anybody's quest to affirm what being Canadian really means. This book is a must-read for the aspiring military professional and every citizen who is concerned about perpetuating into the twenty-first century what we understand to be the Canadian Way."
— Lt.-Col. (ret) Patrick B. Stogran, PPCLI, Veterans' Ombudsman 2007-2010

NOAH RICHLER

WHAT WE TALK ABOUT
WHEN WE TALK ABOUT

Edited by Meg Taylor.
Cover image *"Do I Trust You"* (detail) by Cooper Cantrell, 2010.
Cover and page design by Julie Scriver.
Typeset in Richler, designed by Nick Shinn.
Printed in Canada.
10 9 8 7 6 5 4 3 2 1

Library and Archives Canada Cataloguing in Publication

Richler, Noah
What we talk about when we talk about war / Noah Richler.

Issued also in electronic format. ISBN 978-0-86492-622-7

1. Canada—Military policy—Public opinion. 2. Mass media and war—Canada.
3. War—Public opinion. 4. Public opinion—Canada.
5. National characteristics, Canadian. I. Title.

UA600.R519 2012 355'.033571 C2010-907809-8

Goose Lane Editions acknowledges the financial support of the Canada Council
for the Arts, the Government of Canada through the Canada Book Fund (CBF), and the
Government of New Brunswick through the Department of Wellness, Culture, and Sport.

Goose Lane Editions
500 Beaverbrook Court, Suite 330
Fredericton, New Brunswick
CANADA E3B 5X4
www.gooselane.com

To Sarah

And what can we do here now, for at last we have no notion
of what we might have come to be in America, alternative.
—Dennis Lee, *Civil Elegies*

INTRODUCTION

Achilles' Choice

"The most persistent sound which reverberates through
man's history is the beating of war drums."
—Arthur Koestler, *Janus: A Summing Up* (1978)

War enters the unconscious early.

As children growing up in London, England, in the early 1960s—
about as far away in time from the end of the Second World War as
Canada is today from Jean Chrétien's first turn as prime minister, the
Oka Crisis and the introduction of the GST (which is to say not far at
all)—my sister Emma and I used to collect Action Men, the soldier
dolls called G.I. Joes in North America. We had a lot of them, and
made extra props, clothes and, in our backyard, whole installations of
trenches and a No Man's Land from the broken ones on whose plastic
limbs we'd paint blood using red paint from our model airplane kits
(Spitfires, Messerschmitts, Junkers, Lancasters and B-1 bombers).
We had officers' quarters, a mess tent and, behind the lines, a bar for
time off. When Martha, our younger sister, was silly enough to have
her Barbie doll wander into it—well, the Action Men who'd suffered

at the front, who had lost their friends and drank too much because they didn't know how long they had to live, took turns assaulting her. So ended Barbie's visits.

That bit of shame occurred several years before I came to understand my own sexuality or knew what an erection was, but, no matter, I'd already learned plenty about war and heroism and what it was to be a man from a plethora of comic books, television shows and movies such as *The Battle of Britain*, *Tobruk* and *The Great Escape* down at the Kingston Kinema. On the way home from school, I'd stop in at army surplus stores to buy Allied and German uniform crests and bits of old military junk that were far from useless to me. In one of these shops, I first saw the iconic poster of Steve McQueen on his motorbike making his great escape, the barbed wire over which he'd vaulted safely behind him as he gazed with such serene bravado at the far horizon. I liked it so much I worried I was homosexual, which, of course, would not do in any of the army games we played in the schoolyard.

From the schoolyard we learn so much—and a lot that needs the better part of a lifetime to be *un*learned. Graduating from the schoolyard's various traps of male primitivism is the endgame of a good education in the schoolhouse proper, the point being to civilize young boys and girls (none in our school, damn it) and to teach what it means to be Barbie, victimized, to be the German rather than the Action Man—and, is the hope, why reason and not might is the best arbiter of what is just. The schoolyard's simple animal indoctrination never really disappears from our consciousness but is suppressed through the civilizing process to be managed by the rules of school and family and, later, by laws. We are taught not to bully the fat boy or the kid who stammers or the one who wets his pants and to include these children in our games and rituals. We are taught to recognize the virtues each may have and, in so doing, that folk who appear different or lesser are as entitled as any other to the same privileges and the right not to be at school in fear. But these are hard lessons, the order that is taught a fragile edifice. Under stress, we revert to the natural order of the schoolyard, call it the jungle, easily, and we do so in the barbarous theatre of war most of all.

Such is the lesson of John Rae's *The Custard Boys* (1960), an English novel about a gang of schoolboys evacuated to the countryside during the Second World War. Fallen off the bookshelf now, it is sometimes compared to William Golding's *Lord of the Flies* (1954). In Rae's novel, the children play at games of war even outside their training as cadets at school, zealously imitating real-world action in a pretty "Norfolk village that was so far away from the war in which we longed to play our parts." The boys pick a fight with a rival gang of kids from the village, but their plan of attack goes badly after Mark Stein, the Jew in their midst, runs scared and abandons his post. For punishment, Mark is court-martialled and sentenced by the eldest of the bunch to be shot at dawn.

No one takes the mock trial seriously, only, during the execution that takes place the next day, one of the guns is inadvertently loaded with live rounds and the boy is killed. Again it is proven that war, as the protagonist schoolboy John Curlew's uncle Laurence has described it, is "the universal perversion." A contrarian, he says, "We are all tainted: if we cannot experience our perversion at first hand we spend our time reading war stories, the pornography of war; or seeing war films, the blue films of war; or titillating our senses with the imagination of great deeds, the masturbation of war." Uncle Laurence's debate with the local vicar is a key moment in the novel in which the age-old contradictions of fighting—"All this nonsense about counting the life of battle good"—fire the pair's argument.

"All war is horrible, of course," said the vicar, letting the worn phrase slither through his lips almost unnoticed, "but it is one of the paradoxes of human experience that out of evil comes forth good. War brings out the best in many men."

"It brings out the beast in them, vicar, not the best."

"In some possibly, but men act like animals whether there is a war or not."

"We are all animals, aren't we?" asked my uncle. "We're all murderers at heart. When it comes to the point there are very few men who find it difficult to kill one of their fellow-creatures."

"What you are really saying is that most Englishmen do not shirk their duty. And what is more, they achieve heights of noble self-sacrifice that we ordinary mortals cannot hope to attain."

"Self-sacrifice!" I had never heard my uncle's voice so scornful. "How many genuine cases of self-sacrifice does one find in a war? Men fight because they are told to and because they haven't the moral courage to say 'No.' When they are killed they are not giving their lives for a noble cause—they're dying because they haven't been lucky enough or smart enough to stay alive. I'm not trying to mock the dead; they know the truth better than any of us. But their countrymen and their families weave a tapestry of heroism and self-sacrifice, they colour it with such rubbishy phrases as 'the good die young,' and then when the next generation comes along it cannot see the truth for the tapestry, it cannot see that there is nothing noble or heroic in war, but only man at his most bestial, fulfilling his ancient urge to kill."

Rae was eight years old when war broke out, fourteen when it ended. Later, he performed his national service as a second lieutenant with the Royal Fusiliers. Beyond having come of age in wartime as the fictional John Curlew did, Rae would have witnessed the primitivism of the schoolyard during his time after the war as an enlightened and sometimes controversial headmaster at a prestigious London boys' school. He would have known of the bombing and the rationing. He would have seen soldiers and refugees coming to Britain during the war and others arriving after it. The fact of his having lived through those years provides an authority to the abhorrence of war that he shared, too, with eminent soldiers such as Dwight D. Eisenhower, a veteran of both World Wars and was appointed Supreme Allied Commander of the Allied Expeditionary Force (SHAEF) in 1943. In Ottawa in 1946, Eisenhower told Canadians: "I hate war as only a soldier who has lived it can, only as one who has seen its brutality, its futility and its stupidity." Eisenhower's more flamboyant, outspoken compatriot, Gen. George S. Patton, however, viewed war differently. The "universal perversion" was exhilarating for Patton, who proclaimed in 1945: "I love war and responsibility and excitement. Peace is going to be Hell on me."

Wrote nineteenth-century English novelist Thomas Hardy in *The Dynasts* (1904), "War makes rattling good history; but Peace is poor reading."

Fighting stirs individuals and serves the leaders who organize people into gangs, tribes and states because it provides the responsibility and the thrill of a cause to citizens impassioned by the prospect of their community's defence. And it offers, in the words of Sgt. Ed Wadleigh, a veteran of three tours of Afghanistan with both the British and Canadian armies, the chance to the eager merely "to prove oneself, to play your part in a grand adventure, or simply to get in scraps and gunfights for a few months and fuck shit up." It has always been thus. In Farley Mowat's 1979 memoir of his service in the Allied 1943 campaign in Sicily, *And No Birds Sang*, the Canadian author remembers his father, who had "gone off in 1915 to fight in the Great War, fired by the ideals of Empire—a soldier of the King." The father pulls into the family's Richmond Hill driveway on September 2, 1939, and proclaims, with irrepressible excitement: "Farley, my lad, there's bloody big news! *The war is on!*" ("It's very absurd when a war is imminent," said Bertrand Russell, the British philosopher who was imprisoned during the First World War for his pacifist views. "Immense crowds assemble in Trafalgar Square to applaud. They echo the government's decision to have them killed.")

Wars that must often wait until they have been played out to gain the attribute of having been just typically begun as adventures offering opportunity in far-off lands to professional soldiers but also to men and women from disparate and often less economically fortunate parts of a country. This is certainly the case in Canada, where it has almost always been necessary to travel to the fight because it was never going to cross the water and come to home. This phenomenon of being relegated to territory distant from the action has provided English Canada with one of its most enduring post-colonial creation myths, Vimy Ridge its enduring emblem. It took the First World War, the country is repeatedly told, for Canadians *a mari usque ad mare* to actually meet each other—and, in the mud of the trenches, to bond.

Rallying Quebec to fight for the ideals of Empire during the First World War was harder. The Conscription Crisis of 1917 was provoked by the mounting casualties since the Battle of the Somme and the collapse of voluntary enlistment during the summer of 1916 that left the Canadian Expeditionary Force desperate for fighting men. Conscription became law at the end of August 1917, after the Battle of Vimy Ridge cost Canada 10,602 soldiers, 3,598 of them killed. The draft led to riots in the province, the citizens of which largely regarded the conflict as English Canada's war. Still, the phenomenon of the distant territory applies to Quebec too, and enough French Canadians fought in the Second World War that the enormity of that moment is remembered in several outstanding novels of the period as a moment of high excitement. In Roger Lemelin's comic 1948 family saga, *Les Plouffe*, a French-Canadian bestseller that was later translated as *The Plouffe Family*, Josephine listens to her son Ovide read letters from his younger brother Guillaume, who is fighting with the Allies in Europe and the family has discovered to be safe. In the final scene, Josephine is overcome by Ovide's relaying of Guillaume's battlefront heroics and famously runs to the balcony of their Quebec City home and calls out, "C'est pas croyable! Guillaume, qui tue les hommes!" ("Unbelievable! My Guillaume, he kills men!") At the end of Germaine Guévremont's *Le survenant* (1945), translated together with its sequel, *Marie-Didace* (1947), as *The Outlander* (1991), the stranger—the "survenant"—leaves as mysteriously as he arrived, to fight in the war. The Second World War provides Manitoban francophone novelist Gabrielle Roy's characters the similar prospect of escape from the poverty of Montreal's working-class district of Saint-Henri, and a thrill akin to that which Farley Mowat's father knew. In Roy's most famous novel, *The Tin Flute* (1945), Emmanuel Létourneau is a soldier on leave who wonders why he has joined up at all as his regiment leaves Montreal's Bonaventure train station for the war. "We're going to see the world!" yells one soldier drunkenly. "Tell the boys in France to hold on till we get there!" shouts another.

Roy's Emmanuel, however, feels doubt. A group starts to sing, "There'll Always Be An England," and he tells himself that

they're singing in Germany, in Italy, in France...Just as we
could sing *O Canada!* No, no, no, he thought vehemently.
I'm not going to put myself on any patriotic, national
bandwagon. Am I the only one?

The train pulls away from the crowd, and the troubled soldier decides
that "none of them was going to war with the same goal as the others.
Some were going to the end of the world to preserve their Empire.
Some of them were going to the end of the world to shoot and be shot
at, and that was all they knew."

He sees an old woman, whose lips he imagines he can read, saying,
"There'll be an end. Some day there'll be an end."

Some day there'll be an end, and then another cruel beginning.

War moves in cycles of boom and bust, the bust coming about only
when the exhilaration and the boom of the new war have turned to
punishment. We commit to war, figure out how to "stay the course"
and then, when the key players are defeated or exhausted, how to
find a way out and live in peace for a while. Humankind has found
this cycle and the havoc it wreaks easy to justify and impossible to
arrest. Immutably, we are convinced of war's purpose, seduced by its
gains and beholden to its drama.

For a brief moment at the beginning of the Cold War, the bombing
of Hiroshima and Nagasaki having been the Second World War's epoch-
changing act, it seemed as if the possibility of a nuclear Armageddon
might finally put a halt to this pattern. In April 1951, Gen. Douglas
MacArthur stated in his final address to Congress that the prospect
of nuclear annihilation had rendered war "useless as a method of
settling international disputes." MacArthur was no pacifist, though
his reluctance about atomic weaponry that President Harry Truman
had considered using when, in 1950, war broke out in Korea, is on

record. Four years later, in a speech to the American Legion in Los Angeles, the eloquent but often troubled soldier went further. "The great question is, can war be outlawed from the world?" he asked. Were it to happen, said MacArthur, "it would mark the greatest advance in civilization since the Sermon on the Mount."

The Second World War was an unholy juggernaut of devastation and killing that plowed a road of turmoil not ending at Auschwitz or Nagasaki but wound on through Eastern Europe, Korea, Vietnam and numerous African fronts. In its aftermath, it was appropriate for MacArthur to contemplate how the elimination of war "would not only create new moral and spiritual values, it would produce an economic wave of prosperity that would raise the world's standard of living beyond anything ever dreamed of by man"—as, in Canada, Liberal politician Lester B. Pearson was, in his own distinctive way, also imagining. But a short half-century later, in our own era's climate of numerous and perpetual small conflicts and the "Global War on Terror," MacArthur's expression of hope seems preposterous, so out of touch with today's zeitgeist that statements such as the ambitious general made in his better moments would be dismissed as naive and unpatriotic were anyone other than an officer to express them. The idealism of MacArthur's contemplation is demonstrated no more frustratingly than in the Middle East, where Muslims and Jews continue to feud by the very Mount where Jesus delivered his Sermon. In Israel and Palestine, war has entered a territory beyond exhaustion in which no possibility of peace seems attainable. The spread of nuclear technology and the hostility of neighbouring states make the possibility of apocalyptic devastation terrifyingly real, even ineluctable, and yet the killing is justified because there is not the will to negotiate and fighters, not diplomats, are the players governing the cycle in its mired second stage. We accept the situation and adjust our expectations accordingly. The enemy is a harbour of ideas that cannot be reconciled, and killing—destroying the bodies that are their vessel—becomes the best way to achieve the conflict's ends. Death is the exercise. Soldiers are the means.

Killing is what is required of the soldier, who, in order to perform, must suppress whatever are his or her "human" instincts and do as instructed. "It's just business," said Canadian Katie Hodges, a veteran of two tours of duty in Afghanistan by 2010. The corporal was echoing the view of her erstwhile boss, Chief of Defence Staff (CDS) Gen. Rick Hillier, that the job of the Canadian Forces is "to be able to kill people," and she is right. In war, a soldier's personal views must be left behind; on the battlefield, they are an impediment. "A soldier who is able to see the humanity of the enemy makes a troubled and ineffective killer," wrote Chris Hedges, a divinity student before he became a *New York Times* foreign correspondent and the author of *War Is a Force That Gives Us Meaning* (2002). "We must be transformed into agents of a divinely inspired will, as defined by the state, just as those we fight must be transformed into the personification of unmitigated evil. There is little room for individuality in war."

But suppressing the individualism of human beings is no easy feat. Lt.-Col. Dave Grossman, a former U.S. Army Ranger and now a professor of psychology at West Point, writes in *On Killing* (1995) of soldiers' propensities to shoot high and miss their target. Interviews with Canadian soldiers form a part of Grossman's research that vindicated, across the experience of many nations and wars, the pioneering though often challenged work of U.S. Army combat historian S.L.A. Marshall, who claimed that most soldiers never shoot to kill. Grossman's landmark treatise explores the measures an army must take in order to create the moral distance necessary to counter the empathetic responses of humans to members of their own species that are the cause of this bad aim. "The history of warfare," writes Grossman, "can be seen as a history of increasingly more effective mechanisms for enabling and conditioning men to overcome their innate resistance to killing their fellow human beings."

There continue to be amazing technological advances in this grisly behavioural science, ones permitting snipers to find a human target at 2,430 metres (the record established in 2002 by Canadian sniper Cpl. Rob Furlong before it was broken by Craig Harrison, a British member of the Household Cavalry) and unmanned drones to kill from thousands of kilometres away in air wars in which combatants never have to meet the enemy or register its destruction as anything more than white puffs of smoke on a target screen. "Without warning, without remorse" is the motto tattooed on one Canadian sniper's forearm, though soldiers less clinically inclined may continue to succumb to the sort of individual feelings that hinder the martial enterprise. Even without the incidence of medical conditions such as post-traumatic stress disorder (PTSD) — or, as the condition was called in the First World War, "shell shock" — soldiers may entertain fears, revulsion and objections to their situation. They may be distressed by killing, as not only "war resisters" are, or by torture and its dissonance with the values of the civilization the war is supposed to be defending, as U.S. Army reservist Sgt. Joseph M. Darby was. (Darby copied the photographs of abuse at the Abu Ghraib detention centre, images that eventually found their way into the public arena.)

Most of the time these contrary thoughts exist only as part of what Israeli writer David Grossman, a veteran of the 1973 Yom Kippur War (and no relation to the lieutenant-colonel), calls, in his moving novel *To the End of the Land* (2010), war's "mysterious dance." For Grossman, who lost a son serving in the Israeli Defence Forces two days before a United Nations-brokered ceasefire brought an end to his country's 2006 invasion of Lebanon, these sorts of feelings are but yet more links in "the dark, calculated formal course of the larger system, which comprises thousands of people, soldiers, civilians, vehicles and weapons and field kitchens and battle rations and ammunition stores and crates of equipment and night vision instruments and signaling flares and stretchers and helicopters and canteens and computers and antennae and telephones and large, black, sealed bags." Ora, the Israeli Jewish mother and his novel's central character, walks the length of the country, in an existential rather than belligerent claiming of the territory, preferring not to be at home should a soldier visit with the dreaded notification of her son's death. Her defence against the unthinkable is to refuse to meet it. (The novel's less elegiac title in the original Hebrew translates as *A Woman Running from the News*.) A heartbreaking expression of parental love, the situation Grossman eloquently imagined had undoubtedly manifold real-life expressions after Pte. William Jonathan James Cushley was killed in Afghanistan on September 3, 2006. Speaking with Anna Maria Tremonti, a former foreign correspondent and the host of CBC Radio's flagship news program, *The Current*, Private Cushley's mother, Elaine, recalled the visit of two soldiers surely bringing the news of her son's death to her home in Port Lambton, Ontario: "I wouldn't let them in at first. I heard the doorbell and I looked out the window, and I seen two soldiers there and I just went back to bed. I obviously realized, but I didn't want to. If I opened the door I knew they'd have to tell me."

Such is the reality of war "projecting," said Grossman in Toronto in 2010, "its brutality in the tender bubble of family" while, on the front lines, soldiers stripped of their individuality by the levelling act of the uniform carry out operations determined by authorities making their decisions far from the fulcrum of battle and its primitive contests of survival. The photograph seen all over the world of the incomparably powerful circle of U.S. president Barack Obama and his security advisers sitting with Secretary of State Hillary Clinton and watching, on May 1, 2011, the storming by U.S. Special Forces of Osama bin Laden's Pakistani compound is a testament to what technology can achieve—the reconnaissance, the helicopters, the arms and the live feed of the cameras attached to the soldiers' helmets—though also to the way in which the basic truths of war are unchanged. War is hell, and it is all-consuming, though only for some. To the soldiers who fight wars, the field of vision is narrow and small. Leaders and their acolytes operate in a different space, one large enough in war's first stage for flag-waving and lofty rhetoric, and the ability to urge the young soldiers on without penalty.

As battle persists, distance is diminished. The pity of war finds its way home and risks unsettling a society's martial commitment. Our humanity comes to the fore, the painful recognition of war's nihilism a phenomenon that has been revisited innumerable times over the course of the nearly three millennia that have passed since the seminal, unforgettable scene in *The Iliad* in which Homer describes the noble Trojan warrior Hector's return to his wife, Andromache, and their son, Astyanax. The meeting is a lull in the unrelenting, savage stalemate of Troy's war with the Achaeans—ten years of it already (Canada's turn in Afghanistan has turned out to be as long)—and Hector's reunited family is a symbol of the peaceful and civilized life that the Trojans have been defending. Hector makes the mistake of appearing before his wife and child still clad in full armour and the plumed helmet that he has not thought to remove. In Alexander Pope's eighteenth-century translation, the "illustrious chief of Troy"

> reached down for his son—but the boy recoiled,
> cringing against his nurse's full breast,
> screaming out at the sight of his own father,

> *terrified by the flashing bronze, the horsehair crest,*
> *the great ridge of the helmet nodding, bristling terror.*

Here, so powerfully rendered, is one of the earliest recorded instances of war "projecting its brutality in the tender bubble of family." The sorry truth of it is that our lamenting the poignancy of such scenes is as much a constant as the violence of war is. Not just the works of Homer but those of Goya, Tolstoy, Picasso, Wilfred Owen, Erich Maria Remarque and Michael Herr spring to mind, so that it becomes hard not to conclude that whatever shame, pain and outrage such works stir in their readers constitute, by and large, penance no more exacting than rites of confession in a Catholic church. Our heady undertaking of war and then, afterwards, our hesitation before the horror it engenders are integral but perfunctory rites of passage in its age-old routine. "Even with its destruction and carnage," writes Chris Hedges in *War Is a Force That Gives Us Meaning*, war "can give us what we long for in life. It can give us purpose, meaning, a reason for living."

The remorse some (though far from all) experience, the brief concession to repentant feeling, is less likely to alter human behaviour than to excuse it and permit another go. For a moment we show ourselves to be human before repeating war's cycle of original insult, escalating injury and then destruction before fatigue sets in and peace has a tenuous chance of taking hold again. We move through this cycle acceptingly because a majority considers the pursuit of war to be basic to human nature, evidence of the festering barbarity that burgeons in the jungle and that the 19th century scientists Thomas Henry Huxley and Charles Darwin believed was barely suppressed by civilization's delicate veneer. They are symptoms of the inalienable attributes of the forlorn species that American poet E.E. Cummings called, in 1944, "this busy monster, manunkind."

Cummings, who enlisted with the ambulance corps in the First World War and was imprisoned by the French military for three and a half months on suspicion of espionage (though likely for his anti-war views), expressed his dissent fervently and angrily in the poem "i sing of Olaf glad and big" (1926). Olaf,

> *whose warmest heart recoiled at war:*
> *a conscientious object-or*

was an uncommon hero who paid for his obstinate, courageous stance. "I will not kiss your fucking flag," he tells his commanding officer, a West Point colonel. Defiantly, while his superiors ("a yearning nation's blueeyed pride")

> *egged the firstclassprivates on*
> *his rectum wickedly to tease*
> *by means of skillfully applied*
> *bayonets roasted hot with heat—*
> *Olaf (upon what were once knees)*
> *does almost ceaselessly repeat*
> *"there is some shit I will not eat"*

Perhaps it is a consequence of Canadians having fought other people's wars for so long, of being in their essence volunteers, that outside of Timothy Findley's novel *The Wars* (1977) and the American-born Charles Yale Harrison's short novel *Generals Die in Bed* (1930), that no comparable objector and little such anger exists in our own canon of war literature—or not the anglophone portion of it at any rate. (In Roch Carrier's bawdy *La Guerre, Yes Sir!* [1968], the character Joseph chops his hand off with an axe to avoid having to fight in the Second

World War, but the act is desperate and self-defeating rather than noble.)

Canadians are a stoical and, all too frequently, deferential, lot. "Since the 18th century," wrote military scholar David Bercuson in the *Globe and Mail* in July 2001, "Canada's soldiers have played a central part in shaping the nation we are today. Canada's borders, its French-English constitutional and cultural duality, its unique form of constitutional monarchy, its relationship to the United States, its role in major multinational institutions, its very independence were all shaped by wars that were either forced on Canada (the War of 1812 being the best example) or wars Canada chose to take part in out of higher principles or national self-interest or both (the two world wars)."

Bercuson's contestable historical argument, made weeks before 9/11, is indicative of a vigorous trend that has come to the fore over the course of the last decade. It upholds the idea that Canada is a "war-fighting" nation, but it is a wish for the country more than it is fact. Several thousand Canadians fought in the Second Boer War of 1899-1902, though Quebeckers mostly dissented, foreshadowing the Conscription Crisis of the First World War of 1914-18 (or 1919 if you were a soldier unfortunate enough to have been dispatched to the failed Allied intervention against the Bolsheviks in Siberia). The rest of the country fought en masse, Acadians having joined the "Great War" willingly, as hordes of English Canadians did, to fight for "King, Empire and peace the world over" (words New Brunswick soldier Athanase Poirier wrote home before his death in March 1916), with some four thousand Aboriginal Canadians, about a third of those eligible, also volunteering. (Canadian Aboriginals continue to hold the warrior in high esteem, a phenomenon evident in the annual parade of soldiers at the head of the entry of First Nations into the dancing circle of Winnipeg's November

Manito Ahbee powwow, though many of today's Aboriginal youth, such as the Kahnawake, are encouraged by their elders to enlist with the U.S. Marines, rather than the Canadian Forces.) Canadians also fought, illegally against the Fascists in the Spanish Civil War with the Mackenzie-Papineau Battalion (or "Mac-Paps") of the International Brigade, and then in great and legitimite numbers in the Second World War that followed. They served with the United Nations (UN) in Korea, as volunteers or as drafted dual citizens in Vietnam and then as peacekeepers in a half-century of global conflicts afterwards, but the significance of Canadian troops never having fought, outside of the Fenian Raids of 1866-71, to defend the country's post-colonial boundaries on home soil is easily underestimated. Battle has been, to Canadians, that real but ever distant phenomenon. The claim that the country's borders, its francophone-anglophone duality and its relationships with the United States and abroad were shaped either by wars forced upon it, or by other conflicts that it chose to take part in, is the fantasy of a political lobby that, unchecked over the course of the last decade, has seen the country's ability to fight wars as the truest indicator of its maturity.

In Bercuson's jingoistic schema, government is handmaiden to a military that is essential to Canadian political evolution "because it is the only instrument of government sanctioned to use deadly force—the ultimate policy instrument—to protect Canadian sovereignty." And yet the singularity of Canadian political development is that it has, after 1812 (when the colony was fighting on behalf of the mother country) with only scant exceptions, disdained from using "the ultimate policy instrument" to defend its integrity. Historically, Canadians have addressed what differences they do have in the legislature and in the courts and, furthermore, have exported this practice and made of it the dominant inclination of the country's foreign policy. Ottawa's relationships with Aboriginal peoples are encoded not in a history of conquest and defeat (and massacre) but in a set of treaties, disputed but still binding. The relationship between Quebec and the rest of Canada has been shaped mostly through negotiation, first with Lord Durham and then with an ongoing (and unending) train of Canadian prime ministers. The relationships with the United States and Britain have evolved through discussion rather than the application of "deadly force," the country's very borders the result of discussions at which Canada, unfortunately, did not take part. The country's special, though presently diminished, relationship to the United Nations was similarly the result of Canadian confidence in the country being able to achieve its political ends *without* the use of military force.

Bercuson's unrelenting military boosting (he was making the same point as a guest on CBC Radio's *Cross Country Checkup* exactly a decade later, in July 2011) distorts and downplays the significant roles that Canadian politicians, diplomats, jurists and a variety of other civilians (such as artists) have had in shaping not just the domestic Canadian polity but abstract, universal ideas about statehood that have served as examples internationally—in Scottish constitutional development, for instance, and of course in the development of the UN's Universal Declaration of Human Rights, drafted in 1948. The nature of this contribution is significant specifically because the truth of Canadian history is that our military's stake has not been inordinate. Resolution through discussion and compromise, and the recognition of the interests of others that such an approach entails, is seen to contribute to the greater good and to have characterized not only relationships between the government and Aboriginals, between English and French-speaking Quebeckers (and between the British government and the conquered French colonists before that), but those between Aboriginals and the original Canadians and brokers and fur traders of the Company of Adventurers of England Trading into Hudson's Bay since before the modern nation-state and its apparatus of government was founded. Effectively, the only country Canada has ever sought to colonize has been itself, negotiation mostly the tactic. In 1885, Prime Minister John A. Macdonald sent troops to the end of his incompletely built railroad in order to suppress Louis Riel and the Métis and put an end to the Northwest resistance in present-day Manitoba and Saskatchewan, with the aid of Lt.-Col. "Big Tom" Strange and his rapidly assembled Alberta Field Force, though with only dubious results. Today, it can be argued that the colonization effort continues, most notably in the North and in Quebec, though through economic and not military means. This is not an accidental outcome but a consequence of our history. The legacy of Canada being founded on the back of the business of the Hudson's Bay Company is that the model of the corporation reigns. Rather than the imperatives of the military and a dynamic of conquest, the forces of pragmatism and regulation (and the monopsonistic power of the powerful company that also, to an extent, provides) are what have shaped Canada today. Canada, once Prince Rupert's Land, is a sum of land claims greater than its parts, a country legitimized in courts and boardrooms as much as, if not more than, through soldiering.

Bercuson's bid for the military's pride of place rides roughshod over history but also discounts the particular lesson of twenty-first-century conflict, which is that whatever the borders of the modern state may be, "sovereignty" depends only in the violent short term upon what armed forces do. In the long term, a country relies upon consensus and a deference of a population to the idea of the state in which a people finds itself—something that is displayed, for instance, in a willingness to pay taxes for the broader community's benefit. This dull fact is hard to mythologize, but along with the act of putting on a uniform, this simple but drastically necessary show of civilian commitment to the greater good is the meaningful prof of the national compliance that has "played a central part in shaping the nation we are today." True, Canada has fought wars regularly, but these have always been undertaken on behalf of some greater, multilateral purpose of a higher power or alliance, such as "the British Empire," "the Commonwealth," "Europe," "NATO," the "UN," "the free world" or "the international community," and the democratic ideals that Canadians have invested in these causes. Although the country has fought under the command of other states, and distinguished itself, it has tended to do so in the service of a greater idea that cannot be reduced to narrow self-interest, if only because the altruistic feeling of the general population counts for as much as any government-induced patriotic feeling. Sometimes Canadian governments have contributed troops to these causes zealously, even in craven fashion; at other times (Pearson's, Trudeau's and Chrétien's leaderships spring to mind) with more of a sense of the possibility and the right of the country to choose its own direction and not simply that of the more powerful empire of the day. Whether attained by old-fashioned and now unpopular Canadian peacekeeping or the "war-fighting" that Afghanistan put into the limelight, the truth is that Canadian political principles have provided cause for deploying Canadian troops in the service of other peoples' battles since well before the country's inception. Canada, as Prime Minister Stephen Harper only recently decided to emphasize, is a country that has never invaded another for territorial gain. Even after 9/11, threats to the viability of the nation that typically worry other countries are, in Canada, abstractions. Canadians leave their homes, shops, museums and cinemas and enter into cities, towns and countryside of exceptional stability, safety and calm. In the absence of barbarians at the gates, the task of national security has been, in Canada, a rarefied one—this, even after 9/11, when it became possible to imagine the destruction of office towers and an enemy within.

Still today, the most palpable threats to the integrity of the country felt by Canadians are political—and internal. Outside of the histrionic Hollywood imaginings of an alarmist crop of right-wing militarists in government and academia and their excited acolytes in the media, genuine challenges to Canadian unity are more thoughtfully seen to be derived not from the Strait of Hormuz or the South China Sea but from domestic issues concerning language and land claims or the greater impediments of regional narcissism and greed. Who are you to tell me to speak French or English (this, as the brightest in the world learn several languages as a matter of course), or that this oil or this hydroelectric power is mine, not yours? *Don't mess with it.* These are the typically Canadian phenomena that pose threats to a nation constructed upon a very unusual set of ideas, though still within the bounds of highly civilized ideas about community, peaceful coexistence and a respect for human rights, the parameters of which are constantly being redefined. Even Canadian attitudes to land, the thing that came first, are extraordinarily complex. They have more to do with ideas about identity and belonging and the management of shared resources than they do with personal livelihood—as is the case, say, in the Balkan countries or any number of states with longer histories though less effective systems of taxation, so that the actual possession of land is seen as integral to a family's base prospects of survival.

The Canadian Charter of Rights and Freedoms, the cornerstone of the patriated Constitution of 1982, is the epitome of the Canadian disposition. Like its predecessor, the Universal Declaration of Human Rights, a document drafted for the United Nations by McGill professor of law John Peters Humphrey and proclaimed in 1948, the Charter has been much studied by other countries wanting to institutionalize their own tenets of social justice. The Charter is a refined and principled document even if, in practice, some of the disputes it referees, or the various tribunals it puts into play, seem ridiculous. The preteen seeking lost NHL millions after being dropped by the school hockey coach, the gym in Montreal required to screen its windows so that Hasidic Jews across the alley are not offended by the sight of exercising women in workout wear, the francophone "forced" to ask for a 7UP from an Air Canada flight attendant in English or the condominium board ordered to give the parking space nearest the elevator to an overweight woman—these can all appear trivial causes, easily ridiculed, ones that abuse high-minded Canadian notions of the defence of human rights, jamming the courts and making the country resemble a dysfunctional parody of a utopia as others grapple with infinitely starker realities of torture, persecution and civil unrest quelled by imprisonment and tanks. But, as outrageous and apparently trivial as they can be, legal arguments of this kind are a small price to pay for a society in which the balance of individual and group liberties is constantly being held up to rigorous debate and scrutiny. Even the passing in 2007 of a "code of behaviour" for new immigrants by the small Quebec municipality of Hérouxville, a justifiably derided document that included decrees against stoning and female genital mutilation, against banned face coverings and the carrying of symbolic weapons to school, can either be seen as racist, which it was (Hérouxville had no "immigrants" at the time)—or as proof of the degree to which decades of political barter with Quebec and First Nations have resulted in constitutional debates and the pursuit of good government seeping down and establishing themselves as a fundamental part of the national character.

If the Canadian's world is abidingly prosperous and fair, it is exactly because the country's history has depended for an end to conflicts only rarely on the gun and overwhelmingly on the civil process of which the Charter is the highest expression. But for a few skirmishes—on the Plains of Abraham in 1759, at Queenston Heights in 1812, during the Lower and Upper Canada Rebellions of 1837, the Fenian Raids of 1866-71, in battles with the Métis in the 1885 Northwest resistance, a brush with terrorism during the October 1970 FLQ Crisis and with Aboriginal protesters at Oka twenty years later—the example of Canada really has been of the "peace, order and good government" its departing governors willed for it when that phrase was written into the British North America Act of 1867, defining the standards to which the new country's Parliament should aspire. The history of give and take that characterizes the country called "Canada" stems from the common sense and necessity of Inuit and voyageurs realizing they could not survive the obdurate country alone, so they built caches of food and goods to be shared by consensual, practical agreement with strangers who, in turn, would construct more. It stems from European explorers and early settlers realizing agreements about how best to travel and pursue trade—war's antidote—in territory they could not, in their wildest fantasies of nation-building, ever have expected to govern closely. It is derived from the country's train of inhabitants learning not to regard all-important others, already resident, as an enemy to be vanquished, killed or expelled but as peoples with essential knowledge to impart. Its stems from the fact of a country being founded not on genocide and appropriation but on the back of the Hudson's Bay and North West fur trading companies organizing the territory for trade intended to be profitable despite the impediments of vast distances that can make business, even today, impracticable.

More than how to fight, the lesson of Canadian experience is that it is a lot cheaper and more practical to have peace along thousands of kilometres of sparsely populated river highway than to believe that these routes, and the prosperity they provide, can profitably be managed through force. Canada's legacy of oral and written treaties with Aboriginal peoples and the bugbears of Québecois and now Western and Newfoundland recalcitrance can seem grave challenges in the difficult moment but they are, by and large, petty irritants to a country that historically has possessed the guile and the magnanimity to rise above it all. The country's national boundaries have been peaceful, its territories mostly orderly and its governments, by ordinary standards, good.

The Vancouver novelist and sculptor Douglas Coupland described the chance of being born or raised in Canada after the Second World War as "winning the lottery," a point of view that has a popular Canadian leitmotif. Fourteen-year-old Albertan Samantha Terry is but one of a legion of Canadian high school students discovering early on the urge to "make a difference." Said Terry, who raised $32,000 in 2011 to help sponsor the building of a school in Nepal, "Life is like a lottery and we got the winning ticket, but you should share your prize with everyone."

Through the second half of the twentieth century and into the beginning of this one, Canada can make the reasonable claim, supported by numerous polls and standard-of-living indices, to have been one of the most fortunate countries in the world to live in. For at least fifty of the last sixty years, Canada has been a generally open and welcoming country, one in which a mythology of rescue, human generosity and the possibility of starting anew flourished because the idyllic story has mostly been true. The ordinary Canadian's world is free from the ravages of war, famine, climate change, energy scarcity, poverty, political dictatorship or institutional racism. The country provides universal health care and social welfare programs for citizens when life takes a bad turn. This has been grievously less true for many Aboriginal peoples contending with the vicissitudes of the Indian Act or new immigrants who, qualified professionals in the countries they have left behind, are relegated to driving taxis or washing toilets in hotels and office towers, but even these unfortunate constituencies have significant numbers of concerned Canadians advocating for the improvement of their situations and live far from the penury and racial or gender-based discrimination known to citizens of many other countries that have no courts or charters to which they can turn.

Canadians are not better than others but simply more blessed, not having had to contend with any great amount of hardship to come by their lucky chance or to do much other than be vigilant to maintain it. Their good fortune has been awarded them through birthright or, for some 250,000 new residents per annum, through the second chance of immigration. In Greek mythology, sea nymph Thetis, Achilles' mother, explains to her son that he is able to live either a long but unremarkable life or a shorter one with everlasting glory. On the eve of battle, the vacillating Achilles considers, in Robert Fagles's fine translation of Homer's *The Iliad*,

> *that two fates bear me on to the day of death.*
> *If I hold out here and I lay siege to Troy,*
> *My journey home is gone, but my glory never dies.*
> *If I voyage back to the fatherland I love,*
> *my pride, my glory dies...*
> *true, but the life that's left me will be long*

Had the hero been a Canadian coming of age during the fifty years after the end of the Second World War, there would have been no dilemma. The long and peaceful life was the only one to be had. Canada was the just nation. It kept the peace and promoted development abroad and an equitable society at home. Its governments sought to recognize the equivalent worth to society of different kinds of people with different kinds of abilities doing different kinds of things so that, as Jonathan Swift writes in his long poem of 1713, "Cadenus and Vanessa," it could be said, "Who'er excels in what we prize, appears a hero in our eyes." A host of measures was taken to reward difference and to boost wages and compensation where the market failed to do so in order to make the country even more fair.

Privilege, however, can be hard to bear.

The peaceful country, true to its nature as a twentieth-century paradise, also contained the seeds of its own dysfunction. For Canada was, to too many, the country in which it was also proven, as Tolstoy the political analyst might have said, that all "happy countries are all alike," which is to say not interesting. Without a legacy of hard-fought "wars of existence"—without conquests and glory to be sung, or treachery, brutality and blood spilled for the sake of the country on its own soil—Canada's history can appear to be uneventful and its future can look that way too. The country's fate is the ironic one of utopias imagined throughout the centuries by philosophers from Thomas More to Karl Marx and Dr. Seuss—conceptions of everlasting, better worlds that did not survive prolonged scrutiny, not even in thought, because the social equilibrium upon which their idylls depended were too beatifically good to be true. Humans have appetites, they have failings, and, above all, they resent being bullied into somebody else's grand design. Utopia is an unnatural state, even a modest liberal Canadian one and, because it is, inevitably something will surface to disturb its impossible order and put humankind through the hard work of envisioning the better place again. Life has been lived this way since the Garden: Paradise exists to be spoiled.

For many Canadians, the country's good fortune was something to be decried, an explanation of what for a long time has been characterized as an abundant capacity for failure, mediocrity and apology in the national character. In this representation there are good Canadians and there are bad. Bad Canadians are the descendants of United Empire Loyalists lured north by land grants with their tails between their legs after Britain, the mother country, lost the War of American Independence (and by the promise, not repealed until 1793, to slaveholders among them that their human "property" could be kept). They are Americans dodging the draft during the Vietnam War or "resisting" further tours of duty in President George W. Bush one with Iraq. They are dodgy immigrants who have fled wars in far-off countries or, worse, who have played a dubious part in them and who can therefore be demonized publicly and without trial. They are dual passport holders and others who cannot possibly become good Canadians because they do not speak English or French. They are refugees who have taken the easy way out and who conspire to bring to Canada their aged parents, useless to the labour force and the tax base, in order to take advantage of universal health care and other social benefits. They are freeloaders who speak of rights, not responsibilities, and who revel in asserting differences rather than celebrating common values. They arrive as losers and the second-rate, or they are born into this inferior company and acquire these traits through the complacency of Canadian citizenship apparently making few demands. They are likely Liberal or, worse, from the New Democratic Party, but either way, *socialist*. They do not have the better stuff of Canadians who, loyal to the Queen, rushed to defend the realm in 1899, 1914, 1939, 1950 — and 2002.

History, as has argued Canadian historian Margaret MacMillan, the author of *Paris, 1919: Six Months That Changed the World* (2003), can be used but also abused. "It can be dangerous to question the stories people tell about themselves because so much of our identity is both shaped and bound up with our history," writes MacMillan. "That is why dealing with the past, in deciding on which version we want, or on what we want to remember and to forget, can become so politically charged."

Stories that purport to explain the contemporary, peace-oriented predilection of many Canadians through the suggestion of its being the result of some lesser historical pedigree stick because they are easy to recount. Stories like this may even have a certain historical footing but are generally true only in part. We are influenced by these or others, permitting them a role of "national" explanation only for as long as we desist from offering alternative narratives, factual or mythic, that challenge them. For just as the person living in Canada today cannot be blamed for the internment of Japanese Canadians during the Second World War, nor for having refused ships filled with hundreds of desperate refugees the right to land on safe shores (as the Canadian government did with the Sikhs aboard the *Komagata Maru* in 1914 and the Jews on the MS *St. Louis* in 1939), nor for having oppressed Aboriginals for a couple of centuries before our own (when you and I were not actually agents in these stories), the flight of United Empire Loyalists or any other of the ensemble of cowardly renditions of the Canadian character does not explain the conduct of anyone who did not belong to these groups or live within the sphere of these stories' immediate telling. So too, the kudos derived from inspiring, elevating accounts of the valorous behaviour of troops on the battlefield occurring several generations prior to ours is not automatically an attribute of the present generation's to flaunt.

The only way in which the behaviour of anyone living today is plausibly explained by such stories, positively or negatively, lies in encountering their substantiations of Canadian national identity and condoning them, as we do through ritual and other ways of consciously upholding particular traditions, or by standing to the side and not objecting to their messages. The racism and xenophobia that saw migrant ships turned away from Canadian harbours more than seventy years ago define the failings of our national character only to the point that Canadians (and especially Sikh and Jewish ones, now comfortably landed in this country and forgetting the story of their provenance) are aware of these historical moments and do not act against their being re-enacted with, say, a leaky ship of Tamil immigrants—as arrived in B.C. in 2010. Analogously, the valour of Canadians on the battlefield between 1914 and 1918 or at any other time can only be claimed as an attribute when the example of it is repeated and is consciously the reason for the actions of the person living later. But even then, it is not enough to claim the line.

The implication of our history is that Canadians, good at the job as they are when they do need to fight, are overly cosseted, and disinclined to defending themselves because they do not have to and that they do not want to pay a bill of citizenship that seems out of proportion and unnecessary. Canada, without a legacy of revolution or big wars fought on its own soil, without the sort of rallying tests that are conventionally regarded as forging a national character, has been the safe but also a boring place—soft at the edges and indifferent to any debt to be paid toward society because nobody at home was ever calling it in. At the apogee of its telling, this story says that Canadians forgot their military, did not see the point of it. During the 1990s, the country dispatched her soldiers in the UN's blue-helmets into the very middle of hellish situations rather than keep them on the right side of wars as they have conventionally been fought, with good on one side and bad on the other. While this was happening, believed the impatient and the outraged (or the simply befuddled), the country's diplomats were becoming increasingly tedious guests at the gatherings of nations by making lofty claims about the country's superior, internationalist nature and travelling the so-called "moral high ground." A significant number of Canadians, mostly those who were not Aboriginal or from Quebec or Newfoundland (where different mythologies have reigned), yearned for the chance of another way to see and be seen. It was difficult being a Canadian in this position, being the citizen craving a more old-fashioned idea of a unified, strong country rather than one confused by the more complicated allegiances of multiculturalists. It was difficult being the politician hoping for a seat at the table of international policy-making without the "hard" power to put him there (it is almost always a him). It was difficult being a journalist simply wanting a more consequential beat.

Wars are speedier and more dramatic catalysts of change than are general strikes, social policy and plebiscites, so that without the discombobulation of violence, history strolls more than it is pushed along and the stories that become the cornerstones of the country—that become its "foundation myths"—are slow to be altered. For the Canadian malcontents, a reconfiguring of history was of the essence, and the acclamation of the military was key. It was not so much that the country's history was uneventful but that the country had an *eventful* history of which too few were aware. Here was a position that could puff chests and be aggrandized by including, in its embrace, wars that Canada had fought on behalf of the bigger, better empires of Britain, the United States and the North Atlantic Treaty Organization (NATO).

And yet, in the 1990s, the prospect of a more zealously proactive nation—one with a stronger, more pivotal military doing more than UN peacekeeping—seemed an impossibility in the face of a Liberal Party, still dominant after four decades, and its upholding of a gentler, more accepting, multicultural idea of the country. According to *A Look at Canada*, the study guide for new citizens that was extant then, the country aspired to be

> a peaceful society in which respect for cultural differences, equality, liberty and freedom of expression is a fundamental value. Canada was created through discussion, negotiation and compromise. These characteristics are as important today as in the past.

Any new version of the country would require a complete uprooting of this proposition and for the work to happen forcibly. Such a prospect appeared utterly unlikely, especially after Liberal prime minister Jean Chrétien's return to power in 2000 for a third consecutive term in an election in which the weak opposition of the Reform Party and Progressive Conservatives' newly formed Canadian Alliance, led by Stockwell Day, was summarily defeated. To a right wing becoming ever more extreme, it was clear that in Canada the idea of a broadly inclusive, conflict-averse country had to be wholly etiolated if a more conservative idea of national destiny was ever to have the chance of taking hold. Such a change would demand a ruthless and deliberate razing of a whole packet of myths and stories that were being narrated, through the end of the last century, about the reviled Canada "created through discussion, negotiation and compromise."

This was the job at which Day failed but that the Conservative Party, the phoenix that arose under Stephen Harper out of the ashes of the Canadian Alliance, would manage in a stunningly short time and very well. The change happened speedily between the watershed years of 2001 to 2006 and without the catalyst of a single terrorism-related fatality on Canadian soil. The Conservative Party was able to set about making it happen while in opposition and as its allies in universities, business and its supporters in think-tanks and the media were unhappily in the wilderness. Debates over the meaning of what it is to be Canadian depend upon a knowledge of history and the intrusion of current events as much as nationally binding stories, but this angry cortège was able to effect the transformation because it took the power of foundation myths seriously. To a point, the shift in the public's perception of Canada's role in the world and the rapidity of the change implemented in the brief period of just a few years was the result of a sizable portion (though not a majority) of voters feeling their interests and worldviews had been overlooked for far too long—this a defining part of the Canadian condition no matter where the voter is from—and finally cating their ballots cohesively. But what the Conservative Party and its allies in civil society understood is that for the change to be more than passing, for people's views to be altered more than incrementally, old terms needed to be disgraced and replaced with more expedient others. For fundamental change to occur, there needed to be stories to win not broad consensus but the vitally necessary allegiance of a tactically sufficient number. There needed to be narrative support for governments that deliver troops into battle and afterwards to ensure obeisance toward the politicians and the causes that keep them there. There needed to be an acceptance of mortal threats to soldiers beloved by family and country and an understanding that some of these troops would very likely return injured or that they will make "the ultimate sacrifice" and come home in coffins. There needed to be general agreement that the grief and the loss by soldiers' families and by the larger community of Canada would not be experienced "in vain."

And yet is it really possible that, over the course of one decade, the Canadian worldview changed so dramatically? This is the fundamental question raised by the altered discourse of the last decade and posed by this book. Can it be that the character of a nation becomes something else entirely in such a short period of time, or did it never truly veer much from what it was? These are questions that cannot be answered without deciding what was the character of the nation in the first place. Canada today is ostensibly quite different from the country that existed in the second half of the last century. Its days as a leading power at the UN are ended. A rapprochement with the United States and Israel has replaced its traditionally more multilateral stances. Its welcoming of new Canadians is qualified and sometimes adversarial. The attitude of the Canadian government after 2006 even toward its own citizens is one that reflexively relies on enmities and the cultivation of disputes resolved through the vilification of dissenters, the circumvention of Parliament and an imposition of solutions rather than any reconciliation achieved through "discussion, negotiation and compromise."

In order to understand these changes, we can look for differences or for that which, beneath the surface, has remained the same. For often it is illuminating to see how history puts on different disguises even as the underlying habits of a place are fundamentally unaltered. This is to say either that Canada is today a "warrior nation"—that the peacekeeping version of Canada was a fifty-year aberration and a public that believes otherwise genuinely has ignored Canada's long military history—or that the Canada with an innate disposition toward "soft power," "making a difference" and the sort of peacekeeping work that is now so disparaged is the underlying constant and the "warrior nation" is the fiction.

Whatever is the more lasting Canadian truth, a wholesale revision of Canada's reigning myths of identity has been both the result of and a major factor contributing to the divisive politics of the country during the last decade. Canadians are a healthily skeptical people, and it goes without saying that not everyone bought into the peacekeeping story of the 1990s just as support for today's "warrior-nation" is far from categorical, either. But Canadians are also a reserved lot, so that myths and the particularly vocal can step into the silence and speak for the nation egregiously. The manner in which Canada's new myths of identity have been fostered and narrated has allowed Liberal and then Conservative governments to make decisions and to pass laws that have sent the Canadian Forces into Afghanistan, bolstered them, dictated the terms by which they should operate, be withdrawn, and then swiftly deployed to Libya in another proactive military operation, the last a tendentious demonstration of the "Responsibility to Protect" (RtoP) doctrine that has become the acceptable face of supposedly humanitarian peace operations, today.

Behind the foreground in which politicians, journalists and soldiers provide the theatre, stories provide the means effecting such a turnaround. Not just their vocabulary or content but the various *forms* of narrative play their part in the way a society secures its position in the world and the terms on which it engages with others. The thinking that is shaped by subtly different forms of story such as the myth, the epic and the novel acts as the guarantor of a society through its encouragement of distinct points of view about security, heroism and the nature of good and evil. In following one or another path, a community is able to replicate itself in the world on terms that allow it to survive and even to thrive.

Says South African author Antjie Krog: "We narrate in order to be."

How we choose to do so is of the essence.

This book is a consideration of the phrases and forms of story that Canada has used in order to talk itself into, through and out of the war in Afghanistan. The Canadian commitment to the war required a full-scale eradication of the country's foundation myths as they had been told for half a century. The face that Canada now presents to the world has been profoundly transformed. Much of the change was managed at a banal, mundane level of stories and clichés that were nevertheless so powerful that a previously peaceful society, one in which a respect for the individual distinction of views was paramount, quickly conceded the ground to a more monolithic one fervently embarking on the most destructive of paths and calling such a route "heroic."

And yet, as the Ghanaian is fond of saying, "No condition is permanent." Understanding the dizzying conflict of narratives that has arisen out of Canada's participation in the war in Afghanistan throws a bright light on how we, as a society, convince ourselves that a fight is right, and compels us to ask of ourselves what part the country should properly play in conflicts not yet started.

CHAPTER ONE

The Vimy Effect

From little towns in a far land we came,
To save our honour and a world aflame.
By little towns in a far land we sleep;
And trust that world we won for you to keep!
—Rudyard Kipling, "Epitaphs of the War" (1918)

Between September 2001 and 2006, the recalibration of Canadian ideas about the importance of the military and its role in foreign policy was massive. That the new century's environment of global insecurity would act as a catalyst could not have been foreseen, but there had been the precursors for such a change during the 1990s in the wake of the country's participation in immensely difficult humanitarian interventions in Bosnia, Somalia and Rwanda, the latter two disastrous for Canada. Bosnia had been a complicated exercise of endurance and, in 1993, teenager Shidane Arone was murdered by Canadian soldiers serving as peacekeepers in Somalia. In 1994, Canadian lieutenant-general Roméo Dallaire led the UN peacekeeping force that catastrophically failed to halt the Hutu-led genocide of more than

800,000 Tutsis in Rwanda. The latter two incidents were painfully felt and led to a loosening of the hold that the peacekeeping missions in which the Canada had participated for a half-century had upon the psyche and the aspirations of the country. The implication of the story of Dallaire's warnings ignored at the UN's headquarters was that something could have been done had anyone in New York actually been listening to the good Canadian soldier in the field, and the fact that nothing was led to a lot of Canadians wondering why they were involved in such undertakings. (That another Canadian, Maurice Baril, later Chief of Defence Staff, was a part of the UN management doing the ignoring complicated Canada's injured stake in the story but became, over time, a tangential detail.) The brutal murder of Arone, photographs swiftly circulating of the grinning soldier Clayton Matchee holding back the bloody head of the savagely beaten sixteen-year-old with a baton, sowed the seeds of a different kind of aversion to the UN, one that was rooted in shame rather than pride, but a rupture in the relationship nonetheless. No resorting to codes of honour could have excused the grotesque Somalian incident, and ultimately it led to an embarrassing political inquiry and then to the disbanding of the Canadian Airborne Regiment. It also led to many Canadian soldiers resenting the Liberals who had overseen the process. The resentment would surface in a number of ways, the first of them an antipathy toward the peacekeeping work onto which much of the blame was shifted. Gen. Rick Hillier, appointed by Paul Martin as CDS in February 2005, would memorably come to describe the 1990s as a "decade of darkness." Hillier was refer-ring, ostensibly, to the "rusting out" of the Canadian Forces that had come about as the result of a sequence of decreased military budgets over the course of the twentieth century's last decade. What was also to be understood in the catchy phrase, however, was that the 1990s constituted a very difficult time morally for the military. The shame of the Somalia Affair, the failure of peacekeepers to have prevented the Rwandan genocide and the drawn-out nature of the frustrating UN mission to the Balkans that had started in 1992 with Canadian Maj.-Gen. Lewis MacKenzie in command of Sector Sarajevo led to a lot of soul-searching and regret about the Forces' diminished role in Canadian society and a bitterness toward a bureaucracy regarded as no longer being on the side of the ranks. Today, the diminished budgets of the period are often portrayed as willful acts of retribution against an undervalued military, this detail of spite a necessary part of the story of the Forces' being hard done by, of their being prevented from doing their proper work by a lack of resources and a policy of misguided deployments in peacekeeping missions that were preferred by blithe governments because they could be managed without much kit. The practice, endgame and track record of humanitarian interventions were undergoing drastic revision the world over, but in Canada the dour rethinking was being further prevented by the Canadian military and its advocates needing to salvage a more robust sense of purpose. The quickest way to do this was to retrench and turn back to the much less complex business of "war-fighting."

State funding of armed forces, always one of the heftiest portions of a government's expenditure, waxes and wanes, and it can be argued that the erosion of military budgets were only peripherally the result of the country's commitments to UN peacekeeping operations, at their peak in that decade, however badly they went. The 1990s were a period of monstrous deficits at home and, externally, the thawing of the Cold War that was provided its quintessence in the fall of the Berlin Wall in 1989 and the breakup, two years later, of the Soviet Union and the Warsaw Pact. Unsurprisingly, in that more optimistic time, there was less of a perceived need for conventional armies. A subsequent desire to reap a peace dividend meant, easy enough to fathom, that less money would be put the Canadian Forces' way. But pendulums swing, and then they swing back and, in 1999, under Liberal prime minister Jean Chrétien, military budgets started to be increased again. The reinvestment in the Forces was an acknowledgement of Canadian soldiers being put into impossible situations with inadequate gear, and of years of reduced Department of National Defence (DND) allocations that had come about in part as a result of the astute balancing of government books for which Paul Martin, as minister of finance, would otherwise garner plenty of praise. The reversal of the trend amounted to a recognition of a cumulative shortchanging of the Canadian Forces and the repercussions of a less able military in the global arena but also a first thrust in the mounting debate about how best to outfit Canada's small army for military readiness and just what the Forces should be ready for. Peacekeeping was in disrepute, especially after American might rather than ineffectual UN work was seen to have stopped long episodes of violence—both in the 1995 NATO Operation Deliberate Force, the bombing campaign that brought the warring parties in the Balkans to the negotiating table and swiftly led to the Dayton Peace Agreement and an end to the Yugoslav Wars, and the 1999 NATO Operation Allied Force, the bombing of Serbian forces that ended the Kosovo War and in which Canadian F-18s flew 684 sorties.

Neither support of nor opposition to the country's peacekeeping role, however, was yet a galvanizing Canadian political issue, military history of any kind hardly discussed in universities or the media at all. But then came 9/11, after which the shift in the country's conception of its place in the world, at least insofar as it is determined by government, appeared shocking in its breadth and velocity. The attacks by nineteen al-Qaeda terrorists on the twin towers of the World Trade Center and the Pentagon ripped through the fabric of not only American life. There were no blue skies anymore. Such a perfect morning would afterwards be associated with imminent destruction, with civilian airliners used as bombs and helpless office workers launching themselves from one hundred floors up rather than be incinerated where they were. "We know by instinct," writes the brilliant and idiosyncratic German author W.G. Sebald in his novel *Austerlitz* (ominously published that same month), "that outsize buildings cast the shadow of their own destruction before them and are designed from the first with an eye to their later existence as ruins." Such is the indomitable nature of the American spirit that it is doubtful that architect Minoru Yamasaki and his American partners at Emery Roth & Sons entertained for a moment the Old World thought that their testament to American economic power and reach might ever be felled. But, on 9/11 the 110-storey towers were reduced to molten steel and ash. Resting askew in the smoky dust and debris, the seven-storey narrow Gothic arches of the Towers' decorative facade were transformed by circumstance into a memorial to the innocence, bravura and sense of security of an epoch that was suddenly bygone.The crater of Ground Zero a gateway in the wounded cityscape to a land of new menace. The 9/11 attacks removed oceans and pushed the United States, Canada and the nation-states of Europe right up against the borders of less fortunate countries, ones with constituencies that had been hostile to Western values for a very long time, the threatening possibilities of which did not need to be considered seriously before then. At a stroke, in 2001, conflicts that had appeared to be taking place at a safe remove were brought into the very heart of Western nations. Distance, as North America, Europe, but also Russia and the Antipodes had known it, ceased to exist, the enemy as likely to be hiding in the Muslim suburbs of Adelaide, Bradford, Detroit, Montreal or Moscow as in Saddam Hussein's Iraq, the caves of Afghanistan or, as it turned out, a safe houses in the Pakistani city of Abbottabad.

The evaporation of distance was particularly pertinent in Canada, the archetypically far distant territory. At home, the enforcement—the *creation*—of a secure border between the United States and Canada became a preoccupation as it had not been for almost two hundred years. Canada—to the United States, the vaguely considered country that had historically been the mildly bothersome source of cold winds, bovine encephalitis, subsidized lumber and power cuts—was, it was briefly mooted, the origin of an ill a lot more sinister: the place where the 9/11 bombers came from. When this information was disproved, American congressmen argued that it was where terrorists *would* come from—as Ahmed Ressam, the "Millennium Bomber" who had entered Canada on a fake passport and lived in Montreal for a while before he was arrested at the British Columbia-Washington border in December 2000, had done. Following the attacks, it was evident that along with whatever was going to be the country's military commitment, Canada's approaches to multilateralism and its casual embrace of the open society were also under the spotlight. On October 8, 2001, Chrétien told the nation: "We must insist on living on our own terms according to our values, not on terms dictated from the shadows." It was a maxim the prime minister would follow when, in March 2003, he would decide against sending Canadian troops to Iraq as a part of the American "coalition of the willing," his party's refusal to participate in Ronald Reagan's "Star Wars" space-based defence scheme and then the Ballistic Missile Defence program of the new century only entrenching the Liberals' unpopularity south of the border.

What with the later revelation of Saddam Hussein's Iraqi regime having concealed no weapons of mass destruction, the allegation of their existence the reason that was declared for the U.S. invasion, Chrétien's insistence on not joining the United States' war against Iraq was, after a time, regarded even by Conrad Black, his arch-opponent, as a shrewd, adroit decision. But, in the moment, it was incumbent upon Canada to play some sort of role and within weeks of the terrorist attacks Canada had dispatched four naval vessels offering logistic support to the U.S. offensive against Afghanistan. That October, Canada's minister of national defence, Art Eggleton, alerted the Canadian public that two thousand troops, six ships and six planes were on alert to serve with Operation Apollo in support of United States military operations in Afghanistan. In fact, the country was already serving: Canadian Joint Task Force Two (JTF2) special operations troops were clandestinely fighting alongside the Americans there.

Operation Enduring Freedom, with its mission of routing the Taliban and al-Qaeda, was the precursor to the International Security Assistance Force in Afghanistan (ISAF) mandated by UN Resolution 1386 in December 2001. According to *The Unexpected War: Canada in Kandahar* (2007), an exemplary political history of the country's path to Afghanistan written by Janice Gross Stein, the Director of the Munk Centre for International Studies at the University of Toronto, and Eugene Lang, previously chief of staff to the Liberal ministers of defence John McCallum and Bill Graham, Eggleton had envisioned the Canadian contribution to the ISAF being "not a front-line mission [but] a stabilization mission to assist in opening corridors for humanitarian assistance." As late as 2004, after the Liberals were re-elected that June as a minority government under Paul Martin, the prime minister's intention had been for the military to be employed for "peace and nation-building" in Haiti and Darfur, Sudan. Martin, who took over the helm of the Liberal Party in December 2003, considered Haiti and Darfur to be causes that, true to the character of the country as it had been projected for decades, a majority of Canadians would support. The Progressive Conservative Party, then simply the Conservative

Party of Canada, but also General Hillier and a particularly strident set of academics serving as fellows or on the advisory council of the Canadian Defence and Foreign Affairs Institute (CDFAI) based in Calgary, believed otherwise. Chrétien's talk of Canadian "values" was anathema to this group, its CDFAI component including historian David Bercuson, political scientist Barry Cooper and the ubiquitous Jack Granatstein. Afghanistan was not just the best but the *only* way to move forward. The incipient campaign represented the seizing of a commitment that would improve the country's weakened relationship with the United States and would also have the Forces employed in *combat* again—the job that the military's supporters have always insisted it is best equipped to do. The Canadian "peacekeepers" were stationed in Kabul, where the NATO-led ISAF was under the command of the ambitious Gen. Rick Hillier, previously Canadian Chief of the Land Staff and before that Deputy Commanding General of III Armored Corps of the U.S. Army at Fort Hood, Texas. (Historian Desmond Morton has commented that beyond its description of Canadian actions, Stein and Lang's *The Unexpected War* is also "a marvelous account of U.S. imperialism at work.") European reluctance and a U.S. request for troops to fight alongside theirs, however, swiftly shifted the deployment in Kandahar that constituted the first combat mission for Canadian soldiers since the 1950-53 Korean War. The more proactive role was an undertaking that John McCallum, who had succeeded Eggleton as the Liberal minister of defence in 2002, knew was favoured by a Canadian Forces administration desiring closer relations with American forces and that saw in Afghanistan an opportunity and a way out of the ignominy that had started in 1993 with the Somalia Affair.

On 9/11, Canada had arrived at a fork in the road, one route leading to a continuation of the country's history of peacekeeping and another, more trammelled, to conventional combat work of the kind that the

"Global War on Terror" was demanding. And yet, even as the ashes of 9/11 were settling, convincing the Canadian public of a context in which the country might forgo the rich, marvelously inspiring but also burdensome legacy of Lester B. Pearson and commit troops outside of the blue-beret UN missions it had been engaged in for five decades was difficult. It was an alteration that would require, along with any legislative action, the wholesale revision of a packet of nationally binding stories—from the flowering of the country during the Trudeau years and the idea of the country as a safe haven, to that most enduring of English Canada's creation myths, the Battle of Vimy Ridge. No less needed to happen if the country was to be steered away from the multilateral, UN-oriented policies and open multiculturalism of the previous political era into the more conformist and ultimately bellicose state of being endorsed by the country's rising new establishment. Foundation myths are comfortably ensconced. The about-face was one that many were impatient for but managing it was going to be a formidable project.

The nationally binding stories called "foundation" or "creation" myths serve to explain how a society has come into being and, as cautionary tales, how to behave in it. Creation myths and cautionary tales forge bonds in all sorts of societies—modern and not, scientific and not, where writing exists and does not. The big bang theory is, in the face of our unknowing, as much of a myth of the origin of the universe as is the Book of Genesis. The popular environmental mode of thinking that we speak of as "green" depends, as much as science and medicine do, upon a lattice of cautionary tales to explain how the world as we know it has come into being and, should we wish to survive and to prosper, how best to conduct ourselves in it. "Myths" are stories told to a particular end. Whatever may be the truth of such stories matters less than the pertinence they have acquired in explaining a society's provenance and mores.

In Canada, foundation myths tend to be derived from the stories we tell about the extraordinary endurance of early settlers, about the ingenuity of First Nations that preceded them and about battles and political and historical moments that we deem to be significant because they uphold the country as it is and as we would like it to be in the future. The story that Canada, the modern nation, was forged in the trenches of the First World War when, as the Canadian Corps, all four divisions of the Canadian Expeditionary Force (CEF) fought together for the first time is a story that acts as both a creation myth and a cautionary tale. As a creation myth, the story offers an explanation of the country and present mores as well as the possibility that a population so absurdly dispersed might actually behave as a unified whole. As a cautionary tale, it suggests how best we conduct ourselves in order to navigate our way through the "Global War on Terror" and that a better country will arise out of the ashes of our present, turbulent times. It says we must be selfless and brave, and that we must be nation-builders as the hallowed First World War generation was so that the security of the country is not breached, the territory is defended and a stronger, finer Canada is in place for our children.

But there is another aspect of the myth that is significant. For a myth is not only a story of origins but one that contains within it convictions about good and evil that lead to a specific understanding of the nature of the surrounding world and of the narrating society's place in it. In stories told as myths, human beings occupy a place alongside all the other elements of a contingent universe, the laws of which the narrating society does not expect to be able to surmount. Narratives of the myth world constitute an inherently *humble* form of storytelling in which good and evil are quantities that bear no relation to human morality or any scientific ordering of the world. Their presence exists alongside other qualities and quantities that in their entirety constitute an essentially inexplicable and unchangeable universe. When, for example, Canadians tell the story of the Battle of Vimy Ridge as a creation myth, they tell it in a manner that prompts complicity rather than outrage. Indeed, there is no easier way for Canadians to tell that particular story, as nothing the country did do, or could have done, was ever going to affect its outcome—its duration, perhaps, but not its causes or its resolution. Rather than telling the story of the battle that became the emblem of the many that the CEF fought in some manner that might compel today's Canadian to protest against such absurd, senseless slaughter, it suggests that war is a permanent condition and how to prepare for it's return. War is a situation, the laws of which Canadians could not be expected to surmount.

Another First World War story, that of the Christmas Truce of 1914, in which Allied and German soldiers crossed the terrifying shelled-out landscape of No Man's Land to sing carols together, shows the essentially amoral nature of the myth world. In this story, good and evil are not attributes of the men themselves, but circumstances of an awful and inexplicable situation over which they have no control. For a moment, there is an unlikely halt to the fighting, and then, for reasons of no benefit at all to the men, they must return to the trenches and start killing each other again in a situation rendered even more bizarre and morally inexplicable by the spontaneity of the short truce. The story is an expression of the pity of war in which blame is not apportioned in a way that suggests that one or another party is "evil" and responsible for the ill fortune. Good and evil are quantities that are permanently present in the world and that have entered into it for reasons that the soldiers themselves cannot meaningfully be said to have determined. "A culture forges myths for many reasons," writes American journalist Susan Faludi in *The Terror Dream: Fear and Fantasy in Post-9/11 America* (2007), "but paramount among them is the need to impose order on chaotic and disturbing experience—to resolve haunting contradictions and contain apprehensions, to imagine a way out of the darkness."

Myths, at their most basic, explain how prevailing circumstances have come to be and do so in a manner that promotes human beings' deference to circumstance rather than useless objection to a situation that likely cannot be challenged. As was true of the hunter who stood before the tiger and a jungle of other mysterious, dangerous threats, so was the soldier caught up in monstrous twentieth-century conflicts in need of stories to reconcile himself to situations that neither science nor government has ever successfully been able to explain; where sense and reason falter, myths step in. We accept death and carnage but also mercy, terror, valour and so on as elements of a contingent universe that may happen upon us at any time. Such quantities simply *are*.

The story of Canada as a peacekeeping nation is also a myth, though it is one with a different narrative sensibility. The story of Canadian peacekeeping is an optimistic one that allowed the country to "imagine its way out of the darkness" of the Second World War. Whatever the actual merits of peacekeeping's achievements, the myth prospered because the messages of humanitarian purpose it delivered and others it reinforced served the higher utility of national bonding. Quickly, the story of Canadians as peacekeepers was elevated onto that high plane from which it was able to serve as an inspirational emblem to the country. For more than fifty years, the peacekeeping story flourished. It became an integral part of the national character, a determination of how the country believed its foreign policy should be conducted and of what sort of global citizens Canadians imagined themselves to be. Whether its positive thinking was a true reflection of the nation or no more than a mask for Cold War military strategies; whether the very idea of peacekeeping was, in fact, invented by a Canadian or thrust into the country's lap by chance, for fifty years the peacekeeping story offered a plausible and unchallenged idea of the country as it was, and as it saw its future. It functioned as a wonderfully credible foundation myth for fifty years because it met these criteria of explanation, although its view of good and evil—an essential difference—is, like that of the novel, humanistic. The peacekeeping story sees good and evil not as incontrovertible forces of a hostile world against which, in epic fashion, we must be permanently on guard but as quantities that reside in each one of us that we are able to put into play or to prevent. The universe is a determined and not a contingent place, and human beings are active agents within it. The most nefarious of situations are not to be deferred to but challenged. Circumstances can be altered.

As a creation myth, the peacekeeping story provided a rationalization of Canadian privilege and an explanation of how a lesser power—one that had disbanded its enormous wartime army—might behave. It provided a sense of Canadian singularity and an arrangement of history to complement this conception. After the Second World War, Canada had taken pride in the country's contribution to the execution of the UN's multilateral ideals—to the Universal Declaration of Human Rights that New Brunswicker John Peters Humphrey drafted in 1948 and, during the Suez Crisis of 1956, in the Nobel Peace Prize-winning role that Lester B. Pearson had played in the creation of the United Nations Emergency Force (UNEF), the world's first peacekeeping unit, and in the augmenting number of humanitarian interventions that the UN subsequently conducted around the world. In the wake of the short century's "war to end war," the next one fought by the "Greatest Generation," and the "forgotten" Korean War that came after it, Canadians revelled in the new path its diplomats and soldiers were offering to a tense world in which the proliferation of nuclear technology and the Cold War rivalry of the United States and the Soviet Union were constant threats. Later prime minister, then Liberal Minister for Foreign Affairs, the charismatic Pearson's clever mediation and smart brokering of "soft power" became a symbol of Canadian wiliness and a hallmark of not just Liberal governments for the ensuing decades.

Not until the late 1990s was the story of Canadian peacekeeping as a national foundation myth effectively questioned. After the complications of the UN peacekeeping mission in Bosnia, and the embarrassment and failures of the earlier interventions in Somalia and Rwanda, a groundswell of seething and frustration had started to mount against the tasks that Canadian soldiers were being asked to perform, and the very idea of the country behaving as a benign force in the international arena. But public debate about the point and the viability of peacekeeping operations was still relatively mute, restricted to a small number of critics and proponents that, in today's Canada, would be characterized, contemptuously, as belonging to the nation's "cultural elites." The Canadian public's estimation and even awareness of the country's military was at a noticeable low—to a large extent because of the Somalia Affair but also because the world seemed to be veering to a more peaceful equilibrium after the rise of *perestroika* and the collapse of the Soviet Union. Enough so that when, in May 2000, the remains of an Unknown Soldier were repatriated from France to be interred in the National War Memorial near Parliament Hill in Ottawa, not far from where the peacekeeping monument called *Reconciliation* had been installed by the National Capital Commission and the

Department of National Defence in 1992, David Bercuson was able to write in the *National Post* despairingly of the virtually unnoticed event and of "the disparaging of war of Canadian academics, journalists, the professional peace lobby and the political left [who] have all but removed war as a legitimate part of the process of Canadian national formation." These phenomena, Bercuson declared, were, along with the "annual virtual starvation of the Canadian War Museum budget and series of deep cuts to the Directorate of History, the most obvious signs that Canadian governments were not interested in preserving Canada's military heritage."

Behind the burgeoning allegations was more than a modicum of unsavoury truth. In the fiscal year of 1998-99, Canadian military spending had reached the bottom of the trough of its post-Cold War minimum. The numbers of "boots on the ground" told the story. More than 100,000 Canadians had served under the UN's peacekeeping aegis since its inception, operations in which 142 Canadians had died, but during the watershed month of September 2001, a mere 317 Canadians were being deployed in blue-helmets in small numbers in various UN peace operations, along with 650 troops serving with NATO's stabilization force in Bosnia, where a twelve-year mission that had involved some 40,000 Canadian soldiers over its duration was finally ending. By 2001, the rank of the country's peacekeeping forces had plummeted to thirty-third among contributing nations. The Canadian Forces had shrunk to approximately 21,000 soldiers on active duty—markedly less than the approximately 14,000 infantry, 450 paratroopers and 10,000 sailors involved in Canada's D-Day assault of Juno Beach on June 6th, 1944. Said Gen. Rick Hillier in 2003, not yet CDS, "Any commander who would stand up here and say that we didn't need more soldiers should be tarred and feathered and rode out of town on a rail."

Outside of the country, more so than within, the commitment of successive Canadian governments to peacekeeping duties was dimly regarded. Its military capabilities having been substantially eroded, the country's failure to be able to supply the requisite resources was in the spotlight. This exasperation reached its peak when the UN's failure to muster more than a mere 7,000 troops to protect the six "safe areas" established in Bosnia and Herzegovina (rather than the 36,000 troops that UNPROFOR, the United Nations Protection Force, had requested) led to the massacre in Srebrenica of more than 8,000 Bosnian Muslims in July 1995. Coming as it did after the 1994 Rwandan genocide, the revelation of the atrocity contributed to the widespread impression that UN peacekeeping forces were systemically incapable of doing the work assigned to them. The nature of Canada's involvement was under the microscope. Anthony DePalma of *The New York Times*, then the newspaper's Canadian bureau chief, noted of the United States' northern neighbour, in 1997, that growing controversy was surrounding the struggling, budget-tightened Canadian Forces. "Despite having an army so small it could be seated comfortably in the home arena of the Montreal Canadiens," wrote DePalma, "Canada is on the front line of most peacekeeping missions around the world." But, DePalma warned, "when peacekeeping becomes more like combat, the line between restraint and toughness blurs. And the debate over the proper role of Canada's 21,000 troops and the other 40,000 members of its combined defense forces has left Canadians frustrated and confused." David Rieff, who chronicles the many paradoxes and failures of UNPROFOR in the former Yugoslavia in his 1996 book, *Slaughterhouse: Bosnia and the Failure of the West*, spoke in 2005 of the perennial "mismatch between the countries that actually have quite serious and interesting moral principles, and then actually do it"—the one that actually could, being his own. Rieff, a veteran observer of humanitarian interventions and therefore of Canadian foreign policy, described Canada as "a country that has taken the lead, often very admirably, in calling for things to be done about massacres," but one that "basically doesn't have an army anymore." In Bosnia, Rieff recalled, "we would go up north and we would see their 1957 APCs broken down by the side of the road. It was calamitous." During the Canadian tour of his 2001 collection, *The CEO of the Sofa*, political satirist and *Atlantic Monthly* contributing editor P.J. O'Rourke made more or less the same assessment more caustically, no surprise, describing Americans doing the soldiering and then "handing brooms to Canadian peacekeepers to clean up afterwards."

The criticisms were not only made by foreigners. In 2005, on the eve of his return to Canada, author and human rights scholar Michael Ignatieff decried, before an audience in Dublin, Canada's "entirely bogus reputation as peacekeepers" and its favouring the building of "hospitals and schools and roads" over "paying the bill" of proper international citizenship. "It's disgusting in my own country—and I love my country," said Ignatieff, "but they would rather bitch about their rich neighbour to the south than actually pay the note." The "they," not "we," was a harbinger of the problems Ignatieff would later have convincing Canadians of his patriot's pedigree, the chance of a fissure that the Conservatives would ruthlessly and demagogically exploit, but there was no doubting the intellectual's credentials in the human rights arena. Ignatieff had been a journalist with the BBC before he became, in 2000, the director of the Carr Center for Human Rights Policy at Harvard's John F. Kennedy School of Government. Alongside Jean Chrétien's minister of foreign affairs from 1996 to 2000, Lloyd Axworthy, Ignatieff had been one of the architects of RtoP—the doctrine of the international community's "Responsibility to Protect" the citizens of sovereign states from abuse by their own governments that had been approved at the World Summit of the United Nations in 2005—so the lob from his corner hurt. The implication was that the bill to be paid was in blood and in lives and that having Canadian soldiers wear blue-helmets, but so few of them in the field, belied the seriousness of the country's commitment.

At home, John Manley, Chrétien's minister of foreign affairs at the time, said much the same thing, declaring after 9/11 that "you can't just sit at the G8 table and then, when the bill comes up, go to the washroom." (The use of the metaphor of the unpaid restaurant bill is ironic, coming as it generally does from politicians in the habit of billing to a third party—as they do, in wartime, the costly item of lives to soldiers.) In Ottawa, but outside of Parliament, Jack Granatstein was in the vanguard of the drive for a new Canadian War Museum and blaming the hard time he was having raising funds on the institution's name. "It's clearly a difficult sell," he said in 2000, a year before the Liberal government announced its support of plans for a new building to be constructed at Vimy Place in the LeBreton Flats area of downtown Ottawa. (It opened in May 2005.) "If we were the Canadian Peace Museum, it would be easier." Later, Granatstein would brag in an interview with the *Ottawa Citizen* that he had the museum's "whole third floor ripped out and put in NATO and NORAD" exhibits rather than the peacekeeping ones that had been the gallery's subject. Granatstein became director of the museum in 1998, having published the year before *Who Killed Canadian History?*, a bestseller that faulted educational policies and the country's multicultural permissiveness for the nation not having a more robust sense of its past. Yet to come was *Who Killed the Canadian Military?* in 2004 and *Whose War Is It? How Canada Can Survive in the Post 9/11 World* in 2007, a book that might as easily have been titled *Who's Killing the Canadian Future?* in which Granatstein assails "the harmful idealization of peacekeeping" and imagines a combination of terrorist attacks and natural disasters and blames "peace-loving, incense-burning, pain-feeling, politically correct Canada" for the failure to cope with the aftermath.

The anti-1960s-hippy theme, Pierre Trudeau the miscreant at the heart of it, is a Canadian right-wing constant. Granatstein was one of the most active research fellows of the University of Calgary's Centre for Military and Strategic Studies. Through its Calgary offices, and those of the companion CDFAI, he and his colleagues David Bercuson and Barry Cooper, though also Mark Steyn and others, were repeatedly launching attacks on the peacekeeping notion of Canada—often referred to as the "blue-beret" or "blue-helmet" version because of the colour of the headgear worn by the country's soldiers seconded to UN peace operations for so many years. Like Granatstein, Bercuson and Cooper had been berating Canadians for years for their misguided political views and apparently astonishing naïveté—the country pursuing "hippy-dippy aims of world peace based primarily on unbridled love and unsecured trust"—but also for an alleged anti-Americanism they thought explained, along with such missions having been comparatively cheap, Canada's predilection for peacekeeping work. The mantra of the right was that any of the distinctive policies born in the 1960s heyday of Canadian liberalism are tainted, conceived out of the sublimated envy of the little guy. In the view of this camp, it is impossible that such policies could be the outcome of confident, original minds understanding the singular nature and challenges, though also the responsibility, of their geographical position next to the most powerful nation in the world—and that as much as was possible without resentment. "Multiculturalism, universal health care, soft power diplomacy, economic and cultural nationalism and other [policies] are all, in part, efforts to downplay our own fear that we are an insignificant nation," wrote the *National Post*'s Lorne

Gunter quite typically. They are means of asserting "our national superiority, especially towards the Americans." According to this view, the peacekeeping lobby was seen to be anti-American not only because of the feel-good, incense-burning, hippy-dippy generation of Canadians' horror of wars (and therefore of the United States, the country at the vanguard of fighting them) but because the provision of forces to the UN amounted to a useless, wasteful and ultimately passive-aggressive denial of America's infinitely better capability of being the world's global policeman. Peacekeeping, in other words, was a high-minded way of liberal saps proclaiming Canada's distinct, better nature and had very little if anything at all to do with global geopolitical exigencies. Canadians who supported the pacific idea of the country were simply a self-important bunch of moral narcissists seizing the high ground.

Sean M. Maloney, a professor at Kingston's Royal Military College keen to describe himself as a "rogue military historian," and journalist Mark Steyn were others lambasting the idea of Canada as a viable, peace-oriented society. Maloney had been attacking the country's "feel-goodism" and the "hollow façade" of peacekeeping's "myth-making exercise" for years, irascibly castigating Canadians for being unaware of the country's military history and that the Canadian Forces had major involvements in NATO during the Cold War, sometimes carrying nuclear warheads. "Soft power" was to Maloney and others in his camp a ruse that depended upon the brute (hard) force of America or of NATO for its enforcement, so that in terms of the dismantling of peacekeeping's "hollow façade," the more Canadian Forces were seen to be ready and able to deliver some of the punch, the better. The military, these and other critics repeated whenever they could, had been performing many roles beyond the UN's peacekeeping missions even as it was being run down by successive Liberal governments bilking the Forces to the point that they were no longer available for "heavy lifting." The peacekeeping that Canadian Forces were doing was no more than an extension of Cold War damage control, a job that was, to the knowing, without a humanitarian component at all. How the Canadian public might in good faith have conceived of UN peace operations was an incidental, even contemptible factor of no value to the argument. Peacekeeping missions, retired Col. Sean Henry (a veteran of peacekeeping missions) wrote, were "better defined as international security operations... devised to dampen conflicts that risked sparking a nuclear exchange." Steyn, the doomsaying author of *America Alone: The End of the World as We Know It* (2006), was meanwhile sparing no opportunity to express his bitter contempt for Jean Chrétien, the prime minister in office when Canadian soldiers were serving with UN peacekeeping forces in Bosnia, Somalia and Rwanda and, later, when Canada did not send troops to Iraq. Chrétien was also, not to be discounted, the fella who had done irreparable injury to Steyn's former boss, Conrad Black, by refusing the Canadian newspaper magnate the right to accept British honours and call himself "Sir." Chrétien was, according to Steyn, "smug, complacent, platitudinous, self-absorbed" and upholding a "Trudeaupian" edifice that was a "bald-faced lie."

Ancillary but equally germane to the endeavour of dismantling this aspect of the Liberal legacy so reviled by the Canadian right was the attack of Canadian immigration laws thought of as reprehensibly lax, epitomized most shamefully by the characterization of Tamil migrants arriving, in 2010, after several weeks' dangerous sailing, as terrorists "jumping the queue"—this, from the same Conservative government that would introduce, in 2011, a $7,000 "Super Visa" to push a family of immigrants to the top of the line. Dual citizens regarding their citizenship as a "life-insurance policy" were also in for it, as was the safe haven that Canada had previously been to Vietnam draft dodgers, effectively closed to American "war resisters." The battery of assaults upon the country's Charter of Rights and Freedoms was ongoing, its evangelical substitute being the Harper Government's very Christian promotion in 2011 of an Office of Religious Freedoms. And, of course, essential to the whole enterprise was the dismantling of the Gun Registry on the pretext that having a Canadian seek a licence for his semi-automatic, armour-piercing rifle or other military assault weapons was tantamount to treating owners "like criminals," hindering them in their right to shoot grouse. The unregulated encouragement of Canadian citizens, mostly rural and white, wanting guns and rifles within reach served the project of Canada's militarization in obvious ways, but it was the upending of the myth and the apparatus of Canadian peacekeeping—the pre-eminent emblem of the country's liberal humanitarianism—that was, by the end of the last decade of the twentieth century, the matter of greatest urgency. Canada the Good—the benign soft power with pride of place at the United Nations—became, by 2006, a "warrior nation" exhibiting nothing but disdain for the UN-brokered peace operations that it used to participate in. It became a country in which the *sine qua non* of any assessment at all of the prior version of Canada was a debunking even by sensible moderates of the merits of UN peace operations. "The comforting stereotype of the blue-beret wearing, non-violent Canadian peacekeeper" was, wrote *Calgary Herald* columnist Valerie Fortney, an "antiquated notion at best." The high estimation in which Canadians held their peacekeepers was, wrote Stein and Lang in *The Unexpected War*, "a public perception that ignored Canada's long military history."

This was an astonishing turnaround.

Government and the military but also religious and civilian groups initiate propaganda—the stories that are deployed, or already exist, entrench a message or push a society in a specific direction. In effect, all propaganda follows the same course. An idea is cultivated with a particular objective. The stories that are the vehicles of the idea are seized upon by portions of the public that, convinced by it, spread the information willingly. The new idea takes root all on its own.

In our present hyper-narrated world, social networks and the published views of the media are a useful measure of how not just the content but also the *tone* of stories is used to introduce a new societal message. Journalists, academics, politicians, teachers, clerics, artists and even the odd celebrity make up the "lobby" behind the myths that purport to bind us. They are, in today's terminology of the Web, the "gatekeepers" of the stories and points of view that shape our sense of self and politics. Not only how often but how they choose to express the stories that enable the propagandistic idea, whose opinions are sought out and elevated, matters. Sometimes the members of these professions are evidently allied, acting deliberately and in concert toward the desired political or social end. At other times, the allegiance is inadvertent but acts as a catalyst in the process of "national formation" anyway.

The change of course that Canada took after 2001 was the result of a series of decisions made by government in the face of the "Global War on Terror," the most important of these having been the elevation of the Canadian Forces and the determination to find them combat work. But it was the new emphases on ritual, the idea of the hero and the country's military history that made the Forces' new ascendancy possible. Although the change was politically led, journalists as well as academics, contributing regularly to the editorial pages of Canadian newspapers, played their own significant role. The changes in the way that the country has commemorated Remembrance Day over the course of the last ten years, more so the manner in which they have been reported, provide a benchmark of altered social attitudes (and of others that were imposed), though it is the extolling of the story of the Canadian Expeditionary Force and its troops' performance in the First World War that is the most accurate barometer of the country's turn-of-the-century passage.

A curtailed recollection of Canadian military history of the First World War provided, from 2001, expedient means of eradicating the peacekeeping myth that had lain at the root of the Canadian public persona for so long. As a catalyst of national revisionism and of patriotic fervour, the story of the First World War was so useful that its helpful influence would come, in time, to be known as the "Vimy Effect." The phrase was one that Gen. Rick Hillier coined in 2007 and used before the Conference of Defence Associations and on the speaking circuit. He would again in 2010 in *Leadership: 50 Points of Wisdom for Today's Leaders,* the general's opportune business book follow-up to his 2009 memoir of Afghanistan (*A Soldier First: Bullets, Bureaucrats and the Politics of War*). In that book, Hillier extolled the historical moment as one in which not only did Canadian soldiers perform so admirably, but the leadership of the CEF was "visible, involved and committed." Vimy provided a model for the new Canadian Forces that had previously "meandered aimlessly, perceived as essentially just another department of government." Prior to Vimy, writes Hillier, "Canadians rarely fought as one entity, under one commander" and "did not have the credibility and say in shaping the affairs of the world commensurate with our sacrifice. In Vimy we did, and the consequent signature by Canada on the Treaty of Versailles to end the First World War." This international political clout, rather than the enactment of citizens' ideals, was the peak to be attained—the promise of the old doctrine of Canadian imperialism, in which the country delivers troops to the imperial power for what it imagines to be greater influence on decisions in the foreign policy realm typically concluded elsewhere. No matter, in Hillier's own words, as soon as the Second World War, the Canadians were again being "much ignored by the rest of the world." The delusion persists. Previously, declared Hillier, the country had "frittered away Canadian impact through 'contributions' to larger missions." The Canadian Forces, Hillier complained, "put whole battle groups into the Balkans—thousands of soldiers along with naval and air forces—but we did it in such a way as to be practically invisible." It was the incompletely remembered story of the First World War that was the inspiration and the model. The possibility that, as a perennial mistake of lesser powers, servility would once again be mistaken for a meaningful place at the table was beyond the eager general's reckoning. No matter that the later battles of Amiens and of the Canal du Nord, fought by the CEF during the country's "Hundred Days" offensive, did far more to end the war, Canadians breaking through the German Hindenburg Line, or even that the recollection of Vimy can also be seen to be nationally divisive—and not just inside Quebec. How the Battle of Vimy Ridge was won, and not what it achieved, became the guiding light of Hillier's monumentalist vision for the Canadian Forces.

Accurate or not, after 9/11, accounts of Canadian excellence in the trenches of the First World War attained the status of myth. They would come to flourish in unprecedented manner, all comment upon the war seconded to the story's transformed jingoistic purpose. Generals' and politicians' statements, newspaper punditry, the annual visit of third- and fourth-year students from Kingston's Royal Military College to the battlefields and the commemorative aspect of Remembrance Day invoke the Vimy Effect unrepentantly. Remembrance Day was once a ritual of lament for a horrid war, an honouring of the armistice that was signed on the eleventh hour of the eleventh day of the eleventh month of 1918, a moment that tapped into deep wells of human experience to make its point. The cenotaph that awaits the remains of the unnamed dead so that they may be interred with proper ritual, the wreath that Greeks and Romans offered as laurels to heroic champions and the minute's silence that serves not only as time in which to remember the dead but as a suggestion of wary vigil — of the living attending to the dead and keeping watch so that no looters or enemies dishonour them — are but a few symbolic aspects of the day's ceremonies that reach back to Ancient Greece and further. But as a result of the "Vimy Effect," now the solemn day that was born of the war to end all wars risks being no more than an advertisement and fundraiser for present ones. A politically driven memory of Vimy has been a feature of the First World War since before it was even ended (Max Aitken, not yet Lord Beaverbrook, published the votive history, *Canada in Flanders*, in 1916) and has been deliberately and repeatedly used during the decade of the Canadian Forces' war in Afghanistan to justify the military campaign and also to reconfigure the way present generations of Canadians think about armed conflict generally. The outpouring of belligerent rhetoric facilitating the deployment of Canadian troops in service of the "War on Terror" has drawn its sustenance from a strategically limited remembering of the bloody conflict that inaugurated what British historian Eric Hobsbawm later dubbed the "short century" (one that ended, in his estimation, with the fall of the Berlin Wall in 1989), the war that did not end wars but certainly ended the way they had been previously fought. The First World War introduced industrial technology and method to the job of killing on a scale and with an efficacy that had until then been unimaginable, though, unsurprisingly, arms manufacturers do not use it for PR campaigns celebrating the first of their century's boom decades. The "Great War" was a conflict that never would have been tolerated if, rather than seeping slowly through to the rest of the world through letters and newspapers and, in due course, literature, its violence had been communicated to home fronts with the television imagery and swifter, more pervasive communications that revolutionized the way conflicts have been reported since the Vietnam War.

Or such is the assumption.

Ironically, despite technological advances, the war in Afghanistan has returned to being one that is in the first instance reported in writing: in newspapers and magazines and then, eventually, in movies and books. The digital visual images of the Information Age can be transmitted instantly, but in Canada, with the notable exception of the work of CBC senior correspondent Brian Stewart, the television reporting of the war has generally amounted to little more than a channel for propaganda. Radio has been more inquiring and even subversive — able, under the radar and with the gift of minutes, to explore the views of bereaved families, dissenting soldiers and activists more easily and at length. True of long-form reporting in general, the few decent film or television documentaries that have been produced about the fighting have mostly originated in the United Kingdom (such as Sam Kiley's 2007 documentary about the Canadians in Kandahar, *Afghanistan: The Other War* and, in 2002, *Afghan Massacre: The Convoy of Death* by Irish filmmaker Jamie Doran with Afghan journalist Najibullah Quraishi), the United States (Tim Hetherington and Sebastian Junger's *Restrepo*, released in 2010) and Europe (Denmark's Janus Metz having released *Armadillo* that same year). Canadian documentaries have consistently focused, with the sort of patriotic obsequiousness that is the mark of civilian society's willing complicity with state-generated messages, on the tough work of Canadian troops and the emotional circumstances that they and their families must tolerate. (The CBC's *Life and Death in Kandahar*, a 2008 look at a military hospital, and the National Film Board's *The Van Doos in Afghanistan*, "a rare portrait of soldiers who, far too often, remain nameless," broadcast for Remembrance Day 2011, are a couple of examples.)

This limited imagination is a reflection of the influence of the government's sanctioned point of view regarding the war. It, and a policy of controlling the news through the "embedding" of reporters, is a lot of the reason for television's ineffectiveness, the cost of maintaining and insuring television crews another, but mostly the war is not broadcast (while the "reality" of inane daters, idiot teens, models, dancers, singers and clothes and makeover shoppers is) because Canadians can afford not to be interested. So removed is the experience of the majority of Canadians not just from Afghanistan but from the multitude of places in which wars are being waged that fighting operates on a mythical plane just this side of fantasy. Beyond the families of soldiers and reservists who are immediately affected, Canadians' involvement in the war is so small that an inauthentic nostalgia is one of the first emotions to influence its domestic theatre. *Hockey Night in Canada* commentator Don Cherry is today's Vera Lynn, sports grills and bars from Maple Ridge, British Columbia, to Goose Bay, Labrador (home of 5 Wing and Canada's Unmanned Air Vehicle and low-level tactical flying training) sporting his name. In the invocations that are made to Canadian military history through the language of his "Coach's Corner" tributes to the Canadian war dead between periods of *Hockey Night in Canada*, or in Cherry's appearances in the actual theatre of war, is the implication that Canadians at home, too, are committed and brave and acting as one. Today's Canada is as Olaf's younger America was—a "yearning nation," the social and political leaders of which see in war an opportunity to demonstrate "valour" and prove the "character of the country."

The story of Canada's participation in the First World War may for a long time have furnished one of the country's earliest and most enduring creation myths, but among Quebeckers and other Canadians concerned about the country's new and seemingly laissez-faire attitude towards the military, it is a schema of the country's division. And yet the conventional wisdom that Vimy provided the moment in which a true national spirit was forged, Canadians fighting together side by muddy side in the trenches of Belgium and France, is stirring enough that almost a century after it started to be told, the "Great War" continues to offer a bountiful harvest for not just politicians but painters, filmmakers, novelists and the consumers of these arts wanting to come to terms with the importance of this episode in the nation's history and its bearing upon the present day. Max Aitken, the New Brunswicker turned British MP, then newspaper baron and, in 1917, as Lord Beaverbrook, a peer of the realm, was one of the first to have recognized the mythic usefulness of the war (and not just of a mythic kind, his newspapers having profited by it immensely). Through his friendship with Sam Hughes, Canada's minister of militia and defence, Beaverbrook secured himself a position as Canadian Record Officer—as "Canadian Eye Witness"—to the CEF, publishing *Canada in Flanders* with a preface by British Secretary of State for the Colonies A. Bonar Law in which the Secretary commended his Canadian colleague for having made "the deeds of the soldiers a household word not only in the Dominion, but in the United Kingdom as well." *Canada in Flanders* was one of the very first recountings of the CEF's extraordinary exploits in which it is taught that the Canadians could have served Britain no better. Over the course of a century, this mythic story has persisted and evolved. It says that under their generals, Englishman Sir Julian Byng and Canadians Sir Arthur William Currie, Sir Richard Ernest William Turner, Malcolm Smith Mercer and Sir David Watson (another newspaper man, originally a journalist at the *Quebec Chronicle*), the soldiers of the CEF were brilliantly organized. They scored costly but important victories at the Somme, Vimy Ridge, Passchendaele and Amiens. The Canadians were exemplary soldiers, among the best on the line, distinguishing themselves through their perfection of the "creeping barrage" and other technological advances.

The absurdity of having to fight a distant war on behalf of a nation to which francophone Quebeckers belonged, at best, ambivalently made that province reluctant, but in the English-speaking part of the country, loyalty to the British cause could be assumed. "CANADA'S RALLY TO THE EMPIRE—ANSWERING THE CALL OF THE MOTHERLAND," read a headline in the *Montreal Star* beneath a two-page illustration of the "Canadian army setting sail to join the British Forces operating in Europe against the Germans." The war, said the newspaper, was "an event arousing admiration and enthusiasm throughout the British Empire and described by the British press as 'Unparalleled since William the Conqueror.'" The country's collective memory of a campaign that would eventually claim the lives of some 66, 000 of its sons and daughters (a figure including the dead of the Newfoundland Regiment) was illustrated no more eloquently than in what is, without question, the most famous anglophone Canadian literary inheritance of the First World War, Lt.-Col. John McCrae's "In Flanders Fields." The poem, written in May 1915, is thought to have been inspired by the death of a fellow soldier during the Second Battle of Ypres, and for generations, anglophone schoolchildren have memorized its poignant lines:

We are the Dead. Short days ago
We lived, felt dawn, saw sunset glow,
Loved, and were loved, and now we lie
In Flanders fields.

Today, the much anthologized poem is an integral part of Remembrance Day ceremonies from Canada to Australia. Its reference to blowing poppies inspired a New Yorker, Moina Michael, to campaign in 1920 for the red flower to be worn in memory of the multitudes who had lost their lives in the European carnage. The symbol of the poppy was quickly adopted in Canada and then in Britain, France and the United States on the strength of the poem's indisputably moving qualities. And yet, no matter how affecting, the truth of the poem is that it is not in the least bit subversive. "In Flanders Fields" is a romantic lyric that may deplore the casualties of the war or, in its admonition to the living not to "break faith with us who die" demonstrate a measure of anger, but the overall effect is of a poem that supports the war's cause. This aspect is consistent with the bulk of Canadian poetry of the First World War that Donna Coates, a playwright and scholar of Commonwealth war literature, has argued reflects "a remarkably uniform naïveté, overflowing with expressions of loyalty to Britain and an overriding confidence that the Empire can easily repulse the Germans." The poems, writes Coates, "feature a surfeit of patriotic slogans and an excess of praise—for Canadian soldiers' great deeds on behalf of freedom of liberty; for Canadian victories at Ypres, Vimy Ridge or at Langemarck; for the strength and bravery of the mothers and wives who "give" their sons to battle [and] for the growing self-reliance and maturity of Canada as a nation." Little of the horror of actual trench warfare is portrayed.

There are moments in the Canadian literature of the period in which the experience of war finally does rise above the immediate task of bearing elegiac witness to the consideration of what is at play, to reflections from some more abstract plane. L. Moore Cosgrave, a lieutenant-colonel in the Canadian Field Artillery, shows how the patriotic fire of war as it was experienced by the CEF evolved into pathos and even regret in his *Afterthoughts of Armageddon: The Gamut of Emotions Produced by the War, Pointing a Moral That Is Not Too Obvious* (1919), but such meditations are few and far between. Cosgrave chronicles how the Canadian Corps' "personal hate" for Germans turned, over time, to "impersonal loathing." After the war, he writes that "our souls struggled to present to our frail mortality the true perspective of right and wrong, of that greater humanity which the Supreme Being was struggling to convey to a strangely distorted world." But his belief that the Canadian troops, though numerically inferior, were "infinitely superior in morale—our knowledge of the right and our God-given power of justice, as bearers of the Torch, handed us to carry on, from those martyred comrades of 1914 and 1915," put his work firmly in the camp of anglophone Canadian eulogies, poems, novels and memoirs that made of the First World War the template of valorious experience against which all subsequent Canadian military endeavours should be compared.

If the poetry and journals of the time took a narrow view, later there was a different recounting of events. While no Canadian poet or novelist has come close to inventing a soldier harbouring anything close to the fury of E.E. Cummings's objecting Olaf, there is plenty of troubled feeling in feeling in Harrison's distressing 1930 novel of life in the trenches, *Generals Die in Bed* and, the work of a subsequent generation, the Nova Scotian poet Alden Nowlan's poem "Ypres: 1915." Nowlan, who was born in 1933 and died at the age of fifty, was ambivalent about the role that Canadian soldiers had played in the First World War and described his poem as "a dialogue between the brain and the guts, the cerebral and the visceral." In one of the best Canadian poems ever to have been written, Nowlan's narrator says,

> *I know they were mercenaries*
> *in a war that hardly concerned us*
> *I know all that*

skeptical about the nationalist myths derived from the battle but moved by the courage of his compatriots. They are men such as he would have known in the Atlantic provinces, a region that has continued to provide so many recruits to the Canadian Forces. Soldiers such as —

> *Private MacNally thinking:*
> *You squareheaded sons of bitches,*
> *you want this God damn trench*
> *you're going to have to take it away*
> *from Billy MacNally*
> *of the South end of Saint John, New Brunswick.*

> *And that's ridiculous, too, and nothing*
> *on which to found a country*
> *Still*
> *It makes me feel good, knowing*
> *that in some obscure, conclusive way*
> *they were connected with me*
> *and me with them.*

The muscular musings of Nowlan's narrator express a tension and conflicted feelings that intelligent debate about war should engender, but that is almost nowhere to be found in today's remarkably consensual attitudes toward the country's participation in a conflict occurring, in Afghanistan, too distantly for its repercussions to be felt with any real gravity by Canadians. The ambivalence of "Ypres: 1915," its genuinely human qualities of doubt—and, most of all, the reservation that the quality of might is "nothing on which to found a country"—gives the poem at best a supporting role in the national myth-making enterprise that has helped to pave Canada's path to Afghanistan, though it is disinterred on many websites and blogs every Remembrance Day, nonetheless.

Nowlan's poem and the many novels of the First World War written over the course of the last half-century reflect Canada's evolving view of itself and the role that the ebb and flow of military action has played in the country's political maturation. Timothy Findley's *The Wars* (1977) is still one of the most important of these. The novel tells the story of Robert Ross, a well-to-do Torontonian who enlists out of guilt because of what he imagines to have been his role in his crippled sister's death. It uses Ross's affinity for animals, horses especially, to convey the monstrous brutality of the so-called "Great War." In a plethora of later Canadian novels, the inhuman ghastliness of the war, rather than the "glory" of it, is remembered. The horrors of the front are chronicled along with the disappointments and challenges that confront the soldier when eventually he returns home. In Jack Hodgins's *Broken Ground* (1999), the disappointment of home is cruelly augmented as the demobbed veterans are given the dubious reward of desultory allotments on Vancouver Island needing to be cleared with explosives that remind the returned soldiers of the hell they left behind. In Allan Donaldson's *Maclean* (2005), a soldier returns to his New Brunswick milling town and to the misery of not fitting in, cheap alcohol his escape.

The year of the last book's publication was one in which Canadian troops were first deployed to Kandahar and started to be fully embroiled in a combat role in the war in Afghanistan, saw an extraordinarily artful reworking of Canada's mythic recounting of the First World War in the acclaimed and bestselling *Three Day Road* by part-Ojibwa Joseph Boyden. *Three Day Road* brilliantly interweaves the country's Aboriginal story with the larger and more widely accepted white, Anglo-Saxon Canadian one. The novel owes some of its genesis to the story of Francis Pegahmagabow, a Cree sniper from Northern Ontario who became the most decorated Aboriginal soldier of the Great War but returned home to poverty and bigotry. The terror of the battlefield and the impossibility of return to the prior world are themes the novel shares with much of the Canadian First World War literature that preceded it, but it is the seminal inclusion of Aboriginal accomplishment in his recounting of the war that distinguishes the novel. Boyden's pair of Aboriginal sharpshooters, Xavier and Elijah, take their rightful historical place at the core of the popular foundation myth that tells of Canadians having discovered themselves in the fulcrum of battle, the country's excellence on the battlefield and its selfless contribution to the fighting of "just" wars.

Two years later, the latter notion was reaching its public apogee, the honouring of Canadian soldiers' service in the First World War having attained a grim appropriateness at the ninetieth anniversary of the Battle of Vimy Ridge and the rededication of the Canadian National Vimy Memorial. A towering piece of sculpture designed by Walter Allward, the Memorial took eleven years to build and was finally unveiled in 1936 on a piece of the ridge that had been awarded, after the war, by the grateful French nation to Canada in perpetuity. (The gift was an easy one to make, of devastated forest ground rendered useless by buried ordnance.) The Memorial may well be the most stirring monumental tribute to the military history of the country anywhere, outside of continental Canada certainly. Its restoration was started in May 2001, six months before 9/11, and finished six years later in time for the spring ceremony. The rededication was attended, among others, by Canadian students and a children's choir taking part in the day's activities, Queen Elizabeth II and Prince Philip, Duke of Edinburgh, French prime minister Dominique de Villepin, and Canadian prime minister Stephen Harper, who described Vimy Ridge as "a creation story" explaining the country. Six soldiers having died the day before the memorial's rededication, Harper made a respectable but also martially handy link between the Canadian fatalities in Afghanistan and the commemoration that he was attending—his invocation of the Canadian public's duty to remember, and to act, writes Margaret MacMillan in *The Uses and Abuses of History* (2008), hovering "between praise and condemnation." Dutifully, the media stepped in line. "Bugles both call soldiers to arms and lay them to rest," went the editorial in the *Winnipeg Free Press*. "In Canada today, they sound the battle cry for Afghanistan for the same good reasons that they have always called Canadians into battle. The nation built by those who fell in France so long ago will not today walk away from Afghanistan." The soldiers, said the *Ottawa Citizen*, "were trying to introduce the quintessential Canadian values of peace, order and good government...they were not in Afghanistan as conquerors. That would not be the Canadian way."

The invocation of "quintessential values" served to suggest a righteous war and exoneration from responsibility for the casualties and dangers that, despite the soldiers' death toll, were mostly being suffered by an Afghan civilian population. The invasion of Afghanistan, whatever the "good reasons" for it, was marked from its beginning by a vastly disproportionate rate of Afghan civilian deaths and casualties to those of the ISAF alliance. (Afghan deaths were estimated, by October

2010, to have numbered somewhere between 11,443 and 14,240 and as many as another 20,000 caused indirectly, compared to 153 Canadians and a total of 2,095 coalition dead during the same period.) And yet, no matter how arguable its proposal, the newspapers' appeal to "the Canadian way" was a failsafe. The country's commitment to the new war may have been hard to assess, the reasons for its undertaking altered as the context required, but the old one was a constant, its invocation of an ipso facto branding of the Afghanistan war as "just." The Canadian making the connection could, as even the troubled Alden Nowlan did in "Ypres: 1915,"

> *feel good, knowing*
> *that in some obscure, conclusive way*
> *they were connected with me*
> *and me with them.*

Such were the sentiments behind *Passchendaele*, a feature film based on the eponymous battle that was shooting in Alberta in 2007. (It premiered at the 2008 Toronto International Film Festival.) In time its director, Paul Gross, would be awarded the Order of Canada for his interpretation of the four-month campaign in which 15,000 of the Canadian Corps' approximately 100,000 troops were killed or wounded for their part in a series of battles that took eight kilometres of territory at a total cost of 140,000 Allied soldiers' lives, land won back by the Germans five months later. Gross, who also wrote the script, adhered to the conventional Canadian presentation of the First World War battle, also known as the Third Battle of Ypres, in which the Canadians proved so effective that the Germans dubbed them "storm troops," an accolade generally attributed to British prime minister David Lloyd George. After the Battle of the Somme, Lloyd

George wrote that "the Canadians played a part of such distinction that thenceforward they were marked out as storm troops; for the remainder of the war they were brought along to head the assault in one great battle after another. Whenever the Germans found the Canadian Corps coming into the line they prepared for the worst." The epithet can also be found in a speech made by one Capt. J.B. Paulin, a chaplain from Hamilton, to the Empire Club of Canada in Toronto in May 1918. In his magisterial two-volume work, *At the Sharp End: Canadians Fighting the Great War 1914-1916* (2007) and *Shock Troops: Canadians Fighting the Great War 1917-18* (2008), Tim Cook, the country's premier historian of the military of the period, notes the numerous accounts of the Canadians' "swagger and nonconformity," the humour and better and more varied education of troops that would, at Vimy, put such a thorn in the Germans' side that Crown Prince Rupprecht would wonder, "Is there any sense in continuing the war?" The CEF earned the trust and the admiration of British officers—this to the point that at least one among them, Fourth Army Commander Sir Henry Rawlinson, would write that the Canadians were "my chief anxiety as they have the most difficult job"—performed at a terrible cost. "No Man's Land perfectly symbolized the futility of the Great War," writes Cook. "Only the rotting dead could hold this blasted landscape." The losses at Passchendaele were, said Granatstein, a "black hole" in the nation's memory, though that did not stop him or Paul Gross from jumping into the shallow waters of pap and sloshing around in it. "Who we are was actually forged in those battlefields," Gross told the *Toronto Star*. The country's inadequate teaching, since the 1970s, of its military history was "to our detriment," said Gross to the *National Post*. Reiterating Jack Granatstein's line, the actor-cum-director argued this pedagogical development had contributed to Canada's soldiers becoming peacekeepers rather than infantries when the truth of our legacy was that "we were ferocious fighters, the most feared of the Allied troops."

The movie's championing of such an *un*controversial interpretation of the battle was apparent, too, in what the film chose to omit. In his memoir of the First World War, *Good-Bye to All That*, British writer Robert Graves, a poet, mythologist and essayist (and briefly commander of the young Canadian recruit Lester B. Pearson), remarks that "the troops that had the worst reputation for acts of violence against prisoners were the Canadians." He remembers one Canadian soldier who said, "I was sent back with three bloody prisoners, you see, and one was limping and groaning, so I had to keep kicking the sod down the trench. He was an officer. It was getting dark and I was getting fed up so I thought 'I'll have a bit of a game.' I had them covered with the officer's revolver and I made them open their pockets. Then I dropped a Mills' bomb in each with the pin out and ducked behind a traverse. Bang! Bang! Bang! No more bloody prisoners. No good Fritzes but dead 'uns."

A critic of military culture might have seen in this anecdotal re-membrance, and in other examples of Canadian maltreatment of prisoners corroborated in diaries and suppressed inquiries, in the suggestion of CEF soldiers shooting surrendering Germans at the Battle of Arras in the novel *Generals Die in Bed* or in the allegation of their participation in an (unproven) massacre by Allied troops of some 150 Germans taken prisoner during the Dieppe Raid of the Second World War that Mark Bourrie describes as covered up in his 2011 book, *The Fog of War: Censorship of Canada's Media in World War Two*, incidents that may be peripheral or considered a cultural precedent for Canadian soldiers in Afghanistan handing over detainees rather than bothering with "more bloody prisoners." The darker connection to be made between a series of incidents may not be the "truth," but any myth-making enterprise depends upon a highly selective reading of the past and, in this case, of the Canadians' First World War story. Not just an explanation of valour may be found in it. But in the myth, as Gross and the popular recounting of the present day would have it, neither soldiers' occasional bad behaviour, the dissidence of Québécois, nor the egregiously bloody wasting of the Newfoundland Regiment (fighting for Britain, and not yet as Canadians) is included in the chronicling of an historical moment that, goes the modern lore, defines "who we are." Instead, *Passchendaele* alludes to the Christmas Truce and, in its climactic scene, to the historically dubious story of a Canadian soldier's crucifixion as part of its romantic imagery. (The latter, writes American author Paul Fussell in *The Great War in Modern Memory* [1975], was "a well-known rumour imputing vileness to the Germans" and denied by Currie but inevitably perpetuated in rumour by relatives proclaiming "their" man to have been the Crucified Canadian.) Sgt. Michael Dunne—the character Gross plays—jumps out of the trenches to retrieve a soldier who has been hurled onto a cross of debris erected in No Man's Land, close to the German line, by the force of an exploded shell. Mimicking, also, Christ's stumbling along the Via Dolorosa, Dunne drags the crucified soldier through the water and mud home and to dignity, saving the young man's life (though not his own) as the Germans, moved to silence, hold their fire.

The movie's message of superior Canadian tactics, of the soldiers' valour and ability—and, of course, of the nation being born out of the hell of the trenches of the Great War—was supported in an education guide published by the Dominion Institute as part of its "Passchendaele in the Classroom" initiative for teachers using the film as an educational tool in schools. "Of all the Allied armies, the Canadians were the most feared," Gross writes in it, repeating the popular view that the war represented the country's "coming of age" and that "our notion of what it means to be Canadian was forged in the crucible of the Western Front." The message was an unabashed reflection of the patriotic one that, ever since the start of the war in Afghanistan, has been insisted upon almost anywhere the Canadian turned. Resistance to this quintessential piece of history as propaganda was exceptional, few daring to take issue as, in other countries, historians Niall Ferguson (in *The Pity of War*, 1998) and Adam Hochschild (in *To End All Wars*, 2011) were doing. The credibility of the reigning "master narrative" of the First World War—a hyped story that the Germans do not believe, the Americans pay no attention to and the British are not much interested in—was never in question.

So much, then, for Canadian performance on the battlefield winning the nation kudos, whether in Afghanistan or during the First World War—this sort of reasoning having been offered long before Hillier argued for it as an incentive to fight to a country not quite understanding the challenges of its lesser position in the rivalry of states. Typical of the time, Capt. Alex Ketterson of the CEF writes in his introduction to an anthology of veterans' poetry published in 1918, *On Active Service: Ideals of Canada's Fighting Men* (one that included the work of chaplain Capt. J.B. Paulin), of his companion soldiers having made the "supreme sacrifice." Their deaths, however, would

> solidify and strengthen the sentiments of loyal adhesion to the Motherland. As a result of the present European War, there will be a closer bond of union between Great Britain and her Dominions beyond the seas. Young men from every part of the British Empire have been comrades in arms. They have fought and died in a common cause, and are buried side by side on a foreign field. That will be an indissoluble bond between the various parts of the Empire in years to come. *The noble Dead! Gallant soldiers, what a glorious death; brave Crusaders, you have died in a noble cause!*

Whatever the pronouncements of Lloyd George—who, as a leader of Empire, was very conscious of the benefit to Britain of a willing nation and its armed forces in the Motherland's service—no such thing ever happened. "The Great War was Canada's war of independence," writes Tim Cook in *Shock Troops*, its signature separate from Britain's at the Treaty of Versailles revealing "that something had changed between the two countries"—a judgment with which many other historians, including the reputable Margaret MacMillan, have concurred. But the relationship was one of fealty and economics as much as common cause. Canadians may be buried side by side with Britons in Flanders' foreign field but remain as disregarded by the politicians and media of Britain and the United States as they were a century ago. And yet the "master narrative" persists. Canadian officers imagine their place in Empire, whether one that is British or American or called NATO, believing that their country's "noble dead" will forge an "indissoluble bond for years to come." That Canada might chart its own way and win respect through a course of its own design is a possible future undermined by the narration of a historical episode in which the only reasonable validation of the stupendous waste of young Canadian men and women's lives is to be found in upholding the war, as Hillier does, for "how the fight was won, not necessarily what it achieved"; in and revelling in the *manner* of our soldiers' contribution to various First World War battles' meaningless results, and, later, that of the ISAF campaign in Afghanistan. Not only were the dead noble, gallant and glorious, they were *ingenious*. No matter that only yards were gained and then lost. No matter that our sovereigns in the bloody field do not believe the story, were they even to be interested in it. A story of disgraceful, senseless industrial murder that eventually fatigued even its perpetrators becomes, instead, one of resourcefulness and triumph in which living, Canadians are able to take pride. The result is immaterial.

Maj. John R. Grodzinski, a member of Lord Strathcona's Horse (the Royal Canadians) who teaches at the Royal Military College in Kingston, Ontario, is one of the few Canadians to have challenged the story of Vimy Ridge as it is recounted by Granatstein, Bercuson and innumerable others, such as say, David Houghton, the president of the Vimy Foundation, who describes the battle as "our Bunker Hill, our Alamo." Those two battles were both actually losses—the first by the Americans in their fight with the British and the latter one a devastating defeat in which all but two of some 250 Texan defenders were killed by the Mexican army—but the purpose of mythic stories such as these is inspiration rather than discomfiting truth, and the Canadian battle to which the two were being compared was, in the words of Andrew Powell, one of the Vimy Foundation's patrons, "a ready-made legend, just waiting" for a country in need of them. Grodzinski, less easily swayed, argued in the *Canadian Military Journal* in 2009 that "Britain enjoys a lively scholarship on the Great War that is perhaps more honest and soul-searching than that being conducted in Canada," wondering why Canadians find comfort in such master narratives even when bona fide research contradicts them. He describes the Canadian foundation myth that is so appealing to Gross, Granatstein et al. attributes the First World War slaughter "to the incompetence of senior military commanders, indifferent to the soldier's fate and ignorant of their profession," while at Vimy Ridge, an equally important aspect of the story, "the Canadian Corps demonstrated superior martial skills by taking a feature that had eluded both the French and British armies, and, in doing so...gave birth to a national identity." The Canadian "storm troopers" bested their British colleagues, whose officers are typically characterized as pompous, snobbish and arrogant (as they very likely were).

But these stories of Canadian technical excellence are either disputed by the British or simply not told. The same historical moment demands from Canada's superiors in the hierarchical relationship the country had with Britain that interpreters and myth-makers, serving the motherland's national purpose, downplay anything the former colonies may have achieved because of the postulation of Canada's better ability exists as a kind of subordination. (Where revolutions are not the catalyst, praise such as Lloyd George bestowed—and other rewards such as forgiveness or even independence—are gifts granted by authorities previously denying them. No matter the struggle or, in the Canadian case, the grand demonstration of loyalty that may have led to them, they are acts of largesse awarded by other foreign bodies.) Grodzinski admonishes, very much against the grain, that

> success was achieved, not by "donkeys," but by a hard-
> working leadership determined to overcome the stalemate
> of the trenches. We owe it to those who fell to come to grips
> with what happened. This demands hard work and study,
> discussion and debate, rather than the simplistic popular
> accounts that plague military history. Otherwise, we are
> truly leading ourselves down a very dangerous road...
> We must understand how perspectives have evolved, and
> encourage new and original research, free of nationalistic
> "baggage," in order to gain a better appreciation of what
> actually happened. In that way, we will find some of the
> answers we are looking for that may help guide on [sic]
> the challenges ahead.

We have a duty to be honest and rigorous, with ourselves and with others, and to be able to brook contradiction and argument in our discussions of past wars and the present one in Afghanistan. But instead, in today's Canada, we have arrived at a point where the use of any language that is not euphemistic is greeted as an assault on the work of soldiers, on a singular view of our past, and therefore on the character of the nation itself. Ideology thrives. History hardly comes into it.

To the media and academics that held the keys to the new realm, Canada the war-fighting nation was simply more exciting. Come 2001, the news from Afghanistan loomed, as it did for soldiers, as a great adventure. A lot of force was applied to the impetus of change if only for the banal reason that the altered course that the country took after 9/11 was new. It offered not just a change of political direction but an invigorating array of new takes on overly familiar Canadian leitmotifs, ones previously tried and tested though reported to exhaustion. The old Canadian themes—the Canada of Lester B. Pearson and Pierre Elliot Trudeau, Canada as the place of rescue—had become tedious; the new ones providing purchase to an eager, irrepressible but also acrimonious bunch of academics and journalists offered a way out of their limbo by the fight. War makes reporters feel useful, that their job and their broadcasts might actually be helping. War is the once-in-a-lifetime opportunity that makes careers and reputations. It offers the academic and the stay-at-home columnist the opportunity to opine on matters of grave importance. War provides invigorating opportunity for older, established journalists who would otherwise risk growing stale in a repetitive cycle of news—psychotic killers, cheating celebrities and lying politicians, they all come around—and the possibility of a breakthrough for neophytes and others wanting to stake a reputation. Being able, instead, to reflect on the horrors of war with the authority of a front-line posting is why a plethora of journalists endure years of reporting from City Hall or the courts or writing from some rural backwater until the chance arrival of that special break. Rare, if he or she exists at all, is the foreign correspondent who does not want to report from a war zone and to have experienced, in first person, the character-defining times. War bestows upon the front-line journalist the chance to wear its badges, suffer its extremes of feeling and be able to tell the stories and write the book afterwards. Dangerous as it occassionally is, it offers the opportunity to have had the *fun*. It is work that influential columnist Christie Blatchford, writing for the *National Post* in 2006, declared to be infinitely preferable to the beat in Ottawa, "where politicians blow smoke up one another's bums for a tedious time." (Blatchford moved from the *National Post* to the *Globe and Mail* in 2003 and then back to the *National Post* in 2011.) In Ottawa, wrote Blatchford, "you can always just grab a cab to go wherever you like, whenever you like, and the greatest potential risk you take is that of a latte burn." What, in the capital or in Toronto, where Blatchford lived, was there to compare with the singular thrill of war reporting that would surely leave her, in Afghanistan as it had done in Bosnia, "grateful and trembling to be alive, but desperate to live too, to suck out every last bit of juice, feel every possible feeling." Like a night on the town, only this one a community wrenched by war, Blatchford remembers Bosnia in her book, *Fifteen Days: Stories of Bravery, Friendship, Life and Death from Inside the New Canadian Army* (2007), for feeling "gloriously alive" and wanting "to dance all night in the appalling, glittery disco in the basement of the hotel, drink my face off, smoke like a chimney, lie beside a man and feel arms around me."

War provides its own perverse pleasures: the taste of exceptional experience, the thrill of involvement, a leg-up over the routine experiences of ordinary lives left behind. War, or at least the start of it, is as exciting for journalists as it is for combatants—a *fix*. Most reporters are mum on this score, a couple of exceptions to the trend having been heroin-addicted English journalist Anthony Loyd, author of a memoir of working in Chechnya and Bosnia called *My War Gone By, I Miss It So* (2001), and Canadian photojournalist Paul Watson, whose gripping account of his own manic, adrenalin-addicted and ultimately debilitating years on the front line, *Where War Lives*, was published in 2007. (Watson snapped the iconic photograph of the body of American staff sergent William David Cleveland being dragged through the streets of Mogadishu, Somalia, in 1993 and found himself grievously atoning for his action for years.)

Hence there are exclusive clubs for front-line correspondents and, as with any such clubs, members who cultivate their special aspects and segregate themselves from those who have not undergone the proper matriculation. CBC Radio's off-putting habit of having one journalist speak to another in solemn tones about just how risky and hard on the family front-line reporting is also serves to uphold the exclusivity and adventure of war. As statistics show, the reporting of war really has become a lot more dangerous over the last couple of decades, partly because journalists are no longer thought by combatants to be playing a neutral, let alone helpful, role. And yet most reporters would still jump at battlefield work. At the distant, troubled margins of society is the No (Ordinary) Man's Land in which human character, one's own or that of strangers, is put under a bright, shining light. The war beat is about as close to this illumination and near to being a hero that the reporter gets, the chance of the "something special" that, said Lt.-Col. Pat Stogran of the Princess Patricia's Canadian Light Infantry (PPCLI), should not be seen to be "slipping away." (Stogran was, in later years, appointed to the post of Veterans Affairs ombudsman and would again speak publicly about the war in Afghanistan—though not so positively and so would be heard from less.) In 2002, the PPCLI comprised the first regular troops to have embarked on a Canadian combat mission since the Korean War, a half-century prior. "We were like a pack of rabid pit bulls," said Stogran, "a bunch of crazy Canadians." Said Maj. Mike Blackburn, a fellow officer, "Let's be honest. Some of the training or garrison activities we might be doing when we get home, it's not Kandahar. It's not Afghanistan—it's not *real*."

Many journalists evidently felt the same way. Journalists' relish and high regard for what they are doing is why Andrew Cohen, previously a correspondent with the *Globe and Mail* but executive director of the Historica-Dominion Institute at the time, mocked the unfortunate aspiring Canadian freelance journalist Amanda Lindhout, kidnapped in Somalia in August 2008 and released fifteen months afterwards, in a column in the *Ottawa Citizen* in December 2009. Wrote Cohen: "Perhaps now she'll write a book. Or make a movie. Or become foreign editor of *The New York Times*. You see, she's a journalist. Anyone can do it." His condescension underscored the exclusivity of the club that established correspondents reserve for themselves, even in the digitally enabled social networking age, when just about anyone can crash the front gates.

What Cohen meant, of course, was that *not* anyone can do it—strivers, certainly not. Whatever are the accomplishments of reporters without accreditation and operating without both the security and the restraints that the embedded reporter knows (privileges and restrictions about which the public is not informed), those working outside the rules of conventional journalism merit only reluctant consideration, if any at all, by the Old School. Independent journalist Scott Taylor, an Ontario College of Art & Design graduate and low-ranking soldier in the Canadian Forces for many years before he became publisher of the Ottawa-based military magazine *Esprit de Corps* and author of the war memoir *Unembedded* (2009), is another case in point. Taylor made a documentary, *Afghanistan: Outside the Wire*, with *Ottawa Citizen* defence correspondent David Pugliese, one of the most reputable in his field in Canada. But, working outside of the normal strictures, Taylor tends to be spoken of suspiciously, if not disparagingly, by other journalists so that it is hard not to suspect a certain resentment of the hidebound in their talk.

Short of a tragic outcome, war reporting is as much of a thrill to the correspondent as it is to soldiers such as Sgt. Ed Wadleigh, knowing "that *we were there*—and those who weren't will either forever wish they had been, or at least will never understand what exactly *there* means." Even Michelle Lang, the *Calgary Herald* reporter who died with four soldiers "outside the wire" in Afghanistan in 2009, was "there" because she chose to be, not because she was told to be. She was a "beautiful soul," wrote her former colleague Don Martin of the *National Post* in a piece praising intrepid journalists while excoriating "MPs, Ministers and Governor Generals" who "rarely experience the true grit of combat." Lang, it is fair to assume, *wanted* to be in Afghanistan. "Making a difference" would have been one reason, as it would have been for Tim Hetherington, the award-winning British photojournalist who was killed in Libya during the "Arab Spring" of 2011, a year and a half after making *Restrepo*, an Academy Award-nominated documentary about the life of a U.S. Army platoon in a massively dangerous forward posting in Afghanistan. But this motive would have been inextricable from the certainty that Lang loved her job and found the work special and exciting. Front-line correspondence is traumatic and distinguished and on occasion dangerous. The consequences of journalists finding it so and, in an embedded situation, of their (and their employers') wanting to keep the door open to reporting from the field again, affects the national narrative and therefore political outcomes. It is this thrill of the new beat that, in concert with decision-making in Ottawa, has been the foremost catalyst of Canada's shift away from the country that it had been before the events of September 2001. Politicians were the primary decision-makers, certainly, and well-placed military lobbyists in academia and think-tanks played a major role, but the excitements of journalists were also a major factor.

We are co-opted by institutions—and by ourselves.

If the personal motivations and excitements of journalists proved an inadvertent boon in the selling of the cause of the war in Afghanistan (soldiers' excitements are to be expected), the calendar institution of Remembrance Day was always going to be their organizing moment. Originally Armistice Day, commemorating the end of hostilities of the First World War. Remembrance Day has become, in Canada, Ottawa's primary tool of persuasion, an opportunity of looking forward and of the military's present vindication, more than of the lament for which November 11 was intended. As much was revealed during the first five years of the Afghanistan campaign in which Remembrance Day became an ever more lavish show. The current producers' present staging reached its showy peak in 2011 with Hornet fighter jets flying over the War Memorial as a salute to Canadian soldiers who had participated in Operation Unified Protector, the NATO campaign against Muammar Gaddafi's Libyan regime. The Soviet Union, the countries of the Warsaw Pact and various tin-pot dictatorships have always had parades for this sort of martial tribute, but Remembrance Day in Europe and Canada was meant to have honoured an altogether different kind of sentiment. Remembrance Day, as it is currently staged, and a proliferation of ceremonies ranging from 2010's Navy Centennial Day to the rededication of the Vimy Memorial and the anniversary of 1812 to a host of lesser ones celebrating increasingly arcane moments of the country's military history have showed just how winning is the idea of military "glory," "valour" and "sacrifice" in the new Canadian "warrior nation." But not forgetting, honouring those who chose not to be bystanders at a critical moment in the history of Western civilization, also means not distorting it: looking back with the proper lens. Today, in Canada, the power and destructive capability of war is glorified over peace and the possibility of an end to a sorry paradigm in which the wiping out of nearly all of the 800 soldiers of the Newfoundland Regiment in less than half an hour at Beaumont Hamel (68 survived unscathed, 710 were killed, wounded or went missing) on July 1, 1916, during the Battle of the Somme, a willing procession to the slaughter that is rendered no more comprehensible for the footage that exists of it, is woven into the nation's "tapestry of heroism and self-sacrifice." That the carnage of the fittest of that Newfoundland generation could possibly have been interpreted by the youthful composer Jason Noble, commissioned by the province to write a choral piece for Remembrance Day 2011, as a reminder to today's young people to protect each other as fiercely as the Newfoundland Regiment did is evidence of just how skewed mythic memory can be.

As recently as 2001, the full implications of the war on terror not yet absorbed, Remembrance Day was a muted affair. Social activist and *Toronto Star* columnist Michele Landsberg asked why aid, rather than force, was not being considered in Afghanistan. She noted the $45 billion worth of arms that had been funnelled into Afghanistan during its proxy war with the Soviet Union, and that Unocal, the Union Oil Company of California that was part of a consortium wanting to build a trans-Afghanistan pipeline (and that was absorbed into Chevron, in 2005), had willingly dealt with the Taliban before 9/11. She predicted that when the war ended, the company "will be building its long-lusted after oil pipeline." The peacekeeping story was still an active part of the mythology of the nation, and the ceremony, if conflicted, had a more deferential, humble tenor. The identification of a battlefield enemy had not yet hijacked the mythic, universal aspects of Remembrance Day's commemoration and thrust upon it an epic mantle. The ceremony endeavoured, at the very least, to be inclusive in its commemorative purpose; the valour of Canadians who had lost their lives in UN operations was being mentioned in the same editorial breath as the battles of "Passchendaele and Vimy, Ortona and Juno Beach" and "Hill 677 in Korea." The ceremony had not yet started to shoulder the immediacy and the utility it would acquire during the ensuing decade and was still being used to honour Canadian soldiers in *all* of the campaigns in which they had fought. But, in that pivotal month, 1,382 of the 58,000 soldiers of the Canadian Forces were already deployed overseas, and by April of the following year, when friendly fire would claim the first four of the Afghanistan campaign's Canadian war dead, the calls for Canadians to know their history better, a euphemism for greater—and uncontroversial—public acceptance of the country's military past, were growing progressively louder and changing the way Remembrance Day would be enacted and written about. Even thoughtful, moderately minded columnists such as the *Toronto Star*'s James Travers (who died in March 2011) saw, in Canada in the wake of 9/11, a country that was overly "confident" and sheltering in the "naiveté" of its previous position as a peacekeeper and not a warrior. The country, wrote Travers, was "so smug, in the 80s and early 90s, that it dropped its guard."

On Remembrance Day 2002, the *Toronto Star* was still invoking Canada's "long tradition of contributing to peace missions [that] underscore our nation's commitment to peace" but, of the country's major media outlets, the newspaper stood more or less alone in this regard. In the *National Post*, Christie Blatchford was writing of her yearning "to be among people who love soldiers, who do not go all timorous and squeamish at the very mention of the word 'war.'" The Canadian Forces were, in Blatchford's reckoning, fighting a war on two fronts: against al-Qaeda and the Taliban in Afghanistan and against a sorry league of civilian wets at home and the military's betrayers in Ottawa. It was a marvel that the Forces were even bothering to fight for the country at all, the soldiers being "good men and women who inexplicably and against all odds and particularly despite the poisonous efforts of the federal government to render the Canadian Forces third-rate, continue to serve with bewildering distinction."

By 2003, the view that peacekeeping was the situationally irrelevant, politically useless and overstated activity of an underfunded army had gained traction and was given a credible imprimatur even by John English, the judicious and accomplished historian who may have been the country's premier political biographer, his important prime ministerial subjects including Pierre Trudeau and Lester B. Pearson himself.

"Canadian peacekeeping is not what it used to be," said English. "In truth, it never was." In an assessment of Canadian peacekeeping history presented to the CDFAI in Calgary, English declared that "the Suez dream of UN peacekeepers engaged in non-violent observation and whose presence prevented conflict crumbled in the nineties," as if supporters of peace operations were completely unaware of the setbacks to humanitarian intervention that had been brought into evidence in the Balkans, Rwanda and Somalia or, too, that a new Cold War situation (such as the world is beginning to see again but this time in the Middle East) was unimaginable. English spoke of the *Reconciliation* peacekeeping monument in Ottawa and how it

evokes the image of the peacekeeper that persists in
Canadian memory: the determined professional soldier
possessing skill, civility, and humanity who separates the
irrational forces of destruction, much as a strong referee
would do in a bantamweight boxing match. The soldier
has enough strength to push away the boxers and enough
common sense to label good and evil, danger and safety.

The image pleased Canadians, especially when they
recalled the Nobel Peace Prize that Lester Pearson won
in 1957 and the encomiums that successive UN Secretary-
Generals bestowed upon Canada for beckoning to their
calls of distress.

English was kinder than most—the job of the historian, Margaret
MacMillan has remarked, to "puncture the myths." The UN, said
English, was, in the pivotal decade of the 1990s, "seizing the moment,"
having "defined a highly activist role that would require it to expand
its role in peacemaking and peacebuilding as well as peacekeeping."
English pointed out the failures of what has come to be known as
"traditional" peacekeeping—that is, the placing of peacekeepers
between and to separate hostile forces, usually with a form of consent,
operating under a strict UN Charter Chapter VI mandate stipulating,
among other rules of engagement, that soldiers do not fire until fired
upon. In his address, English noted the bureaucratic impediments
at the UN and in Canada that hinder the making of intelligent
choices about deployment, though he recognized the goodwill and
internationalist tendencies of Canadians even as he criticized these
ideas in practice. But it was English's opening sentence, "Canadian
peacekeeping is not what it used to be; in truth, it never was," that has
proved so useful to the detractors of everything about the old Canada
that the "blue-helmet" had come to represent.

Peacekeeping is not simply about expediting a bunch of soldiers at their peril in the middle of an unsettled conflict with guns that cannot be used. It is not the blithe practice of a view of conflict resolution that has not changed in more than fifty years and not recognized that the Cold War, the global political environment that was a significant but not the sole determinant of peacekeeping's evolution, is, if only in its 1950s incarnation, ended. And yet, repeatedly, the charges have been made by a legion of critics that, in English's words, "the peacekeeper on the Sinai in 1960 faced much simpler times and tasks," that "peacekeeping has evolved to the point where demands placed on peacekeepers transcend their traditional role, rendering it virtually unrecognizable to its founders."

That the "Suez Dream" of UN peacekeepers crumbled during the 1990s—when, despite their failures, the number of operations and the international will to "make a difference" were at their height—is contestable, though it is certainly the case that Western dedication to the UN-administered style of conflict resolution faltered. By the close of the twentieth century, Canada's actual commitment to peace operations was both underwhelming and being taken for granted. Enough so that when it would come time to defend the purpose and the record of peacekeeping, few were up to the task. Enough so that the Battle of Medak Pocket that took place in Serbian-held Croatia in 1993, an engagement in which Canadian peacekeepers took fire and, contrary to the UN's "rules of engagement," fired back, was described as "Canada's secret battle" by *Ottawa Citizen* reporter David Pugliese and afterwards by CBC correspondent Carol Off in her 2005 book, *The Ghost of Medak Pocket: The Story of Canada's Secret War.* The battle was "secret" because, as Gen. Rick Hillier and many others were pointing out, the Canadian Forces had lost their connection with Canadians, and the government and the media were not paying much attention to military matters. It would take a war in Afghanistan to make people interested in Canadian war-fighting again, but even then only marginally.

For practitioners of peace operations to regard their fighting manual as static and in no need of revision, however, would be tactical idiocy. And yet this allegation was the deception at the heart of the caricature of peacekeeping that has persistently and bombastically been put forward by critics intent on endowing the country with a larger, more powerful and more proactive military. Canada, wrote Sean M. Maloney, had become "just another adjunct to a blue-helmeted, would-be world government," its descent into "irrelevancy" having taken it from a time and a place when "the UN and NATO were Canada's to use for its own interests, not the other way around." The Canadian Forces, far from the quiet but pivotal role Maloney argued they had played during the Cold War, had "drifted from their military focus to conducting fisheries patrols or counting caribou in the Arctic." From the end of the 1990s, the damning of peacekeeping became, among a coterie of military historians and fellow travellers in the media, something of a blood sport, and the game in their sights was liberal Canada, slaughtered in a moment of being caught off-guard in the clearing. It is next to impossible to find anything good at all being said about the entire history of Canadian peacekeeping in the first few years after 9/11, such was the invidious nature of this period of revisionism. Peacekeeping, where it existed, was no more and no less than an extension of the Cold War, argued Maloney, playing with Prussian Carl von Clausewitz's famous early nineteenth-century dictum in the title of his book, *Canada and UN Peacekeeping: Cold War by Other Means 1945-1970* (2002). The post-Cold War operations that Canada had undertaken in the ensuing decades were, claims Maloney, "in the main, not UN peacekeeping missions. They were mostly armed humanitarian interventions and stabilization missions, and even open warfare." The Canadian military, declared Jack Granatstein in the *Toronto Star* (typically the repository of more left wing views), "hates peacekeeping because it hurts training, it's not a fit job for a soldier in the eyes of many soldiers and because it's so unrealistic in public's expectations." Today, the prevalent slang of the Canadian Forces describes peacekeeping work as OOTW (operations other than war), though for Granatstein and his camp, the task does not even exist. "When Canada does peacekeeping," said Granatstein, "it's really doing peacemaking or peace enforcement, both of which are just synonyms for war."

But war and peace operations are discrete military ventures—because of the innately different intentions behind them and because of the nature of the army's practical involvement. In war, the military is implicated and a player in the conflict. In peace operations, the military is a third and tempering, adjudicating and sometimes (though not always) neutral force. The former is, in the words of respected international law expert Michael Byers, "a combat-oriented approach," the latter "one that focuses on negotiation, peacemaking and nation-building." This essential difference is one militarists strive to obfuscate in order to maintain the gorging viability of the war machine and aggressively expand its franchise. (The recent NATO intervention in Libya, during the 2011 Arab Spring, can be seen, what with its fortuitous promotion of the ability of Canadian fighter pilots in the skies and all the free publicity surrounding their nearly one thousand sorties, as a brilliant and timely de facto argument for Canada's planned purchase of new and controversially expensive F-35 jets.)

Beyond this distinction, however, what is in evidence in the debate that the proponents of a more nuanced role for the Canadian military appear for the time being to have lost are the optics of humanitarian interventions as they are presented in the three intimately related terms of peace*keeping*, peace-*building* and peace*making*. These three overlapping and somewhat nebulous terms have come to describe various forms of conflict resolution and the degree of force used in their execution. Peace*keeping* suggests a fragile entente, or none at all; peace-*building* describes a minimally stable society and the development work that must be done to improve it; and peace*making* suggests that there is as yet "no peace to keep" and stability is something to be wrought out of a situation through fighting. Peacemaking and peace enforcement exist as separate doctrines that may sometimes use the tools and the resources of combat. But to lump all together and call each a synonym of war is to render not just these more particular terms but also the very word *war* meaningless.

The failure to have been specific in the realm of language (peace-*making* was a lot of the work that the UN was doing in the 1990s) has not served the cause of the supporters of the Canadian commitment to multilateral and generally UN-led missions of conflict resolution at all. The use of the term *peace operations* to describe the full variety of the work in question would be a good start. By allowing the debate to be even nominally one solely about *peacekeeping*, the fiction of a dichotomy in which it is implied that peace operations and warfighting exist as incompatible undertakings in a sort of zero-sum game has been allowed to persist. The truth of the matter is that there is not a single advocate of the resumption, in some form or other, of Canada's erstwhile commitment to peace operations who believes that their pursuit should exist at the expense of a conventional standing army. And yet this continues to be the impression successfully conveyed by the militarist camp, its caricature of the naive Canadian besotted with Canada's peacekeeping legacy one of the lobby's most effective means of denying its opponents any credibility. Peacekeeping is discredited by acknowledging its history, though in tight-fisted paltry ways, and by using the lexicon to stringently, impossibly, narrow the definition of the range of work. Peace operations, in this paradigm, are not proactive as, in fact, the UN Charter's Chapters VII and VIII allow them to be. They do not involve the training of other nations' armies and officers of law enforcement, such as the Canadian Forces are presently committed to doing beyond 2011 with the Afghan National Army and Afghan National Police. They do not involve reconstruction or development tasks conducted by the military through the advancement of the Provincial Reconstruction Team (PRT)—an alliance, such as existed in Kandahar, of soldiers, diplomats and civilian workers from aid organizations (NGOs) working, under a military commander, on the "Three Ds" of defence, development and diplomacy as one coordinated group in one region. Using a word that narrows the range of peace operations to the one discredited UN Chapter VI kind has served the adversaries of "blue-helmet" work handily, as any arguments to be made about the operation that is OTW (other than war) are undermined through their very erasure. Not just peacekeeping, but an entire school of thought seeking an alternative to the bludgeon use of military force—and, most importantly of all, the popular will supporting this attitude to conflict—is whited out with the same heavy brush. Peacekeeping becomes, instead of one of an arsenal of multilateral approaches to conflict resolution, a moniker of political futility, dysfunction of the UN and the misapplication of the strengths, resources and precious lives of the Canadian Forces. The broad range of peace operations as envisioned by the UN Charter and furthered for half a century by Canada has been so constricted by denials of what it was, and also what it might have moved toward, that a gelding of UN ambition is achieved at the very same time that the definition of what the Canadian Forces have it in them to do is expanded. For, according to its critics, peacekeeping, where it operates, is something the soldier does best, though, on the other hand, nothing the soldier does can legitimately be called peacekeeping anyway. In this way, the peacekeeper is defined out of existence, for if peacekeeping does not exist and peace-building and peacemaking are no more than "synonyms for war," then war is all there is to speak of and any deference that the Department of National Defence pays toward peace operations, from conventional Chapter VI work to the RtoP kind, is a lie.

The discrediting of Canadians as peacekeepers was regarded by the military lobby as a necessary condition to send the Forces to war and to be able to restore the military's "connection" with civilians that Hillier and others believed to have been lost. Deploying troops to Afghanistan, ran the argument, would improve Canada's reputation on the international stage, restore a greater sense of purpose to the Forces and return, to the country, the robust character that critics imagined had been wasted away by fifty years of apparently useless humanitarian interventions.

By 2006, when the resurgence of the Taliban resistance in the province of Kandahar was at its peak, the effect of the fighting was to reinforce the militarists' arguments and to diminish the nature of the contribution, before the Canadian public, of soldiers in blue-helmets. Said Stephen Harper to CBC Radio One's parliamentary review program, *The House*, in September that year: "The fact of the matter is we are fighting a war in Afghanistan. We need to beat the Taliban on the battlefield." During the preceding five years, Remembrance Day mention had still been made, though with increasing difficulty, of the actions of Canadian peacekeepers. Come November 2006, David Bercuson was able to confidently announce in the *Globe and Mail* that this year the ceremony "would be different," saluting Canadian Forces "engaged in two rituals that bind them to soldiers from eons past and warriors from almost every nation on earth—they deliberately go into harm's way at the bidding of their community to kill or be killed by others whom they do not know, and whom they have nothing personal against."

How much *failure* in such military ventures binds the Canadian soldier and the ordinary citizen is uninteresting to Bercuson. The clear implication of his article is that "those who deliberately go into harm's way at the bidding of their community" without being prepared to "kill or be killed" were the country's peacekeepers. In the new construction of the Conservative, pro-Afghanistan war lobby, the Canadian soldiers who had fought in peace operations were, by the middle of the decade after 9/11, being brandished as symbols of the complacent Canada free-riding on the coat-tails of other countries' more bona fide commitments to global conflict resolution. They were a part of a country left behind by events that, wrote Bercuson, was experiencing a "new melancholy" due to a "reawakening to the world of fang and claw," unable to accept "the irony that our peaceful and democratic way of life must sometimes resort to the organized brutality of war as the ultimate means of our self-protection." A bunch of shirkers and softies, "Trudeaupian" hippies for sure, this portion of the country was still under "the long-held post-Korean War illusion that we are somehow uniquely blessed on this Earth to live in a safe nation, far from any conceivable source of danger, protected from harm by geography and the goodwill of allies." Inevitably, Bercuson's column reiterated familiar charges, and did so with an invidiousness and a ferocity typical of Conservative posturing during the first five years of the war especially. The efficacy of soldiers seconded to peace operations under the UN Charter's Chapter VI directives was derided, and these missions' supporters in civil society were blamed for putting Canadian troops in hopeless and dangerous binds and sending them into places where, according to the prevalent expression, there was "no peace to keep." The more proactive peacemaking that Chapters VII and VIII, the very next clauses of the same UN document, open the way for, was inconvenient knowledge. The revival of the Canadian military demanded a total abnegation of the liberal, humanitarian, multilateral and multicultural views that have given such impetus to peacekeeping over the preceding fifty years.

The most obnoxious of this set of beliefs was the liberal's openness to supranational government bodies of which the UN was the first and biggest emblem, its multilateral peacekeeping forces the earliest examples of such odious internationalism in practice. The openness needed to be no more than the mildest of abstract contemplations for it to arouse the ire of the military's more ardent supporters, their fury bringing to mind the hysterically funny plots about world government in fundamentalist Christian movies such as the United States' alarmingly successful Cloud Ten Pictures' *Left Behind* series, in which the UN president is, of course, the Antichrist. Along with its hallmark of hateful vitriol, the right-wing invective can be so marvellously childish as to merit a visit. Here, for instance, is what Sean M. Maloney wrote of the Canadian peace operations versus war-fighting debate:

> In one corner, with the light blue and white trunks, is the UN Supremacist. He is motivated by a belief that the UN has and should be the arbiter over how much military force should be used, and by whom, against whom. All nations should bow to the might of the UN bureaucracy, the Security Council, or, if necessary the General Assembly. He has a Canadian flag sewn on his trunks and his underwear

is made up of maple leaves, so his Canadian fans in the
crowd, many of who wear pin stripes, will champion him.
His brain has been damaged from too many shots to the
head lately from little bullies like Serbia and Iraq, and, when
he was younger, from big bullies like the Soviet Union.
Consequently, his vision is impaired. He *thinks* his opponent
is wearing a top hat, beard, and trunks spangled with the
stars and alternating bars of the United States.

In the other corner is the man in the red and white
trunks, Canada: the *real* Canada. The one who, as a young
man, beat the Kaiser's Germany, who pummeled the Third
Reich, and who stood alongside others shoulder to shoulder
for 25 years to contain the street fighter in the red jacket
with the shiv who was trying to interfere with the game and
to intimidate the audience. Though he was forcibly retired
by his owner and manager back in 1970 because he wasn't
a box office draw, and because the street fighter scared his
handlers, the man in red and white is finally back, tanned,
and fit. This boxer once saw his current UN opponent as a
tag-team fighter against the back alley hoods, fight fixers
and gangsters, but has become dismayed with the myopia
of late, especially when the UN Supremacist refused a fight
with the guy in the black turban and constantly quoted
rules and regulations to excuse himself from the ring.

And so on.

The corollaries of the dressing down of Canadians' attachment to
peace operations were the unrelenting assault upon the credibility
of the UN itself and familiar accusations that peacekeeping's liberal
proponents were inherently biased against the only state that, at the

turn of the century (this, before the 2008 economic crash and the massive expenditure in Iraq that contributed to it), was thought to be able to play the same role of global policeman, though without the dystopian bureaucracy and wrangling. The UN's Canadian proponents were, in other words, ipso facto "anti-American"—and the force suggesting the equivalence of two sentiments was the rising conservative Canadian establishment's antipathy toward any multilateral organization greater than NATO. (By 2011, even an organization with as few partners as NATO was falling into disfavour at the CDFAI, Bercuson and Granatstein at it again, praising the Canadians at the expense of other members of the ISAF and NATO alliances in "Lessons Learned? What Canada Should Learn From Afghanistan.") The International Criminal Court (ICC) used to be the prime emblem of UN internationalism operating at the expense of national sovereignty run amok though, later, the global recession thrusting economic circumstances into the fore, UN efforts at controlling climate change and the 2005 Kyoto Protocol became it. Whether in the economic realm or that of justice, panaceas for humanitarian problems of populations in which their Canada could see neither a strategic interest nor the possibility of a resolution by a body as complicated as the UN were simply to be abandoned. The effects of climate change upon migration, physical habitat and the availability of food; the surfeit of problems arising out of ethnic and regional differences are arguments for humanitarian engagement concerning democratic practice, physical security, clean water and standards of basic human decency such as are guaranteed in hospitals, schools and roads; and seemingly lesser issues such as fair trade and the need for the more equitable treatment of workers by Canadian mining companies operating in the developing world in a manner that would never be accepted on home turf: none of these merited serious consideration. In the face of these encroaching and ultimately ineluctable issues, the antagonists of the "blue-beret" version of Canada were circling the wagons and rejecting the more progressive and multilateral view of the world that, far more than "war-fighting," had been Canadians' destictive legacy in international politics and provided the country good standing. The peacekeeping idea was anathema, as was the aegis of the United Nations, the institution organizing it. The UN, declared Granatstein, was an "abject failure."

The former director's quip about being able to raise money more easily had the word *peace* been a part of the War Museum's title reverberates. In remarks such as not just Granatstein was making lay an intolerance of the UN but an evangelical hatred of anyone or any organization that dared to use the word *peace* in its formula. Peacekeeping is detestable to the supporters of an old-fashioned military because it is complicated and because it opens the door to reasonable doubt and to the sort of moral propinquity that Lt.-Col. Dave Grossman identified in *On Killing* as encouraging soldiers' "innate resistance to killing their fellow human beings." If the idea of fighting for peace was to be eradicated; if, as was stated at the beginning of the Afghanistan engagement, fighting for political advantage and a better trade relationship with the United States rather than for "Canadian values" (another detested term) was to be the war's outcome, then the liberal views that underpinned the old humanitarian tendencies needed to be destroyed, outright, and wrecking all aspects of the myths and beliefs supporting them in civil society was a necessary part of the operation. The military lobby needed the public to believe not merely that peacekeeping as it continued to be practised in so many countries was no longer appropriate but that it would *never* be appropriate. War was the task at hand, and it needed to be embarked upon with nothing less than total commitment.

As arguments about "security" and the Canadian public's negligence of the military and its apparently flagrant misunderstanding of its history failed to convince the nation at large, some historians and commentators sought to discredit peacekeeping through more specious arguments seeking to diminish the iconic figure of Lester B. Pearson in the public eye. These pundits declared, as Sean Maloney did, that when the United Nations Expeditionary Force was created in 1956 to resolve the Suez Crisis, Pearson, then the Liberal minister of external affairs, had played only a minor part in its invention—that in fact a Canadian *soldier*, Gen. E.L.M. Burns, had come up with the idea, thus putting the strategic credit back with the Forces. Or, as John English and Andrew Cohen have chronicled in their biographies, it was argued that Pearson's crisis-defusing motion to create a United Nations police force large enough to keep these borders at peace while a political settlement was being worked out was, in part, attributable to chance—that Washington had conceived of the resolution but knew that it would not be accepted by the UN were the United States to propose it. American ambassador Henry Cabot Lodge Jr., this account goes, was on his way to find the Brazilian representative, Joao Carlos Muniz, so that the non-American other might put the motion forward when, the lucky Canadian stepping out of his office at the fortuitous moment, he ran into Pearson instead.

The Liberal, habitually voted one of the top ten Canadian prime ministers—by *Maclean's* magazine, by the CBC's "Greatest Canadian" competition, by CanadianWild.ca and numerous other bloggers and list-mad websites—was, it could be said, *Pearsona non grata*. But foundation myths are stubborn things that can take generations to revise, and where these obliterating measures failed, the tactic was to press-gang Pearson into the cause—to remind Canadians, as Andrew Cohen did in *While Canada Slept, How We Lost Our Place in the World* (2004), that "Pearson was no pacifist" and had consented, during the Cuban Missile Crisis, to American nuclear warheads being stationed on Canadian soil; that, according to Sean Maloney, Pearson not only did not invent peacekeeping, the career politician taking the credit for a good soldier's work, but that the UN "did not beguile him." The relationship Pearson had with the UN was, apparently, meaningless. The truth of his close relationship with the Canadian military, one that he relied upon "to protect Canadian global interests," was that it spoke "volumes about the sophisticated outlook Canada had during a time of maximum danger." In 2008, after the Manley Report condoned Canada's extended involvement in Afghanistan, Granatstein resorted to the same subtler tactics of appropriation. Pearson wanted "Canada to play a strong role, and he understood that this favoured land had to work with its friends to guarantee its security," wrote Granatstein in the *National Post*. "He understood that Canada had to be prepared to fight in defence of its national interests." Truly, in the face of such analyses, it should come as a surprise that Pearson, the prime minister whose legacy was becoming a battleground, was an icon to the proponents of Canadian participation in UN peace operations in anyway at all—rather than, say, that British prime minister Neville Chamberlain, promising "peace in our time" in the face of a terrible war that would arrive anyway, insisting upon the resolution of disputes "by discussion instead of by force of arms." Pearson, ran the argument, would have been as much of a hawk in Afghanistan and continental partner with the United States as Harper showed himself to be, and not an advocate of blue-helmets at all.

And yet it is hard to reconcile the belligerent rhetoric swirling around the campaign in Afghanistan, with Pearson's deeply felt and thoughtful consideration of peace and "our failures since 1914 to establish it." Whether insisting that the UN "should not be the instrument of any one nation" (i.e. the United States), dreading "the psychological and political consequences of the employment of the Bomb," or realizing, well ahead of Samuel P. Huntington, that "the most far-reaching problems" would "arise no longer between nations...but between civilizations themselves." Pearson's ruminations were of an altogether finer calibre than we have heard from any politician, military figure or civic leader in Canada in the last decade. In his 1957 Nobel Prize acceptance speech, Pearson solemnly described a choice that was "as clear now for nations as it was once for the individual: peace or extinction." The life of states, Pearson told the world, "cannot, any more than the life of individuals, be conditioned by the force and will of a unit, however powerful, but by the consensus of a group, which must one day include all states."

Pearson was not condoning the narrow alliance of just a few. He was not defining the national self-interest, in the sort of "you're with us or against us" frame of mind of militarists and conservatives, parochially. He would have understood the threat posed by al-Qaeda, or indeed terrorism of any kind, but Pearson tempered his political judgment—the brokering of soft power demands it—with humanitarian decency and the sort of high aspirations conspicuously absent from twenty-first-century Conservative Canadian politics. Pearson had a vision of social progress that his detractors continue to paste as foolish and unworldly when, as a substitute for "impossible to achieve" or "naively pursued," they use words such as *noble* and superior or describe its provenance in the "moral high ground" to dismiss it. True, Pearson went against his own position on the issue of atomic weaponry, agreeing to accept U.S. nuclear warheads in Canada in 1963, but to characterize Pearson as belonging to the militarist camp when he so eloquently and unhesitatingly spoke of the essential and vital nature of peace is to bend the many and often conflicting messages of the historical record, as suits. "The best defense of peace is not power, but the removal of the causes of war," said Pearson, who used his Nobel Peace Prize address to speak of prosperity, power, policy and the people as the "four faces" of peace. He warned, "The stark and inescapable fact is that today we cannot defend our society by war since total war is total destruction, and if war is used as an instrument of policy, eventually we will have total war."

Pearson was concerned, in other words, with *root causes*, another liberal term that sends the conservative camp into paroxysms, and he considered the absence of prosperity to be one. He believed, as any sane person does, that a "state has not only the right, but the duty, to make adequate provision for its own defence" but specified that it had no right to do so "at the expense of any other state." He recognized, in the umbrage of the spectre of a nuclear Armageddon that is today *more* rather than less likely for being "terrorist" in nature, that "in modern warfare, fought on any considerable scale, there can be no possible economic gain for any side. Win or lose, there is nothing but waste and destruction." He understood, a quintessentially Canadian sentiment, that social and economic deprivation needed to be addressed globally, and, as is true of any meaningful endeavour, that the magnitude of the task is not an excuse for not trying. "You do not have to have poverty and economic instability; people do not have to be fearful about their crops or their jobs, in order to create the fears and frustrations and tensions through which wars are made," he said, "but poverty and distress—especially with the awakening of the submerged millions of Asia and Africa—make the risks of war greater."

It is a gauge of how seriously the war's proponents understood the task of unravelling the country's peacekeeping persona that the job of contending with it was undertaken on a variety of levels. With the Conservative prohibition in 2006 of the photographing or filming of the repatriated dead and the accompanying decision not to lower flags for each new soldier's death, alongside other measures such as the government's endorsement of "Red Fridays," the way was being laid for there to be no confusion about the war that the nation was fighting and the likelihood that there would, after the acceptance of the role in Kandahar, be more losses. (The stipulation of no media recording of the returning dead was later modified by the Prime Minister's Office to permit images taken by the media with the permission of the bereaved, upholding the impression that the government was merely seeking to protect the grief-stricken families.) Red Fridays were a component of Operation Connection, described by its expositor, CBC veteran reporter Brian Stewart, as a "highly skilled sales campaign to sell the mission" to the Canadian public with a budget, in 2007, upwards of $23 million and employing 500 military and civilian personnel worldwide. Stewart, host of CBC-TV's foreign affairs magazine, *Our World*, described the "information machine" behind Operation Connection as "a public affairs unit that dwarfs all other government promotion offices." (Lara Ryckewaert of *The Hill Times* estimated in 2011 the number of communications specialists working in cabinet ministers' offices to be 1,500, with 87 serving in the Prime Minister's and Privy Council Offices.) The DND generated "a hive of publicity supporting the whole Afghanistan force and the military's overall image" and was headed by the forthright General Hillier seizing with relish upon that unwritten aspect of the top soldier's job, to be its "key architect and salesman."

This job of national transformation was also taken on in the recruitment advertisements that the DND was using in cinemas in 2006, when not just the war but also the battle to fight it on the propaganda front was at its peak. Russian advertisements from the period have the same production values and veneer as the Canadian ones but do not shy away from showing soldiers shooting at people. At the key point in the narrative, the eager Russian conscripts' discussion of good pay, vacation and benefits is interrupted by a battle alarm. Off they run, enthusiastically, to battle. Australian advertisements make the link to Gallipoli, Vietnam and Iraq and, when it comes to the feel-good humanitarian work, show women, not men, doing it. British Royal Marines Commando ads uphold the yobbish excitement of a soldier's shoot-'em-up vocation as "something else," pitting the sheer excitement of being in the army against the indolent and purposeless life those staying behind lead, of too much fast food and sitting on the couch watching game shows and so on.

The Canadian advertisements, however, are markedly different. War does not feature. The recruitment ads show Canadian soldiers herding citizens toward a Red Cross truck that could but as easily might not be in Afghanistan, rescuing the survivors of a winter plane crash, forest fires and flooding. They show them saving boat people from the Pacific and fishers off the coast of Nova Scotia and clearing a building seemingly demolished by an earthquake. Had the advertisements been any longer, it would not have been a surprise to see the soldiers, as Maloney would have it, "conducting fisheries patrols or counting caribou in the Arctic." Only in one less-than-a-second scene is a shot fired at any thing, let alone at a person—either at short range or from the insentient long distances at which much of present-day wars are now fought. There is no death. No maiming. No blood.

The titles across the final frames of the short videos read "FIGHT

FEAR. FIGHT DISTRESS. FIGHT CHAOS" and, ultimately, "FIGHT WITH THE CANADIAN FORCES." But the tasks portrayed in these advertise- ments—of soldiers, according to the thumping narration, "across Canada and around the world, making a difference"—are ones that the 2006 viewing public would almost categorically have associated with peacekeeping or search-and-rescue work. The transition between the image of Canada that existed before 9/11 and the requirements of the country it was becoming was so smooth as to have constituted a deception. The sleight of the recruiter's hand, however, is altogether necessary because the foundation of a national character is what it is for good reasons—ones that are neither ephemeral nor accidental but rooted in the history and the geography of a place. Advertisements that said, instead, "KILL OR BE KILLED BY PEOPLE YOU DO NOT KNOW AND HAVE NOTHING PERSONAL AGAINST" would not have worked nearly so well, as they would have come right up against the peacekeeping character of the country of the day that the broadcast advertisements recognized.

If, as Granatstein has complained exasperatedly time and again over the last decade, "the peacekeeping mythology never dies," it could well be because the set of ideas it reflects, whatever the variants of the terms that are used to describe them, has deep roots—deeper ones than whatever spin is put on history for the purposes of a particular campaign, deep enough that as late as the autumn of 2010, Canada's mission in Afghanistan at an end, a Nanos poll found 52 percent of Canadians favouring a peacekeeping role for Canada and only 21 percent favouring further combat missions. Hence the 2006 Canadian Forces recruitment advertisement depended for its efficacy on not being very militaristic at all. It cannot be forgotten, and certainly was not by the ad's designers, that the basic Canadian impulse has always been one of generosity, of the unambiguous wish to assist in the improvement of other people's lives. The film advertisement needed to acknowledge the habits and fundamental character of a majority of Canadians even as the government was seeking to alter these traits. It needed to be sly. It needed to deceive.

By 2006, even the perfunctory nods that had been offered in Remembrance Day editorials toward Canadians abiding by the increasingly discredited idea of Canada as a peace-oriented nation had been replaced by one of outright hostility. In the new paradigm, Canadian soldiers were warriors and nothing else, and anyone who deigned to imagine alternative roles for the Canadian Forces such as they had pursued for fifty years (the video recruiters notwithstanding) was almost certainly without the moral authority derived from either combat experience or supporting the troops without qualification. In 2007, Jack Granatstein closed the shop of the ad hoc think-tank Council for Canadian Security in the Twenty-first Century that he had co-founded with Eric Boisvert and Roger Sarty in November 2001, the bye-bye note on its website's homepage: "Mission accomplished...The Council has been heard." Come Remembrance Day 2009, the CBC was using Granatstein, previously finding war "a difficult sell," as its establishment commentator. The battle to raze the prior version of Canada's mythology of peacekeeping looked, effectively, to have been won.

By January 2010, Canada's rank among nations contributing to UN stabilization operations had plummeted to fifty-seventh position, with just 17 actual troops among its 142 personnel serving in peacekeeping roles. By September 2011—the latest figures available at time of writing—Canada's ranking had risen, but only slightly, having managed the small climb to the fifty-third rung, with a mere 22 troops, 155 police and 20 "military experts" making up its total of 197 peacekeepers in the field. The Pearson Peacekeeping Centre that had been established in Cornwallis, Nova Scotia, in 1994, its headquarters moved to Ottawa in 2006, was a pathetic shadow of itself, its insignificance an insult to the memory of the man after whom it had been named. Canadian participation in peacekeeping missions had become utterly token, while enrolment in the military continued its burgeoning path. By January, 2012, the uniformed ranks of the Canadian Forces amounted to more than 90,000, including some 25,000 reserves, a sum that was 8 percent greater than in 2001 but still considerably less than the approximately 116,000 combined forces and more than 53,000 reserves enlisted in 1956 and nowhere near the 1.1 million who served during the course of the Second World War—when, despite our relatively meagre population, this country provided the Allies with their third-largest navy, their fourth-largest air force and five land divisions overseas and two in Canada. But, unquestionably, by 2011 the Canadian Forces were enjoying a higher and more visible profile than at any time since the Korean War. The solemnity with which Canadian military fatalities in Afghanistan were honoured was noticed by the armies of other countries fighting in the International Security Assistance Force and reported with envy in British tabloid newspapers. We'd come a long way even before this opening to the *Globe and Mail*'s November 11, 2009, editorial:

> What do you see on the faces of aging Canadian war veterans who stand at attention, bright red poppies on their lapels, while the Last Post is played just before 11 a.m. on Remembrance Day each year? Do you see fear? No. These . are the men and women who could have hidden, or feigned an injury, or simply refused to fight, but who instead went willingly to the trenches in both world wars, the Korean War and in recent conflicts such as Afghanistan. Do you

see anger or bitterness? No. They are men and women who lived through horrors beyond imagining and would do it again. Do you see the preening vanity of people seeking their 15 minutes of fame? No. They would be there, even if no one else was.

No mention of Canadian peacekeepers' valour was made in an admonishment that seized the opportunity to put the boot to another of the prior version of Canada's attendant myths—this time, of the country as a safe haven for American war resisters during the Vietnam years. On the front page of the paper, the by now routine insult was made to Canadians displaying "a marked disinclination to their armed forces, or [who] see them solely as peacekeepers."

In 2010, the prominence that had been given to Canada's "non-violent society and our international role as peacekeepers," and to the "country created through discussion, negotiation and compromise" was nowhere to be found in the new version of *A Look at Canada*, the country's new guide to citizenship, called, instead, *Discover Canada*. A bid for recruits highlighted on the page describes serving in the Canadian Forces as "a noble way to contribute to Canada and an excellent career choice." In the new document, the military is mentioned thirty-five times, peacekeeping once. The advertisement is but a small part of a revamped portrait of the country that puts the role of the military first and foremost in its conception of the country. A list of advisers to the booklet includes eminent Canadian historians Margaret MacMillan and Desmond Morton; Rudyard Griffiths, the co-founder and then director of the Dominion Institute (now the Historica-Dominion Institute); Andrew Cohen, the first president of the Historica-Dominion Institute; and, inevitably, Jack Granatstein.

"At last, Canada has a guide for prospective citizens that is not an embarrassment," proclaimed Granatstein, praising his own good work and lauding the revised guide as one that would "help newcomers and Canadians better understand Canada"—Canada, the "warrior nation," that is.

On May 27, 2011, a press release whipped off before the weekend by the Department of Foreign Affairs paid an absolute minimum of perfunctory attention to the annual International Day of UN Peacekeepers to be held on the Sunday, an occasion of which no mention was made in any of the national papers or broadcast media. On his department's website, the new foreign affairs minister, John Baird, wrote, "In Canada and around the world, Sunday will be a day to acknowledge the men and women who serve in United Nations peacekeeping operations. We will also honour the memory of those who have lost their lives in the cause of peace. This year, we will honour 45 more brave souls than last year. Canada will continue to work with the UN Secretariat, the Security Council and our fellow member states to further the progress made in recent years in supporting our peacekeepers and their vital work."

Just who were those "45 souls," whether they included any Canadians or not, what were the circumstances of their deaths or even the nature of the UN peace operations they had died for, was not stated. Settling into his new office as plans were being finalized for the successful visit to Canada of the Royal newlyweds, Prince William and Catherine, Duchess of Cambridge, Baird would quickly issue an edict demanding that a portrait of the Queen hang in Canadian embassies worldwide and, in due course, order gold-embossed business cards with the name of the building in which the Department of Foreign Affairs is housed—the Lester B. Pearson Building—removed.

These petty moves, so denigrating of Canadian sovereignty, would reach their servile apogee in the August 2011 decision of Defence

Minister Peter MacKay to reinstate the navy and air force's title of "Royal," discarded in 1968 by Paul Hellyer, the minister of national defence in Lester B. Pearson's Liberal government. To hell with Canada determining its own post-colonial path. The Conservative genuflection to "tradition" and, in particular, to one subservient to the British monarchy, was a way of hearkening back to a romantic idea of Canadian heroism and sacrifice that preceded and denied the independent course that the country's military had pursued for fifty years, of which the country's peacekeeping activities were the extant emblem.

The truth about peacekeepers is that, far from "supporting our peacekeepers and their vital work," the government is ashamed of them and the Canada they have come to represent. Old-fashioned war-making by a willing, subservient Canada zealously eager to please is the endgame. Anything else is confusion.

CHAPTER TWO

Warrior Nation

"The real existence of an enemy upon whom one can foist
off everything evil is an enormous relief to one's conscience.
You can then at least say, without hesitation, who the devil
is; you are quite certain that the cause of your misfortune is
outside, and not in your own attitude."
   —Carl Jung, *The Structure and Dynamics of the Psyche* (1916)

On October 17, 2001, Jean Chrétien's government saw off the HMCS
Charlottetown, Preserver and *Iroquois*, their flagship, as part of Operation
Apollo, the naval task group on its way to the North Arabian Sea in
support of the U.S.-led Operation Enduring Freedom.

On the eve of the warships' departure from Halifax Harbour,
Governor General Adrienne Clarkson paid tribute to the peacekeeping
role that she and many other Canadians were finding hard to align
with the exigencies of the "War on Terror."

"We do what we can, and that is very good indeed," said the Governor General. She spoke of Canada as a country that had "lurched and
lunged, sprinted and sauntered through a forest of ignorance, hatred

and bigotry and hacked out for ourselves a path towards a clearing, a lighted place which, make no mistake, can only remain a clearing if we maintain it, if we agree to enlarge, if we promise ourselves and pledge to each other that it is worth our efforts. If we fail in this, the forest will take over and the darkness will come and envelop us."

As the country's press corps looked on, Clarkson implored that the Canadian Forces not "hate; we must not hate. You must not despise; we must not despise. You must not fear, we must not fear. No matter what we are called upon to witness, fight or reconcile, we must remain what we are."

"There is no escape from these people," wrote Christie Blatchford in the *National Post*. Angrily, she pilloried "Canadians in the grand experiment of a multicultural, immigrant, aboriginal and bilingual community," railing against military send-offs such as she was witnessing incomplete without some "messiah from the Liberal Party, summoning up half-baked rhetoric and half-truths." The incongruity, to her mind, of not just the Governor General but also elected politicians and CBC-TV's Peter Mansbridge (or "Pastor" Mansbridge, as John Doyle of the *Globe and Mail* would later call him, "oozing a we're-all-in-this-together attitude") including, in their acclamation of the conflict's "heroes," the wives and children of the soldiers imminently to be left behind struck *Blatchford* as contemptible. The message of the Governor General's adieu would be one that the country would return to nearly ten years later, but no mater. In the war's first stage, what Blatchford was conveying was that for Canada to succeed in Afghanistan, the "warrior nation" needed to have the martial commitment of Spartans. The legacy of peacekeeping needed to become one of "war-fighting" and the country to be stoical. Mollifying phenomena such as the "grand experiment" of peaceful, tolerant and undemanding Canadian multiculturalism and the extolling of weepy, attendant families left behind needed to be halted. (It was an old habit, this putting on of a brave face; during the Second World War, notes Mark Bourrie in *The Fog of War*, censors demanded that the tears of women and girlfriends in press photographs be airbrushed out.)

What Canadians had been told during the onset of the country's participation in the war in Afghanistan was that the country needed to commit to the campaign for reasons of "security" and to protect our special relationship with the United States. In a lecture for the C.D. Howe Institute published in *Commentary* magazine in 2002, Jack Granatstein wrote that the country was fighting in Afghanistan because "Canada has no choice but to cooperate. Since the 1940 Canada-U.S. defence alliance, the two countries have become inextricably linked. Canada's refusal to support the United States would thus carry with it real costs, in terms of reducing its leverage in future negotiations with Washington on obtaining more secure access to the U.S. market, as well as its sovereignty if the United States acted to protect itself from attack without working with the Canadian government and the Canadian Forces."

Granatstein's dour intoning of a possible North American *Anschluss* should the country fail to act had much in common with the now forgotten arguments, before 9/11, of a host of agitated right-wing pundits foreseeing a Canadian monetary union with the United States as inevitable—speakers whose views concerning the country were, as the *National Post*'s Lorne Gunter and others had alleged of the peacekeeping faction, rooted in a conception of Canadian statehood as a fundamentally "insignificant nation." Later, the country's emergence as a petrocurrency and the disastrous economic slide of the United States after 2008 would put an end to these mercenary, fawning ideas about a best possible economy for Canada being guaranteed by union with Washington, but the idea of ingratiating military partnership with the United States would persist. The argument that Canada must pay heed to its relations with the United States must be taken seriously, as their salubriousness cannot be anything less than a primary consideration of Canadian governments, but Granatstein's *Commentary* article was based on the premise that the country was "part of a vast and powerful if informal U.S. empire now, just as a century ago Canada belonged to the British Empire," the author trading in "Canadian obsequiousness to Britain and the Crown" for a new fealty to America that was more suitable to the times but no less unctuous. The military historian's craven genuflection before the greater powers—such a Canadian habit—was taken even further by others in the same fear-mongering camp, notably retired Lt.-Col. Douglas Bland, a Queen's University professor and chair of its Defence Management Studies Program. In "Canada and Military Coalitions: Where, How and with Whom?" an article written for the Institute for Research on Public Policy during the same agitated year, Bland ominously cautioned that "should Canada hesitate or seek to avoid these new obligations, it seems likely that the United States will blockade its northern border, undertake covert intelligence operations in Canada and act unilaterally to defend itself by deploying its armed forces in Canada whenever the President deems it necessary."

Dire predictions are as much of a hobby for this camp as utopian pacifism can be for the extreme left—Granatstein seeing the worst in the fictive first chapter to *Whose War Is It? How Canada Can Survive in the Post 9/11 World* and Bland in his 2010 novel *Uprising*, in which he imagines rebellious Aboriginals committing Hollywood-scale terrorist acts and Canada without the requisite soldiers to fight them. As dilettantish dabblings in fiction, the professors' projections are harmless enough. In a spirit of generosity, it might even be suggested that Bland's novel, with its clackety datelines communicating urgency at the head of chapters, is in line with the work of that legendary Canadian commercial self-publishing polyglot, the former D-Day air force pilot, Maj.-Gen. Richard Rohmer, author of such memorable political and military thrillers as *Exxoneration*, *Ultimatum* and *Periscope Red*. Their "chilling visions of a world of military conflict, legal and political entanglements, and Canada's role in domestic and international spheres" are, says his publisher, Dundurn, "as important to Canada today as when the books were first written." Indeed, Barry Cooper, the CDFAI fellow and University of Calgary colleague of David Bercuson and Granatstein, who a plays tireless lock in the Canadian academic defence analysts' alarmist scrum, announced, in his laughable review of his colleague Bland's novel in the *C2C Journal*, that "for my money he deserves the Giller Prize." (Friendships evidently do not pose ethical questions for Cooper, who wrote in one of his *Calgary Herald* columns plugging more of the CDFAI's work that his relationships with the authors were merely "a happenstance that fades into irrelevance beside the significance of their argument.") But as papers in serious journals, Granatstein and Bland's gloomy forebodings amount to howling academic idiocy of the first order, puerile and overexcited doomsaying that only proves how little the predictions of our "experts" should be depended upon. The fantasy that the United States might invade and seek to occupy Canada shows a staggering ignorance not only of the present—the United States more or less has its way in Canada, anyway—but also of history and, specifically, just how difficult it is to occupy a foreign country at all.

The last ten years have rendered these postulations especially absurd, given that a decade of war in Afghanistan against a rag-tag band of ill-equipped militants and suicide bombers cost the United States more than $432 billion since 2001 and Canada somewhere between $18 billion (the Office of the Parliamentary Budget Officer) and $29 billion (the Rideau Institute) and 158 soldiers' and four civilians' lives by November 2011—and this with only dubious results. It almost begins to be interesting to contemplate the ridiculous Bland-Granatstein scenario, properly belonging in comic books, if only to calculate at what cost an American annexation of Canada might possibly be achieved.

But the warnings have a more sinister aspect. Comments such as Granatstein and Bland make are designed to provoke; they are intended to facilitate the path to war and depend upon arguments about the country as hopelessly permissive. A unified nation built on the bedrock of a powerful military, its civilian population deferentially stepping in line, is the ambition, one that requires the relentless dismissal of skeptics and a garrison mentality that in turn serves to promote its enabling culture of fear and secrecy. (The phrase *garrison mentality* is one that great literary critic Northrop Frye uses in his seminal 1971 collection, *The Bush Garden: Essays on the Canadian Imagination*, to describe the fear of Canadians nervously bunkered down before the dangers that lurked in the vast, threatening spaces beyond the limits of isolated towns. Now the Canadian literary imagination has grown up and is comfortably internationalist. But the militarists linger in the Canada Frye thought to be a backwater and, in the garrisons of their DND and university offices, see dangers everywhere.) The object of the militarists' threatening predictions was to denigrate the peaceful country that Canada's multicultural society had been for half a century. And in their dissatisfaction with the country as they knew it, this lot do as previous generations of like-minded Canadians used to, gazing wistfully back across the Atlantic—only this time looking south and expressing their Canadian discomfort by envying the greater power in Washington and the Pentagon and wanting to be a part of it.

Others made the point of Canada's needing to participate in the "War on Terror" without quite needing to resort to such rhetorical histrionics. We were in Afghanistan, wrote David Bercuson in the *National Post*, because we'd "[ducked] out of the war in Iraq." "Canada," wrote Christie Blatchford, had joined the fight in Afghanistan "because the 9/11 terrorists trained there." We were there, according to Michael Ignatieff, not yet the leader of the Liberal Party, to settle the bill, still unpaid, of our being an international citizen. We were there, said Barry Cooper, "to show that we were no longer free riders." In the minds of some, simple revenge also played its part. "This government will not allow Canadians to be killed without retribution," said Defence Minister Gordon O'Connor in 2007 in one of a series of "misspoken" moments for which he would subsequently be ousted. "If our country is attacked, we are not going to stand blandly by and not do anything about it."

Building the impetus for a conflict being fought 10,000 kilometres away was the endgame, and it required the uprooting of the Canadian public's reigning understanding of the country to put it about. At the federal level, funding for the Veterans Affairs' "Canada Remembers" program was being augmented, and the Department of Heritage's "Celebration, Commemoration and Learning" program, seeking to "generate pride in Canada's heritage by giving citizens an opportunity to share their experiences, background, myths and symbols," benefitted from a tenfold increase in special funding, from approximately $300,000 in 2003 to about $3 million in 2007, when the DND's separate Operation Connection was at its height, for activities promoting knowledge of the country's military history. New initiatives used the technology of the Digital Age to build easily accessed portals to information propounding the country's true, and apparently neglected, heroic history. Some of these, such as the "Heroes Remember" section of the "Canada Remembers" archive of

Canadian troops' memoirs, produced in partnership with the CBC in 2005 (the "Year of the Veteran"), were initiated by the Liberal Party, endeavouring to define a new mood for the country—but late. Others, such as the two-decades old initiative of the *Historica* minutes for television; the Memory Project, which collected and archived oral testimonies of soldiers who had fought in the two World Wars; and the now defunct Council for Canadian Security in the Twenty-first Century, had been put into gear in the private sphere. From the benches of the opposition, Stephen Harper's contempt for the liberal, peace-oriented Canadian constituency that had rejected him at the polls in 2004 was still on petulant display, but the military lobby was without a doubt gaining traction and the press corps, exulting in its new, post-9/11 beat, was exerting more influence. Canada, true to revived though also contestable ideas about its past, was becoming a war-fighting nation again. Under the headline "ENOUGH WITH PEACEKEEPING," *Toronto Star* columnist Rosie DiManno declared in 2003 that it was time to "make righteous war, not la-la peace." The UN, embroiled at the time in the long aftermath of civil war in the Democratic Republic of the Congo (previously Zaire), needed "commandos, not peacekeepers" and "snarly, vigorous intervention." During the first years of the war, the drum-thumping sloganeering of a number of influential columnists in the anglophone Canadian media continued to mount. This bellicose nationalist view, one with little room for reconciliation or tolerance of any kind, was extending even into the realm of battles long settled. In spring 2004 in the *National Post*, David Bercuson wrote with vitriol of the French plan for Germany to be invited to Europe's commemorations for the sixtieth anniversary of D-Day, excoriating the tendency of liberal society "to mix forgiveness with forgetfulness" that the invitation signalled. The following year, the *National Post*'s Christie Blatchford was writing wistfully, as she would many times, of soldiers "who grasp that a just battle is better than a false peace born of fear."

The reasons that were offered for Canada's entry into the fight trumpeted, first of all, the cause of national security, that catch-all twenty-first-century codeword permitting not just torture and the curtailing of personal political freedoms but cost-cutting, bigotry and evasions of all kinds. (In Toronto, "security" is used to explain anything from the removal of seats from streetcars and thus of hypothetical bombs beneath them, to social restrictions at the city's elitist private high schools not wanting public school rabble at their proms as their students' dates, to the refusal of city councillors to release construction plans affecting residents—as happened on the street behind my own when one owner's cowboy contractor's construction gaffes threatened to bring the neighbour's house down. When the beleaguered owner asked to see the plans for the site on which no work had taken place for months, he was told he could not. Why? For *security* reasons. Do not let your guard drop. The terrorists are everywhere.) Mostly, however, the war effort was being driven by the Department of National Defence and its acolytes declaring the point of deployment to be the proper restoration of good relations with Washington. The United States was the country's largest trading partner, and the job in Afghanistan a perfect mission for a wanting easy byes along the border and to win pride of place in the halls of the Pentagon. After Chrétien's decision not to send troops to Iraq, there had been a widespread feeling that the Liberals were precariously governing from the pinnacle of an "anti-American" nation and that the country had been letting down its closest ally for far too long. A number of Liberal gaffes, notably a few by MP Carolyn Parrish, then chair of the Canadian-NATO Parliamentary Association, contributed to this testy political climate and kept the idea of a fundamental fissure between the North American neighbours active ("Damn Americans, I hate those bastards," muttered Parrish as she left Parliament in February 2003. Then, after George W. Bush election victory of November 2004, she said, "I wouldn't guess what's next on his agenda, but it's probably not peace and love," though it was the crushing of a George Bush figurine on CBC's current affairs comedy, *This Hour Has 22 Minutes*, in 2005 that finally saw her booted from caucus.) On the Canadian side, Bush's failure to have mentioned Canada as an ally in the speech he made after 9/11—an omission that David Frum, the Canadian writer of his "axis of evil" speech, described as an oversight—but also high border tariffs on Canadian softwood lumber and, most of all, the United States' seeming indifference to the first Canadian fatalities of the war—four soldiers killed by American friendly fire in April 2002—were irksome. Many Canadians felt, contrary to charges of anti-Americanism so easily and frequently made against them, that the country had demonstrated an unquestionable allegiance during and after 9/11 that had, effectively, been ignored—it was certainly not rewarded. Alternative undertakings such as ongoing UN missions in Haiti or the Middle East, or the possibility of new ones such as Darfur, Sudan, where President Omar Hassan Ahmad al-Bashir was conducting atrocities that the UN's International Criminal Court would later describe as genocide in 2008, were not going to cut it.

This was true despite the urging of Prime Minister Paul Martin, who thought of Darfur as an exemplarily Liberal cause. Roméo Dallaire was another who had UN peacekeeping missions in his sights, even if his views about how such operations should be conducted had evolved away from the relatively powerless position he had been straitjacketed by in Africa. But Martin was resented within the Liberal Party, beginning its rapid decline, and Dallaire had become, to the opponents of Canada's blue-beret days, a critic that no Conservative needed to take seriously. Dallaire had played a tragic role in the Rwandan genocide of the Tutsis and suffered a devastating nervous breakdown afterwards. These events, chronicled in his 2003 memoir, *Shake Hands With the Devil*, his statesman's pleading on behalf of Darfur; and, above all, the case he repeatedly tried to make for teenaged fighter Omar Khadr, after his capture by American forces in July 2002, to be treated as a child soldier and therefore not guilty of the murder charge he was facing while incarcerated in the U.S. detention facility in Guantanamo, allowed those who would have none of any of the general's proposed reforms the pleasure of believing that, in tolerating the old soldier, they were being good humanitarians despite not having to embark upon the slightest change of course. (In cognitive psychology applied, to the habits of conspiracy theorists on the Internet, this sort of behaviour is known as "selective exposure": people are able to convince themselves of views they already hold by seeking out conforming arguments or, as the Conservatives were doing with Dallaire, by selecting an opponent whose views are believed to be fundamentally weak, therefore pose no threat.)

The commitment to Afghanistan was infinitely preferable to Sudan or any of the old files and so it was not long before Paul Martin, prime minister between 2004 and 2006, gave in to the demands of his new Chief of Defence Staff, Gen. Rick Hillier, appointed in February 2005. Hillier was convinced that putting "boots on the ground" in Afghanistan would win Canadian support for the military and restore its broken bond with the Canadian public. In 2003, the Chrétien government sent 2,000 soldiers to Kabul for a year, it did so calling them peacekeepers. When the choice fell to Martin, he consented, with a similiar proviso that the Canadian Forces do peacemaking and reconstruction and win hearts and minds. In *The Unexpected War* (2007), Stein and Lang describe Martin insisting that neither potential humanitarian interventions in Darfur nor Haiti missions "could be constrained by Afghanistan or I wouldn't agree to the mission." But the tide was turning, and the new impulse behind Canada, the warrior nation, was replacing the commitment to peace operations and diplomatic soft power as cornerstones of the country's dominant, nation-building mythology. The deployment of troops to Afghanistan would hone the military. It would not just maintain but bolster trade with the United States and open doors at the Pentagon. The phrases *insurgency* and *counterinsurgency warfare* were only rarely used, if at all, by DND officials then briefing Minister of Foreign Affairs Bill Graham as the war was one that no one was yet suggesting would be lost (or not won). "We needed combat troops because there was trouble, we had to pacify the region," said Graham. "We needed lightly equipped, agile soldiers who would go into the villages, 'make love to the people' and 'kill the bad guys.'" Canada was travelling down the road to vanquishing at Vimy again. The country's history of valorous and innovative performance in combat, its selfless readiness to perform and the ability of the country to "punch above its weight" were the new leitmotifs beginning to surface.

"When a single Canadian soldier walks on soil in a foreign, hostile land, every single Canadian walks with him or her," said Gen. Rick Hillier, then Chief of the Land Staff, to the *National Post* in June 2003. Canadians, Hillier told the troops, "need to pay attention to their army. They need to visibly support you, and they need to ensure that you are set up for success." The Canadian Forces, Hillier would later (famously, rather than notoriously) say, are "not the public service of Canada. We're not just another department. We are the Canadian Forces, and our job is to be able to kill people."

Hillier proved adept at wresting better procurement for the Canadian Forces from Ottawa bureaucrats, though the changes in the nation's approach that took force so vehemently after 2001 were achieved through language, ritual and the upholding of mythic accounts of Canadian valour, the story of the Battle of Vimy Ridge chief among them. The promotion of these helpful means to the new ends of the "warrior nation" occurred alongside the obstruction of stories likely to impede such revisionism and the suppression of groups and incidents likely to prompt contrary tales—such as, for instance, the stories told by the coffins of the fallen arriving home. If Canada was to be able to fight effectively in Afghanistan, if the Forces were to benefit from their turn away from the low budgets, piecemeal public attention and generally ignominious standing that had been their lot since the reversals in Somalia and Rwanda and the exhausting and not altogether understood war in the Balkans, then the new leitmotifs were going to have to come into effect, ones supported by the venerable, enduring language of heroism. Whatever dialogue of common humanity had existed prior to 9/11 needed to concede its place to an epic form of storytelling in which evil was absolute and had a face. The enemy wore a kaffiyeh and a black beard and, like the monster Grendel in the story *Beowulf*, lived in a cave; "good" was the property of a country rushing back into a majestically unsubtle narrative of the frontier. No longer were the more complex narratives of novel thinking—with its curiosities, its openness to arguments of "root causes" and, as significantly, its capacity for humour though, above all, its capacity to expand the sphere of our moral concern through the imaginative leap it demands of its readers—entertained. In a country in an epic state of mind, a narrow, regimented and intolerant polarity reigns: simple opposites of good and evil, strength and weakness, male and female, dominate. There can be no argument, no confusion (an exquisite concept that describes, in science, a mixing of substances that need not be chaotic or perplexing). "Victory" is the end, and patriotism is the means. In support of the war effort, an allegiance to territory and to property, rather than some more vague set of transnational ideas about rights and identity, is paramount. Home is all that is good, and at the border lurks the enemy. Other countries are "with us or against us," and to challenge the simplicity of this idea is to be a traitor and to prevaricate as only a dithering (surely liberal) or a contract-breaking cowardly soldier might—and as the *hero*, most of all, would never do.

Heroes serve a purpose. If a threat to a nation is legitimate, if it is one that is reasonably thought to imperil the physical security of its citizens or the integrity of its borders, then the military is called in to do its work of killing. At such moments, the fear of a state or of a community is deemed to be warranted. War is undertaken as a matter of survival—rather than, say, as an opportunity for a military keen on what it has decided is an appropriate assignment or, inexcusably, as a means of acquiring territory or resources or of causing deliberate harm to some other group. A war may be described as "just," though the response to whatever is the perceived threat must not be disproportionate for it to retain that important epithet. We retain armed forces for such moments, and consider it a success when life is peaceful and soldiers are idle.

This phenomenon runs contrary to what is the case in most of the jobs of civil society, in which the work a person does is legitimizing and to prevent him doing it is to deny a great part of his *raison d'être*. When it comes to war, the civilized country should be elated when the standing army at its disposal is not used at all. An army must be kept, however, and an inactive one creates problems of its own. In peacetime, or a period of less palpable threats (as was the case in the "decade of darkness" that was the waning of the Cold War), in a nation that is not using conscription to otherwise occupy its unemployed, either the number of troops must be drastically reduced or work must be found to keep them busy. What army leaders fear is that "rusting out" of skills, as much as the depreciation of gear, so that the military administration even of a relatively unthreatened and peaceful country such as Canada, especially under the administration of a war enthusiast such as Hillier, is constantly on the lookout for missions. This is hardly difficult, today's world constantly offering a great variety of military undertakings to choose from. In spring 2011, a list of assignments, actual and potential, would have included work in Afghanistan, the Congo, Haiti, Ivory Coast, Libya, Sudan and Syria, to name just a few places. The use of the words *security* and *terror* that made Afghanistan a war of survival, and a "just" cause, though the moral argument, that explained NATO's decision to embark on its "just" mission to aid the popular uprising in Libya during the Arab Spring appeared mostly a matter of choice, "Why Libya and not Syria or Yemen?" being a question with generally unsatisfactory answers.

Libya was a safe, easy operation, where ousting dictators in Syria and Yemen would not have been. We attend, in the grave matter of conflict, to the homeland's national security and, on occasion, to the interests of less fortunate states. Canadians understand the obvious need for troops to defend the nation and to see to the first, though with regard to the latter, too often we reveal ourselves to be consumers of war with arbitrary tastes. The militarists will not have it, but there is actually no contradiction in citizens holding those who commit their lives to the military in high esteem while, at the same time, wanting to determine a say in the work soldiers do in their country's name. Whether that job is hunting down the Taliban in Afghanistan or carrying out peace operations in Darfur or the Congo, the public is entitled to have a view. It is entitled to be a part of the discussion of what the military does *in its service*, though the erosion of any possibility of civilians challenging the course of action that government and its military leaders undertake is the point of the onus Hillier places on ordinary Canadians to "pay attention" and make sure the army is "set up for success." To that end, a particular kind of story needs to be mobilized for the high readiness of an army or the execution of a conflict to be permissible. In narrative terms, the stories that were beginning to be used in Canada to facilitate the new war were ones transforming the country away from the humanism of the novel and the peace operations that were its kindred endeavour into the simpler, more easily nationalistic categories of the epic.

The "epic" is not simply a story that is long (though it may be), or written in verse (though it may be), or a tale that, in today's high school lexicon, suggests something "awesome." The epic is a form of narrative that emphasizes the difference of a community and does so chauvinistically. In epic storytelling, history bolsters the tribe and militates against whatever are the threats perceived at the borders of the territory. It is the narration of a period in which storytelling is at its most explicitly righteous, a time when accounts of treason as much as stories of valour enter into the fray. It is the storytelling of a society in a high state of insecurity, the kind it chooses to ensure its survival by justifying the infallibility of its position through the invocation of history and divine right—and, when all other means are expended, by force of arms.

So, in epic stories, when the hero is on the point of being vanquished, when there is neither the point of nor the time for moral argument anymore, he is vindicated by the strength of a special weapon that has been delivered to him by the gods or the powers that be: Achilles' shield, Thor's hammer, Darth Vader's lightsaber, B-2 bombers and even "Little Boy" and "Fat Man," the nuclear bombs that the United States dropped on Hiroshima and Nagasaki in August 1945 to end the war in the Pacific, are all weapons that are essential to the epic story. Without the accompanying, mobilizing narrative, the conviction that at some dire point we might actually use such weapons in reality proves no more than "might makes right." What the existence of invincible weaponry in an epic story does is to imbue the cause of the narrating society—the "good guys"—with moral purpose in a venture that may in fact be "just" or, as invading Troy for the sake of the lover Paris's humiliation of Menelaus was (when he absconded with Helen), be wildly reprehensible and outrageously silly. Using the formidable weapons in our arsenal that we would rather not have to—drones, missiles, nukes—becomes permissible. Might is blinding and seductive, enough so that even after the dubious success, more likely failure, of the war in Afghanistan, MPs in Ottawa voted unanimously, in March 2011, to send the Canadian Forces to join NATO against Muammar Gaddafi's Libya. Fortunately, the Libyan campaign was an easy one for Canada to support, the mad dictator's crumbling regime in disarray and no match for NATO might. Several members of Parliament absented themselves, but not one deigned to debate the entry into another conflict, not least, because there was actually hardly a threat. As the justification of the use of force becomes more commonplace (force swiftly becoming a habit), it is worth remembering that, in epic stories, there is usually a cost associated with using the divine weapon of last resort. Achilles dies. Darth Vader sacrifices himself. The ring that seduces J.R.R. Tolkien's hobbit Frodo is one that Gandalf, who appears to die after using his own great power, will not use. The lesson is that inordinate might should not be turned to complacently, but with gravity and seriousness. Winning a quick and complete victory with overwhelming force may inflict less harm on the defeated and, in compliance with the debate that the Dutch lawyer Hugo Grotius started in 1631 with *De Jure Belli ac Pacis*, may even be "just." But even "just" wars must be undertaken with remorse.

It is through story that the use of brute force is sanctified. With a decently swaying epic story, the use of overwhelming force is, no matter how disproportionate, not seen to constitute a measure annulling a war's "just" aspect. So, since the first Gulf War of 1990-91, but especially with the NATO bombings of Bosnia-Herzegovina in 1995 and, during the Kosovo War, of Serbia in 1999, even when Western nations' physical security has not been the issue, the language of extending "liberty" is appropriated so that the case can be made for a "just" war, today's imprimatur of moral acceptability being one that is sanctioned by the UN. This was the significant advance of post-Second World War twentieth century thinking, the attribute of "just" having evolved from its early incarnation as the right to defend oneself against injury or the loss of property to notions of universal human rights and expectations. If the engagement can be portrayed as one in which the point is to create the democratic conditions in which a fairer society might exist—to "nation-build," in other words—then, regardless of intent, the language of humanitarianism is of tremendous strategic utility. Protecting nations' physical security has provided incentives not only for defensive wars but also for pre-emptive, aggressive strikes such as President George W. Bush exercised in Iraq, and Israel resorted to in its attack on a Syrian nuclear reactor in 2007 (and was threatening to do against Iran in 2012), but the legality or even common sense of these unilateral moves is highly debatable. As the advocates of humanitarian interventions and generally more liberal views are many, and influential, it makes sense for battling powers acting provocatively to pay lip service to their concerns and even to be able to appropriate them. Broad notions about universal human rights and the well-being of the "international community," ones that burgeoned during the second half of the last century, are today routinely conflated with the idea of the "just" fight so that wars undertaken by Western coalitions typically have the language of humanitarian intervention appended to their cause. So, for instance, at the outset of Operation Iraqi Freedom—the codename for the 2003 invasion of Iraq by British and U.S. forces on the pretext of eradicating Saddam Hussein's stock of non-existent weapons of mass destruction—President George W. Bush declared of the United States that "our cause is just, the security of the nations we serve and the peace of the world." The mission was clear. The aim of the war was not just "to disarm Iraq of weapons of mass destruction [and] to end Saddam Hussein's support for terrorism" but "free the Iraqi people," an argument many Canadians and certainly Prime Minister Jean Chrétien did not find convincing.

Wars may be fought for reasons of existence, as an obligation to allies though also for honour or simple conquest. Sometimes, as was the case during the Second World War, outrages against humanity provide a *casus belli*, though in many instances these incontrovertible reasons are only arrived at afterwards. Grotius decided upon three grounds for the just war—self-defense, reparation of injury and punishment. But much of the time, wars described as "just" are about no more than the defence of the status quo of societies as they experience friction in the face of others. As one society comes into contact with another, there is the possibility of trade and a surplus but also of violent contest. The surplus is whatever the society has too much of. The surplus is the wealth that accrues after the mere replication of the society is achieved from one day to the next, a quantity that is by its very nature hoarded and distributed unequally. Strictly speaking, the defence of a surplus—of property and the right to it—is insufficient cause for a "just" war. The "just" war must belong to Grotius's categories or be the "war of existence," types of conflict that certainly occur and that are undertaken when all other means of settlement are exhausted. A community's peaceful existence is not the issue. If a communty's peaceful existence is not the issue—if, in fact, the disequilibrium of the economic surplus that comes into being with the encounter of two or more communities is the thing that is being protected—then it is much harder to argue that the war is "just." The surplus may be necessary to the security of the society, but that is not enough to warrant war's vindication. The result may be a war being waged to protect a morally indefensible order, a case of one society seeking to protect a disproportionate economic benefit, such as access to oil, as was often charged during the United States' invasion of Iraq. (This sort of economic self-interest has also been alleged regarding the war in Afghanistan. As Michele Landsberg anticipated, the construction of a Trans-Afghanistan Oil Pipeline out of Azerbaijan and Central Asia is a going concern, and in 2010, the year in which it was revealed that U.S. surveyors had mapped a potential trillion dollars in "vast mineral riches," an agreement was signed for a gas pipeline to Pakistan and India.)

In our present age it has become harder and harder to justify wars on a simple basis of "existence" as, what with the shrinking of distances within the global village, the status quo pits the vastly wealthy against the impecunious, neighbours in a social order that becomes harder and harder to accept as morally defensible. Conservatives are more prone toward an epic view because they depend upon the surplus and its unequal distribution for the tension between the classes that is the engine of their society's prosperity. When Prime Minister Stephen Harper attends the World Economic Forum in Davos, Switzerland, as he did in January 2012, and speaks of Western nations having become "complacent about their prosperity," he is really talking about their relative economic *position*. Conservatives regard property—that is, their economic security—as an unassailable right and see those who question or may detract from it as the enemy and a monster. To be "complacent" is to be responsible for the poverty that is the result of being an individual or a state performing less well, and therefore not deserving of government action. It was British prime minister Margaret Thatcher's conviction that to be poor, a criminal or simply in need was the disadvantaged individual's or the criminal's fault that provided twentieth-century Conservative ideology with its great leap forward. The bond between the rich and powerful and the outrageously poor, of the 1 and the 99 percent, is broken by an absence of empathy that means care does not have to happen.

Liberals (though also "red" conservatives), by contrast, do not break that bond. They are uneasy with disproportionate differences and, by and large, consider the deprived and the disadvantaged as merely less fortunate in life's game of chance. The poor are underprivileged, but they are not monsters. Because, in the liberal paradigm, they are seen to be as human and alike in nature as the prosperous rest, it is the liberals' responsibility to help and protect and encourage them out of their relative misfortune. The fundamental aim of their politics is to help those who cannot help themselves, and so liberals pay heed to the enabling or debilitating effects of circumstance—to "root causes." They are not radical in their point of view, and although this principle of understanding, or the more generous disposition to their fellow human of which it is indicative, is not the sole determinant of their worldview, it is nevertheless the ever-present one, and it applies whether the focus of the issue is domestic or lies in the realm of foreign policy. "We cannot in this day have a stable national democracy without progress in living standards, without too great extremes of wealth and poverty," said Lester B. Pearson in his 1957 Nobel Prize acceptance speech. "Likewise we cannot have one world at peace without a general social and economic progress in the same direction. We must have rising living standards in which all nations are participating to such a degree that existing inequalities in the international division of wealth are, at least, not increased."

Where the arch conservative remain mired and comfortable within the epic's more hostile and defensive worldview, the attitude of the liberal and "red" Tory is akin to that of the novel. Theirs is the more sophisticated and humanizing form of story. Their thinking is the highest expression of the Enlightenment and of the egalitarian and inclusive principles of liberal democracy. If, in the myth world, no surplus exists and all things are shared, and in the epic, the surplus exists as something to be hoarded and protected, then in the novel's view, a surplus exists but carries with it an onus to be redistributed more fairly. A lot of political energy is directed toward the problem of just how to do that in largely urbanized societies in which the notion of "community" is abstract and no longer depends on blood ties or upon the likelihood of a majority of its members actually knowing one another. Today's world is distinguished not by shocking social inequities that have always existed in some form or other but by our increasing awareness of them, so that ignorance of another's bad situation can no longer be an excuse for doing nothing about it.

And yet economic and social inequities, especially as they are institutionalized in property, are deeply entrenched and accumulate enormous weight and political arguments of their own. Consider, during the 2011 Occupy movements, the multitude of arguments that were made on behalf of the right of the rich simply to *be* rich. Or the resistance, in America, of even Warren Buffett's 2011 argument that he, a multibillionaire, really should be paying more income tax than his secretary, a straightforward and logical proposition that the IRS chose not to press. Without a meaningful social compact, without some credible form of the redistribution of wealth that can even take place over generations to be acceptable, the status quo cannot be seen as moral. If hoarding economic privilege is perceived to be the reason for a conflict, then the language of the "just" war is problematic and the enemy is entitled to fight or to resist, to defend against social inequities, as the young and the disenfranchised did throughout North Africa and the Middle East during the Arab Spring, because ordinary laws have failed them. Creation myths—the stories that explain a society as it is—are no longer convincing, what with the existence of a surplus that breeds feelings of anger in those who resent it and insecurity in those who would defend it. If these sentiments cannot be assuaged politically, then war or rebellion ensues.

Epic storytelling is a response to these phenomena, a form of narrative that mobilizes a particular order to its defence through a distinct conception of good and evil and a justification of the offending surplus. In a society operating at a level of subsistence, all citizens are necessary to its reproduction from one day to the next and there is no "surplus" to speak of. In Canada—or at least in the Canada that does not resort to the extremes of epic thought for nation-building purposes—society's guiding principles are generous and inclusive and at least the ideal of good government says that citizens are equally necessary and potentially able to contribute to the nation's prosperity. The aim is that all of the state's constituents should fare better than preceding generations have done and that all people abiding by the laws of the country have a place. If Canada, a secure society with its particular history of negotiation, enters into the trade that comes about when two different societies recognize their surpluses and deficits and barter them, the country does so from a position of equanimity exactly because it does not feel threatened. Trade, in such an atmosphere, bolsters peace because it creates common interests.

At least in theory, the mechanism of trade levels the comparative advantage of rival societies by offsetting, say, their surpluses (of oil and labour) against their deficits (of labour and oil) so that ultimately each is better off. Even the foreign aid, NGOs and volunteerism that are expressions of so-called "Canadian values" are a part of the trade of bounties and shortcomings in which a surplus of Canadian good fortune—whether of wheat, of school-builders or educational or engineering skills—is offered at a price far below its domestic worth to countries in greater need in which these goods or services have more value, and what is received in the exchange is a greater sense of community and purpose.

Free trade is a liberal argument and should be an easy conservative one too, though it ceases to be when its levelling mechanism begins to detract from the hoarded power and surplus of the inordinately wealthy (whether people or states). In the epic society, the existence of the surplus must be rationalized as it is not, as in the myth world, shared. It demands a form of storytelling that enables the defence of the community and paves the way for the *necessity* and not just the likelihood of violence. The complaisance of myth-telling is no longer sufficient and the epic is the different kind of narrative that arises to reflect and to justify this new order. To that end, the epic rests on assumptions about the inherent superiority of a particular society or of a group. It is a form of storytelling that exists in opposition to, say, the mythic humility of environmentalism, in which nature is the good being defended but as common wealth, rather than as a surplus to be managed by a particular party or corporation—as, for instance, the resource economy would have it. Nature exists to be shared and sustained because, according to environmentalism's tenets, there is no waste within the natural order to expend. By contrast, the epic sings the virtues of a particular society to its members, typically managing to do so through carefully constructed renditions of the history of the society in question. It upholds a community's singularity and merits, and does so in a manner that makes the safeguarding of the property in its possession easier—and, too, the rights of certain bodies within the community (kings, corporations) to oversee the process and amply reward themselves for doing so. Whether the society that is being defended is Agamemnon's Greece, Boudica's Britannia, Roland's France or Stephen Harper's Canada, the perception of an enemy, real or imagined, demands a specific recounting of the birth and true identity of the nation and a rearrangement of the social order into structured hierarchies with the demigod figure of the hero on top.

But the truth about surpluses is that some gain value and are hoarded or sought after—think fossil fuels and their rising price as reflected in stock markets and then at the pumps—while others, such as Canada's young men and women sent to fight on low wages, can be expended. A U.S. diplomatic cable released by WikiLeaks in 2009 put on the record the view of Edmonton Conservative MP Laurie Hawn, subsequently nominated to sit on the Canada-United States Permanent Joint Board on Defence, that "rising unemployment rates at home...would help the Canadian Forces to recruit and retain troops, at least in 2009 and 2010." A less offensive way of making the military attractive to the surplus of young people in the labour market that permits a military's healthy recruitment (though certainly in Canada, men and women join the military for a variety of reasons other than penury) is to extol the work that armed forces do and to speak with admiration, as David Bercuson did, of soldiers who "deliberately go into harm's way at the bidding of their community to kill or be killed." Soldiers are to be applauded and their deaths are to be honoured as necessary sacrifices on behalf of the community and its continued sustenance. In this way, the society in an epic narrative frame of mind uses fear and honour to maintain readiness in the face of threats and enemies it knows, imagines or pretends are constant and close. The enemy may be "evil," as Hitler and Stalin and Cambodia's Pol Pot (to name just a few) indubitably were, or no more than a false and convenient construction. Either way, when it comes to upholding the epic narrative, no method is too base. The preservation of society, more than individual rights or dignity, is the epic narrative's objective. Hence, the demarcation of moral qualities within its structure is clear. The hero is absolutely good. The enemy is wholly monstrous and bad. Whether a terrorist hijacker or a Jew, an American, a member of the Taliban or a native doubter, the monster is not just threatening to good members of the community that must be protected at all costs but utterly different in kind, so that when it is slain, there is no penalty—quite the opposite, in fact. Selling the epic cause requires a story of blatant and unprovoked injury such as occurred on 9/11, or the spectre of it happening in the future, as the language of the "War on Terror" supplies. The retreat into an epic frame of mind reflects a community's movement back into a primordial state of fear, and the first trick of its language is to imbue the oratory of war with a lexicon of absolute good and evil, sanctifying the host and demonizing the enemy and appealing to base tribal instinct to make the fight easier. This dynamic operates at all levels. The obnoxious environmentalist meddling in the oil sands is a "foreigner," not to be considered, though the more terrifying is the monster, the more his removal elevates the hero and justifies him.

So with regards to the war on terror then "counterinsurgency" and its Canadian theatre in Afghanistan, the epic draws conflicts along strict lines of, on the one side, soldiers as indubitable heroes and, on the other, the enemy as "detestable murderers and scumbags"—strategic words that, drowning out the more tempered views less appealing to the media of other generals (Lt.-Gen. Andrew Leslie or Maj.-Gen. David Fraser, to name but two), Gen. Rick Hillier purposefully chose to describe al-Qaeda and the Taliban's militant fighters in July 2005. The Canadian is infallible, and the al-Qaeda or Taliban member is utterly alien and a monster, and therefore not deserving of any kind of humanitarian consideration. The idea that humanitarian consideration brings benefit to society as a whole—that it is, in fact, the mark of the civilization being defended—is relegated to the sidelines in the heat of the epic struggle. The Taliban or al-Qaeda member, the "other" in this situation, is an enemy and a threat, and it is incumbent upon the home side to destroy it without lament. Speaking after the July 7, 2005, tube bombings in London, England, about whether Canada might become a terrorism target, Hillier, then Chief of Defence Staff, extended the scope and the gravity of the enemy threat beyond the territory of the detestable murderers and scumbags as much as he could. The fight in Afghanistan may have been taking place in a foreign field but was predicated upon the defence of home. "It doesn't matter whether we are in Afghanistan or anywhere else in the world," said Hillier. "They detest our freedoms. They detest our society. They detest our liberties. They want to break our society. I actually believe that."

Vile enemies are necessary, but the *sine qua non* of the epic, that form of story zealously and chauvinistically singing the virtues of one society over another, is the hero. The hero is a figure, as the great Homeric scholar Cedric H. Whitman said of Achilles, who has his head in the heavens but his feet on earth. His job is to bridge the gap between gods and mortals. ("The absolute and the human meet," writes Whitman, "but only after death.") As the hero irrupts into the epic story, so, too, does his foil, the enemy, who does the same for hell and all that is evil.

The introduction of the hero promotes and fosters the allegiances that support one state, or a portion of its population, over another. The hero is the emblem of the highest values of the society. He is a figure who is better than others. In effect, a caste system has been introduced. The hero is the leader, real or moral. He is the general or the warrior, the "titan of business" or the corporation, the vision and imagination of which must be allowed to operate unhindered (and untaxed) in whatever battlefield it finds itself—of commerce, of dirty streets, of actual war. To do otherwise is to impede the hero from doing his job and to curtail the qualities and abilities that permit rather than skew the good society. Ordinary civilians are lesser beings and exist to be protected. They are the "women and children" invoked both as the helpless and vulnerable and, through procreation, as the guarantors of the society's future.

The word *hero* is derived from the Greek word ηρως ("heros"). In the mythology of the Greeks, the hero is someone who watches over or protects and is likely to be a demigod. He is typically the offspring of some illicit liaison or a figure in whom a divinity had a special interest that was often sexual so that he is different in his essential nature from ordinary mortals. He is, due to lineage, superior in kind and usually destined to be noticed. (In the Ancient Greek world, this was not generally a good thing.) As civilization has come to be more humanist, more anthropocentric, the word *hero* has come to describe not just the warrior but a man or woman of exceptional qualities in any realm whose conduct provides a model to which the ordinary rest should aspire. In the liberal Canadian paradigm, the hero may be someone other than a figure with exceptional martial attributes. He is likely to display noble and exemplary qualities in any number of roles in a society that offers up a much more varied panoply of parts to play, whereas in the conservative epic view heroes are of a more traditional line. The hero is likely in uniform and typified, in wartime, by the men and women of the military. In the epic society, soldiers are the most valuable of citizens. They are, as Minister of Defence Peter MacKay described Canadian troops upon their exit from Afghanistan in July 2011, a country's "best," even if, as a surplus of labour, they are also expendable.

Much of the appeal of the epic lies in the narrative simplicity that the hero and the theme of mortal chase, constructs archetypal in their character, supply. This atavistic aspect of the epic story is evident in the plethora of technologically advanced but otherwise primitive vehicles of storytelling profuse in our new Digital Age, and in electronic games especially. In June 2011, the top ten bestselling Xbox 360 video games, each having sold more than three million copies—titles including *Halo*, *Call of Duty* and *Gears of War* but also James Cameron's *Avatar* (the highest-grossing movie of all time)—rested on the same epic paradigm of almighty heroes and their struggle in stories in which the game is categorically one of hunt and elimination. The world of these games is reduced to a simple one of fields of battle and simple categories of good and evil that we learn as children and then cling to in epic storytelling and fantasy. In today's strangely refracted world, the cast of a sci-fi action movie such as *Battle: Los Angeles* can speak of their multimillion-dollar experience as "boot camp" and find reporters to take them seriously ("BATTLE-WEARY CAST AND CREW SHARE THEIR WAR STORIES," headlined the *Toronto Star* in March 2011). The computer and video game experience affects even popular ideas of what constitutes the "news," action from the front lines likely to reach the home front most immediately through social networks such as Twitter and to reappear in so-called "newsgames" such as 2011's *Bin*

Laden Raid, in which players were able to assassinate the al-Qaeda leader for themselves, seizing property from the Abbottabad safe house, just as U.S. Navy Seals had done two weeks before. The game's creator, Jeremy Alessi, told *The New York Times* that such games can "be created quickly enough to be relevant in the news space."

Illusions of fantasy, play and, evidently, journalistic seriousness reign in video games so that Ian Bogost, a professor of game theory at Georgia Tech and a games designer, was credibly able to describe "newsgames" as a new form of journalism that, depending on player interaction, "involves more than just revisiting old forms of news production." They can do so because the technology does not yet allow for the subtlety of character and the more curious, empathetic and *true* reflection of the world that is achieved in the more sophisticated narrative form of the novel. Our predilection for the atavistic simplicity of epic stories is unchanging, even as its guises are constantly reiterated and adapted to keep up with the times. So, barring the odd Quentin Tarantino flick, the villain who used to be a Nazi with an English accent is, today, a bearded Pakistani or Afghan, and there's a whole lot of work out there if you are one or look the part.

Stripped of its martial complication, the instinct to heroism is wondrous and basic to human beings. Its selflessness has challenged scientists wanting to explain it, inspired artists and politicians seeking to honour and commemorate it and touched those who have benefitted by it. Philosophers seeking to understand heroism have dedicated centuries of thought to solving the mystery of such action and what is usually, though not always, its valiant nature. Indeed, community recognition of "heroes" is an age-old phenomenon, great warriors and performers of all kinds having been awarded kudos—honour, glory and acclaim—by state leaders and in literature and art ever since Homer implored the Muse to "Sing the rage of Peleus' son,

Achilles," who, in Western culture, is perhaps the most famous hero of all. Millennia of statuary stand as evidence of the cult of the hero that, in the twentieth century, took a more plebeian turn. Military medals were first issued by the French under Napoleon, and the British have been awarding the Victoria Cross since 1854, though after 1917, Communist Russia awarded medals to Heroes of the Soviet Union, a category including both soldiers and civilians for extraordinary acts protecting the motherland but also for promoting socialism and peace. The Communist Party decorated Heroes of Socialist Labour for their industry and awarded a Mother Heroine medal, no quarrel there, to women who had borne the state ten or more children. In the United States, steel magnate Andrew Carnegie, a man who never quite got over the role he and another less remorseful industrialist, Henry Clay Frick, had played in breaking the notoriously violent 1892 Homestead Strike, set up a fund to recognize, philanthropically rather than for patriotic advantage, extraordinary acts of courage by ordinary people. (The Carnegie Awards are still given out today.) Canada had its own system of civilian and military honours that, despite the 1917 Nickle Resolution forbidding the granting of British titles to Canadians, mimicked that of the old colonial master until a bill established the Order of Canada in 1967. Between the Korean War and 9/11, ribbons and medals recognizing military heroism in soldiers were awarded for long service or by the UN to members of the Canadian military who had served in peacekeeping missions. Since 1972, the Order of Military Merit and sundry medals for bravery and courage have been awarded by the Governor General to soldiers and civilians alike. For most of the last century, the epithet of "hero" was bestowed quite democratically. In the North American panoply of peacetime, heroic acts could be performed by anybody—and even by pets, the Purina dog food company having its own hall of fame and awards for bravery.

The Purina Hall of Fame is easy to mock but, scientifically speaking, not at all contemptible. Ever since Charles Darwin published his revolutionary treatise *On the Origin of Species* in 1859 and thrust the new field of evolutionary biology into prominence, scientists have turned to animals for illumination of the heroic question. For Darwin, there was essentially no difference between the adaptive evolution of humankind and that of any other animal species, the genes being chosen through "natural selection" those with the properties that served the prospect of its survival best. For his intellectual heir, British scientist and author of *The Selfish Gene* (1976) Richard Dawkins, the process of natural selection of our DNA is even more extreme. According to Dawkins—who, a notable atheist, also wrote *The God Delusion* (2006)—our bodies are merely organisms acting as vessels for the competing genes that, governing our evolution as a species, constitute the more legitimate focus not only of evolutionary biology but also of philosophical questions such as the existence of God. Within these ruthless parameters there is not much room for heroism, often involving self-sacrifice, to be rationally explained. Darwinism and many of the philosophies of mind that are the great nineteenth-century biologist's legacy take an amoral, if not outright pessimistic, view of human nature that discounts much possibility of altruism in "selfless" acts.

Such views are born out of the belief, pioneered by Charles Darwin and his contemporary Thomas Henry Huxley, that humankind's moral tendencies are inherited and therefore subject to evolutionary laws though their details are a product of the culture and a matter of choice and therefore free will. Still, Huxley's view of humankind's underlying animal nature is dire. Morality, for Huxley, depends upon the tenuous and often unsuccessful suppression of our baser instincts. Frans de Waal is one of the few contemporary biologists to have challenged a school of thought in which human beings are regarded as innately selfish and our few decent acts as the product of what the director of Living Links, the Yerkes Primate Centre at Emory University in Atlanta, characterizes as "a thin veneer hiding an otherwise selfish and brutish nature." De Waal, one of the world's leading primatologists, has conducted many behavioural experiments proving that envy but also generosity, trust and a framework of morality exist in primates' nature and, by extension, in us. De Waal sees plenty of precedents in the animals he studies—in the action, for instance, of chimpanzees, averse to water, willfully drowning in order to save others, or in the ape taking on a "policing" role and protecting the community from itself. To de Waal, humans are, in their essence, *good*.

Stanley Coren, a professor of psychology at the University of British Columbia and author of a number of popular books about dogs (*The Intelligence of Dogs, Why Does My Dog Act That Way*), has chronicled more than a thousand plausible cases in which the actions of dogs have saved the lives of their owners, either by sounding the alarm, bringing assistance, pushing or pulling people to safety (sometimes out of broken ice) or doing battle against aggressors, sometimes armed. Coren, like Darwin before him, has wrestled with the apparent contradiction that the heroic impulse to self-sacrifice poses to the theory of natural selection, for while the survival of the person who is rescued through such noble action may be ensured, whatever genes are in the "superior" rescuing animal, including the presumably valuable heroic ones, are, through death, lost. Darwin resolved the contradiction of heroic action and its persistence in the species by concluding that the presence of heroic individuals improves the chances of survival of the whole family or community of which the hero is a part. Coren quotes Darwin: "He who was ready to sacrifice his life, as many a savage has been, rather than betray his

comrades, would often leave no offspring to inherit his noble nature."
And yet, Darwin observes, "a tribe including many members who were
always ready to give aid to each other and to sacrifice themselves
for the common good, would be victorious over most other tribes:
and this would be natural selection." Such incidents display the
"kinship" that Coren believes to be fundamental to heroic acts, and
that First World War officers, consciously or not, thought too when
the early battles of World War One were perceived of as weeding out
the weak. Heroic self-sacrifice is often made for the sake of family
through blood but, as dogs' relationships with humans (or soldiers
to their 'band of brothers') demonstrate, these ties are not necessary
to its flourishing. We establish kinship and a sense of community
through other means — through the promise of protection that owners
and dogs offer to each other, or that soldiers offer to the citizens
of their homeland and that "peacekeepers" and the proponents of
humanitarian intervention offer to a family of even broader definition.

Authentic acts of heroism are ones by which the whole community benefits. The society is stronger for the heroic acts that only
a few are able to perform, whether as citizens, as Canadian Forces
deployed in conventional wars or as others wearing the "blue beret."
Beyond the immediate result of the successful heroic action, such
demonstrations of self-sacrifice make further ones more likely through
their recollection in collective memory. The survival of the species is
ensured by genes carried in the body but also by stories of heroism
that affect the DNA, so to speak, of society rather than the individual.
That benefit may well be inadvertent. It may stem out of base instincts
such as Sgt. Ed Wadleigh's desire "to get in scraps and gunfights for
a few months and fuck shit up." The heroism of Achilles, recall, was
really no more than one man's rage, prompted by a relationship
with his charge, Patroklos, that was romantic and sexually vague. A
celebrated Attic vase by the Sosias painter shows Achilles lovingly

tending an injury his mortal friend has suffered. In Homer's *The Iliad*, Patroklos goes to the fight dressed in his best friend's armour and dies pretending to be the demigod that he was not, instigating the wrath of Achilles, famous across the ages, and the end of the Greek hero's recalcitrance. When the Achaean hero finally enters the battle, he does so not because he supports Agamemnon's troops but in order to avenge his friend Patroklos. Effective motivational symbols that militaries use, in particular the insignias of regiments, make the best of these contiguous emotions, conflating heroic accomplishments, no matter their origin, with the national purpose. (When a soldier believes himself to be fighting "for Queen and country," the Queen is his Patroklos, the country the entity that benefits.)

The victory Achilles delivers to the Greeks is the derivative outcome of the anger and inordinate sense of insult that sees the morose, reluctant, self-absorbed and politically disinterested soldier finally, devastatingly, enter the fray. Relieved as the Achaeans, dying in droves, must have been, what rendered Achilles' actions "heroic" had everything to do with his excellence as a warrior but little to do with altruistic motives such as the patriotism of the soldier that the the society mobilized for war makes a point of repeatedly invoking. Achilles did not give a toss about Agamemnon or Ajax or Odysseus or any of the Greeks but himself, but finally he does go to battle and the combination of his temper and ability lays waste to the Trojans on the battlefield and their valiant prince Hector and sets into motion the Greek victory that was sealed, eventually, by the wily Odysseus and the ithacan hero's sneaky qualities that saw him put into play the ingenious Trojan Horse. Virtue, as we define it now, was a lesser detail in either of these heroes' successes. The Trojan War was an aggressive one waged by a flotilla of marauding Greeks over a more civilized opponent and in it anything was fair. In *The Iliad*, it is Hector who is by far the most humanly decent warrior and "hero" fighting

on either side of a conflict that in no way could be classified as "just."
(Imagine how many times the United States, Britain or France might
have been assaulted if some celebrity's cuckolding of a foreigner had
been the cause.) From Troy to Afghanistan, the truth about battle is
that contests between rival societies provide the backdrop against
which wars are fought, but the "heroic" performance of troops that
settles these conflicts is usually the consequence of a soldier's love of
his colleagues—of his dedication to the pack on whom his life, in the
fulcrum of battle, depends; of his extraordinary capacity for survival;
or merely of his refined bloodlust.

Thus, in the eulogies offered to Canadian soldiers who were killed
early on in the Afghanistan campaign, before 2006 when the fighting
was at its toughest and no end of it was in sight, homages to Canada
took a back seat to tributes to the soldiers' character as one of a band
of brothers. The phrase is not a television invention, or even one of
Stephen E. Ambrose, the popular American historian upon whose book
the HBO miniseries was based, but taken from William Shakespeare's
stirring lines in *Henry V*, delivered by the king on St. Crispin's Day,
their sentiment still germane.

Says Henry:

> From this day to the ending of the world,
> But we in it shall be remember'd;
> We few, we happy few, we band of brothers;
> For he to-day that sheds his blood with me
> Shall be my brother; be he ne'er so vile,
> This day shall gentle his condition:
> And gentlemen in England now a-bed
> Shall think themselves accursed they were not here,
> And hold their manhoods cheap whiles any speaks

That fought with us upon Saint Crispin's day.

In the early days of a conflict, as the drama of the new cause carries the soldier along, the lost are eulogized in a manner that emphasizes the stoic singularity and toughness that distinguishes them from the ordinary citizens who are being protected and languish in their beds. They are perfect troops—who, like Cpl. Ainsworth Dyer (died April 2002), are "always ready to step up to the plate"; who, like Sgt. Robert Short and Cpl. Robbie Beerenfenger (died October 2003), "loved what they were doing and they were brave in the execution of their duties"; or who, like Pte. Robert Costall (died March 2006), "when most people would run away from the sound of gunfire, [he would] run towards it."

Later obituaries would pay homage to the nature of soldiers' motivations in more personal ways, while crediting the "Canadian values" that all exemplified but were disparaged in the war's first stage. Initially, the country needing to be gathered around its new role, the courage and bravery of companionable soldiers entering into the fire of combat, rather than altruistic motives were upheld. Hockey arenas, sports bars and Tim Hortons coffee shops were often the venues in which dead soldiers' qualities were applauded as heroic because at the same time it was essential that these special attributes appeared within reach of ordinary people wondering how to place themselves in regard to the conflict. The cult of the hero is the centrepiece around which all the other terms and images, all the inferences and invocations of the epic narrative, swirl with centripetal force. Writes American religious scholar Karen Armstrong in *A Short History of Myth* (2005), "The myth of the hero was not intended to provide us with icons to admire, but was designed to tap into the vein of heroism within ourselves."

The fighting hero, of course, is put into relief by the prospect of the death he is defying. The ingredient that is most vital to the heroic story, therefore, is the memory of death and a master narrative that warns of the likelihood—indeed, the *inevitability*—of righteous, "ultimate" sacrifice. The concomitant point of epic thinking is to ready the public for the prospect of casualties. So, in 2005, the first Canadian troops having arrived in Kandahar, the Liberal minister of national defence, Bill Graham, warned that the Canadian "public needs to be prepared for the sight of body bags coming back from Afghanistan" on what would later be described as his "pre-body bag tour." In the state at war, it is important to honour the dead with ritual—with gravitas and ceremony that position the loss in the greater narrative of the nation in its just fight.

Ritual breeds consolation but also distance. It substitutes public for private feeling by conflating the mourning of a community of strangers with the more personal devastation that immediate kin will naturally feel. Ritual encourages the public to count itself among the bereaved in the epic story of the fight of good against evil being played out at a national level. By putting these two different kinds of grief on an equivalent, the greater pain that the smaller number of family and friends feel is elevated onto the more public but also abstract plane. On the one hand, genuine succour is derived there from the sympathy of the masses, but, on the other, the singularity of the family's pain is subsumed to the needs of the state and the greater population as the point of the ritual is diverted toward other ends. The anger and existential outrage that loved ones are likely to feel are seconded to public and political interests and, to that more tried, enduring and appropriating narrative. Death becomes Duty; Pain becomes Patriotism. In the solemnity and details of the ramp ceremony, messages from public officials and, in special cases, the pomp of a state funeral, what is being formalized is consideration for the bereaved family, due recognition of the soldier's "ultimate sacrifice" and the army's loss, but a link is also being made to past deaths and others that will occur in the future. Death is an occasion of mourning but also a galvanizing public relations opportunity. The gravity of the struggle in Afghanistan, but also the country's resolute and (in the view of the state) unequivocal return to a previous set of more orthodox ideas about nationhood and the rights and responsibilities of the citizen in civil society is being amplified. Funeral ceremonies make their point by relying immeasurably upon the lexicon of the hero—of courage, bravery, selflessness, "making a difference" and not "dying in vain." Ritual works, brilliantly. What chance does dissidence have when monolithic acclamation is the order of the day? State purpose trumps personal anguish even when the lesser story is one with its own compelling reach.

In Canada, the cult of the hero provided a point of fusion in which domestic actions and those in the realm of foreign policy were combined to alter and then to reinforce the new, more martial state. Well before the events of 9/11 there had been initiatives to commemorate heroes in uniform, but it was from that watershed moment that the word *hero* took on a heightened importance. In deference to the firefighters and police officers who lost their lives in the World Trade Center towers, and the passengers of United Airlines flight 93 that crashed near Shanksville, Pennsylvania, the idea of the hero attained a new gravitas in the United States. Out of the smoking ashes of the World Trade Center rose a cult of the hero willed on by an angry, injured and impassioned nation—one that saw an enemy and wished to slay it. In Canada, too, courageous actions by Canadians in uniform achieved prominence. Standing side by side with the United States despite Prime Minister Jean Chrétien's later decision not to send soldiers into Iraq, the selflessness of the fire and police services at Ground Zero resonated and the cult of the hero burgeoned. After Canada suffered its own first casualties, on April 18, 2002, the qualification of "hero" was awarded to soldiers and police officers with fervour. The Ontario Police Memorial is a tulip garden at Toronto's Queen's Park where more than two hundred officers who have died in the line of duty are remembered. HEROES IN LIFE NOT DEATH, reads the dedication on the plaque. "The names on this memorial remind us that we can never take for granted the contributions of our police officers," Ontario premier Ernie Eves said there in May 2003 as the deaths of two more police officers were mourned. "They are routinely asked to put themselves in harm's way to protect our families and our communities. They are, in fact, putting their lives on the line for you and I and society."

After 2006, the dangerous peak of the country's commitment to the war in Afghanistan, the phenomenon reached new but also less discriminating heights. In 2008, more than a half-century after their deaths, the names of two more policemen, one a constable and one a highway traffic officer, were added to the Ontario Police Memorial's "Wall of Honour," with Premier Dalton McGuinty telling the assembled crowd that "it takes a special kind of person to face danger, to take speeders off our highways, to protect our kids from drug dealers, to keep our communities safe." Both members of the police had died in traffic accidents—one, in 1927, on his motorcycle and the other, in 1935, in a head-on collision with a delivery truck running an intersection. Nevertheless, the epithets of the new age were invoked, McGuinty remembering the new inductees as "extraordinary."

That the officers' deaths were a loss was not in question, but their automatic elevation to heroic status when the circumstances of their deaths were only dubiously so speaks to the sensibility of a country (or at least of its guiding forces) that is covetous for laurels. New mythic requirements had been brought on by the war. Both men may well have been heroic, and many times—this, over the course of careers in which the mere fact of their having chosen police service can be seen as evidence of heroic selflessness. In the case of those who die "in the line of duty," theirs becomes the tragic choice that is another of the classical prerequisites of heroism. Except that by either of these standards, but for the presence of the uniform, the hard-working single mother who comes off the night shift and, desperately tired, dies in an accident driving her children to school can also be described as "heroic." She performed selflessly. She made the tragic choice. All sorts of unknown heroes "make a difference" in myriad unacknowledged ways.

The veneration of "heroic" sacrifices that started, in the new century, after 9/11, became routine with the deaths occurring in distant Afghanistan. The funerals and ceremonies accorded police officers assert a trend in which, more than the actual circumstances of the death, the uniform is the thing that is being honoured. They uphold, a condition of the narrative, the ideological contention that a person in uniform can do no wrong. Certainly, heroic acts exist, and a great many of these are enacted by the army, the police and others who put on uniforms or carry arms, for the very reason that these people hold jobs inherently more dangerous than, say, dentistry or writing. No one disputes that bravery on the battlefield or in the defence of others should be viewed with tremendous respect and many times in awe. But there is a fundamental distinction to be made between what are often politically expedient attributions of heroic praise and the nature of the acts themselves, a bit of scrutiny that goes a long way to granting or denying credence to the suggestion that a soldier may have been injured or died "in vain."

If, after Osama bin Laden was killed on May 2, 2011, or due to any other military action, the war in Afghanistan can meaningfully be said to be over—as opposed to over for us—its mandates fullfilled and mission achieved, then the 158 Canadian soldiers and four civilians who lost their lives in Afghanistan by the end of 2011 can rightly be said not to have "died in vain." They can unequivocally be said to have contributed to the cause, as the DND website honouring them puts it, of "serving Canada and helping the people of Afghanistan." If, however, some other path—of diplomacy, say, or of massive aid and reconstruction such as Germany knew during the years of the Marshall Plan—might credibly have brought Afghanistan and even the state of international "security" to the same level, if Canadians fought in Afghanistan for a decade to be noticed on the international stage and the country was no differently viewed, or to maintain a trade relationship with the United States that was mostly unaffected, or to bring a lasting peace to Afghanistan and permanently improve the lives of schoolgirls there, and these objectives were not achieved, then the retrospective nature of their heroism takes on a different quality. Regardless of the nature of the brave act, the argument can be made that these soldiers really did "die in vain." They become martyrs to a political cause that may be viewed as misconstrued, and even cynical or whimsical, rather than the deaths that came about as part of the profoundly regrettable but necessary cost of a better social outcome that could not have come to pass without their regretted deaths. (In the King James Bible, a source of literary precedent, not incontrovertible truth, Paul says of Christ's crucifixion that "if righteousness come by the law, then Christ is dead in vain." What Paul is saying is that were humankind to reach that point of emancipation anyway, there would have been no need for Christ's death.)

Being unaware of the vagaries of heroic appraisals can put the nature of the act itself into the fog. Inordinate meaning is derived from a logic that is convenient to the national mythology but also false: the regular occurrence of heroic acts committed by men and women in uniform does not mean that all those who put on a uniform are heroes. It does not mean that only *people who wear uniforms* commit heroic acts, or—the dangerous extension of this idea—that men and women in uniform commit *only heroic acts*. The height of ridiculousness, this contrary logic was displayed shortly after the February 2010 arrest of Trenton base commander Col. Russell Williams for murders and pedophiliac acts he would promptly confess to, when the mayor of Quinte West, John Williams (no relation), organized a rally to "support our troops." The insinuation was that citizens expressing horror and shame at the sex crimes of a high-ranking officer were ipso facto making a traitorous attack on the entire mission in Afghanistan. The very fact that the former colonel had evaded notice, let alone capture, for so long could in itself be seen as a symptom of the sometimes problematic confusion of heroes and uniforms, but to doubt either in any way is to question the veracity of the whole epic story of the soldier or the police officer's "mission," his "ultimate sacrifice," his "making a difference" and the "price paid" in the line of duty.

The cult of heroism, efficiently practised, negates any chance of imperfection. The valorous qualities of the hero excuse others that, in peacetime, would be reprehensible. No matter how violent, bad-tempered, lascivious or otherwise flawed, the hero is likely to be excused. From the time of the Greek myths to today's shallow elevation of the hero in sports and celebrity culture (the mischief and fripperies are kindred to those gods of Olympus), this has been true. The failings of ordinary people are forgiven in heroes because their exceptional qualities are necessary to the fight. The rules are different for heroes are different because they are the emblems of

168 | CHAPTER TWO

rare, singular virtues that a society in distress holds in high esteem.
So, in *The Iliad*, when Homer introduces Thersites, a commoner who
objects to Odysseus's war and accuses his leaders of greed and self-
interest in the Achaeans' long campaign against the Trojans (one
that is not going very well), the objector is rebuked because he is a
plain, expendable man and questioning the heroic venture is beyond
his station. Or when, in 2009, diplomat Richard Colvin attested that
Afghan detainees were handed to Afghan prisons and tortured there
or, in 2011, WikiLeaks mastermind Julian Assange making his own
disturbing allegations was the thorn in the warring leaders' side, the
whistleblowers were humiliated. Colvin was described by Defence
Minister Peter MacKay as a "suspect source" likely duped by the
Taliban, this at the kinder end of the invective hurled his way, and
Assange by his detractors as a sexual criminal and as physically ugly.
The material that each of the dissenters brought to the fore mattered,
and may well have been true, but in the epic construct what each was
doing contradicted the state and its heroes and needed therefore to
be undermined.

Where Colvin and Assange proceeded to languish in a sort of
purgatory, their transgressions the thing that each would be remembered for, Achilles' petulance, narcissism and self-pity (though not
his temper) were, in the end, forgotten. The Greek hero ultimately
took his place among the immortals for his feats on the battlefield
conducted in the prince's armour that was the uniform of the day. The
uniform conceals all those untidy, complicating but also distinguishing
aspects of a soldier's individuality, from long hair to an unidentified
predilection to murder women and file their panties in neat rows in
the attic. The medals, ribbons, aiguillettes and assorted denotations
of rank that are allowed merely emphasize the degree to which, in
various bodies, the virtuosic qualities of the soldier — of heroism

and of "selflessness" (i.e., of the soldier being loyal to the unit, and not himself, and putting aside any of the distinctive traits that would give him an identity)—are achieved. To allow the hero to convey some more complete impression is to take off the uniform, or to put creases in it. It is to raise the possibility that some aspect of the police officer's or the soldier's character might be human; that the hero might be civilian, fallible or even common. It was the evocation of the more universally appealing possibility of heroism in ordinary civilian life that made President Barack Obama's address to mourners after the January 2011 shooting of Congresswoman Gabrielle Giffords in Tucson, Arizona, so stirring. The constitutional right to bear arms was the cleaver, but in a speech surmounting political differences that at a tense moment of national schism was praised by Democrats and Republicans alike, Obama said:

> Our hearts are full of gratitude for those who saved others. We are grateful for Daniel Hernandez, a volunteer in Gabby's office who ran through the chaos to minister to his boss, tending to her wounds to keep her alive. We are grateful for the men who tackled the gunman as he stopped to reload. We are grateful for a petite, 61-year-old Patricia Maisch, who wrestled away the killer's ammunition, undoubtedly saving some lives. And we are grateful for the doctors and nurses and emergency medics who worked wonders to heal those who'd been hurt. These men and women remind us that heroism is found not only on the fields of battle. They remind us that heroism does not require special training or physical strength. Heroism is here, all around us, in the hearts of so many of our fellow citizens, just waiting to be summoned.

The idea of the ordinary person as capable hero belongs to the novel rather than the epic. It envisions, with grace, the hero as someone who may not be in uniform, as someone who is potentially any one of us. The complicated flip side of such a construction, the pill that is hard to swallow, is a concomitant imagining of the enemy as not distant from what circumstance might have any person be. Beneath his monster's uniform, the enemy is someone who in his essence is no different from any one of us. He is someone bound by the universal laws of our common humanity. Writes American playwright William Saroyan in the prologue to his Pulitzer Prize-winning play, *The Time of Your Life*, that opened on Broadway in October 1939 — a month after the Second World War started, "Remember that every man is a variation of yourself. No man's guilt is not yours, nor is any man's innocence a thing apart. Despise evil and ungodliness, but not men of ungodliness or evil. These, understand."

The search for a hero, any hero, attained its zenith in the 2006 initiative of Rudyard Griffiths, then director of the Dominion Institute, to provide a state funeral for the last Canadian First World War veteran, John Babcock. In 2009, the initiative to honour Babcock was repeated by the Historica-Dominion Institute and once again rebuffed. It expired after the veteran died in February 2010, at the age of 109. That year's "Vimy Ridge Day," commemorated since 2003, was marked with a heightened public ceremony in Ottawa at which both the prime minister and Governor General spoke, but the state funeral did not come to pass.

John Babcock was born on July 23, 1900, and left the farm to join the army at age fifteen. He never fought in the war. The authorities discovered that he was underage and held him back. He was stationed in the United Kingdom with the Boys Battalion in 1917 and was under two-week house arrest after a brawl with a bunch of British soldiers outside a dance hall in Wales when the Armistice was declared. His story is comic, really, and a latter-day Evelyn Waugh would have had great fun with it. But in Canada, divided about the point of the war, only earnest adulation will do. Humour rankles. (It does not "support our troops.") In 1921, Babcock emigrated to America, joined the United States Army, and spent most of his life there. In 2008, after a visit by Veterans Affairs Minister Greg Thompson to Spokane, Washington, where Babcock was living, he was re-awarded Canadian citizenship at a swearing-in that took place in his American home. A press opportunity was made of the note of appreciation Thompson had encouraged him to write and how much the prime minister and the Governor General, Michaëlle Jean, were moved by it.

Babcock, who was a modest man, died on February 18, 2010. He himself had no illusions about the incidental role he had played in the war or the way in which the fact of his being "the last living Canadian veteran" was so powerfully emblematic that it had some scrambling for a kind of remembering he did not want. "I really didn't accomplish very much," said Babcock in one of the last interviews of the many that the chance of longevity awarded him in his final years. When he learned of plans to hold a state funeral for him, Babcock was clear about where the honour lay. "I think it should be for the fellows who spent time in the front lines and were actually in the fighting," he said.

In light of the vitriol that was regularly intoned against Canadian citizens who had "never known war" by columnists such as Christie Blatchford and Rosie DiManno, or by the editorial team of the *Globe and Mail*, the campaign for a state funeral for John Babcock appears all the more ironic. Babcock had not served on the front lines either, but he wore the uniform, so to make such an observation was not patriotic. If ritual processions are an integral part of the appropriation of soldiers' deaths and the primary means of their elevation to heroic status, then with John Babcock the phenomenon breached the absurd.

He had not even died yet, but neither this nor his lack of interest in being specially honoured, nor any of the other affecting comments that he made, mattered much. "I think it would be nice if all the different people in the world could get along together so we weren't having wars," said Babcock. "I don't suppose that'll ever happen, though."

We are all tainted: the old soldier's views were patently ones that it was not convenient for a fighting society in the thrall of war's perversion to adopt. Babcock, said a relative attending the funeral, would have been upset by all the "falderal," but the last veteran was, according to Griffiths, "both an individual and a symbol" and, in the battle to win hearts and minds, the symbolic moment a funeral provides mattered more, as usual, than the feelings of any of the individuals involved. Thus Babcock was constantly being spoken for—by politicians or by citizens such as Andrew Cohen and Griffiths, whose professional lives were invested in the amplification of his story. "The duty not to forget now falls on a generation who has never known war," said Griffiths after the death of a veteran who had patently done everything he could to avoid becoming a myth. "As long as John Babcock lived and breathed, he reminded us, by virtue of his service, that Canada didn't just arrive here yesterday. It didn't fall from the heavens, fully formed. His message: We built. We sacrificed. We came from somewhere," wrote Cohen in the *Toronto Star*. "Whatever Babcock represented as a veteran—duty, courage, honour, and perhaps adolescent exuberance and recklessness, too—he is no longer a tribune of his time. Now the memory is ours to preserve. Alone."

This was an astonishing subsuming of a life to some imagined higher purpose, a quarrelling over inheritance that was aggressive and unseemly. But Cohen, during his tenure as executive director of the Historica-Dominion Institute, was fervently engaged in the job of national myth-making. The organization, with its mandate to extend the historical education of Canadians, had made a point of revealing, through a number of surveys, many Canadians' ignorance of their country's past, a lack that certainly needed addressing. It had published books, documents and interactive websites on issues concerning Canadian national identity and embarked upon the Memory Project, an unquestionably important archive of Canadian soldiers' remembrances supported by the Department of Canadian Heritage. Cohen, who had attacked what he believed to be the complacency of the nation in *While Canada Slept: How We Lost Our Place in the World*, shared the widespread view that the First World War had provided Canada its "governing mythology" and, even after Babcock's death, was arguing for "a national day of commemoration" to remember the man who was described as the country's last "living link" to the "Great War" and, a later concession, the veteran's generation's part in it.

Griffiths, afterwards the organizer and host of the prestigious international political series of theatrically staged Munk Debates, had already had a go. The online petition he had issued through the Dominion Institute in 2006 was eventually signed by 90,000 Canadians and led to the unanimous consent of an easily persuaded Parliament that it should honour Babcock with a state funeral when that day came. The unexpected spanner in the works was that Babcock did not want it. He could not quite put it out of mind that he did not fight and felt that such a ceremony would, in its disproportion, dishonour those who did and celebrate a war that should be lamented. "It may become necessary for a young man or woman to join the military to defend their country," said Babcock—but regretfully. "I hope countries think long and hard before engaging in war, as many people get killed. What a waste—not to mention the relatives who are left to mourn."

In choosing to obstruct, no matter how deferentially, those who would aggrandize the role of our military at every turn, John Babcock had not acted alone. Charles Coules, the oldest living British veteran,

106 years old at the time, refused an official invitation to participate in the November 2011 Remembrance Day commemorations in Europe because, said his daughter, he was against the glorification of war. How inconvenient these men's wishes are to the story that we are trying to write.

Unless, that is, you ignore them and bully on anyway.

"Canadians," wrote Cohen, "should respect the wishes of Mr. Babcock's family during this sad time, but the Government of Canada should extend the offer." The Prime Minister's Office, needing no coaxing, promised that the government "has plans to respectfully mark this moment in our history," ensuring that "Canadians will have the opportunity to pay their respect and honour all those who served our country in the First World War." The *Globe and Mail* demanded a "large public event" very soon. With the 2010 Vancouver Games on the horizon, Griffiths suggested with quite extraordinary gall that "it would be well deserved if we could find a way to honour Mr. Babcock and his generation at the Olympics," and that "it would be a fitting tribute if the next gold medal that was won by our athletes was given to his family." Anyone who doubted after Leni Riefenstahl that sports could possibly become the extension of politics by other means, even in such a placid democracy such as Canada's is, no longer needed to be uncertain. (Would Canadians have participated comfortably in an Olympics at which China or the former Yugoslavia celebrated their national heroes? It is doubtful, though Canada has started doing it.) Anyone who wondered just how Babcock's family might have been able to cope with an "offer" from 90,000 people, one that the late soldier repeatedly said he did not want, had to step to the back.

Cohen, fervently, likened Canada to "a nation of amnesiacs stumbling about in a poetic fog." A catchy phrase, but one that was not true or, if so, in a way he did not intend, as Joseph Boyden, Alan Cumyn,

Allan Donaldson, Timothy Findley, Jack Hodgins, Frances Itani, Andrea Nann, R.H. Thompson and Jane Urquhart constituted but a few of Canadian authors, performers and poets who were keeping the memory alive even before propagandists got at this actually quite controversial founding Canadian myth for their own purposes—a little more funding, an easier war. The institute's purpose in calling for a "national day of commemoration" was, wrote Cohen later, "less to honour him than the 600,000 Canadians who fought in Europe and the 60,000 who died," was "not to romanticize his role or glorify his war. It is to offer a teachable moment to Canadians, for whom the Great War is ancient history, so they might have a better understanding of what it was, in all its horror, and what it meant to us as a nation." In fact, the propagation of the Afghanistan era's version of the constantly revised First World War story had already been tremendously successful. The Canadian hockey teams' success at the Vancouver 2010 Winter Olympics was, inevitably, compared to Vimy "in the pride it fosters in us as a people," its rite of passage as important as "that hallowed victory of the Great War" (Andrew Cohen), the moment that, as when "all four divisions of the Canadian Expeditionary Force fought together for the first time and overwhelmed a massive German stronghold.... our nation will be seen to have become fully grown up" (Lorne Gunter). No one died, and the gold medals were not conceded to the Americans a couple of weeks later as the ground at Passchendaele had been to the Germans (and, too, it has to be asked how many times a nation gets to grow up), but no matter. Vimy could be used to explain just about any Canadian success unabashedly. It was during the controversy surrounding Babcock's death and its proper commemoration that I overheard a grade nine student, doing much better in history than she expected, proclaim, "I'm storming the ridge, Mom—just like the Canadians at Vimy." Eventually propaganda drains meaning from even the best stories in its arsenal.

In truth, Canadians already had "the opportunity to pay their respect and honour all those who served our country in the First World War" through public institutions that, before any short-term political convenience have existed to satisfy Canadians' very decent and understandable desire to want to commemorate events that should not pass unnoticed. One of these is Remembrance Day. Another is Parliament, where a minute's silence would have been appropriate and would have most effectively expressed the sorrow of all Canadians upon John Babcock's passing—had Parliament not, at the time, been prorogued. But instead, "Vimy Ridge Day"—that, although not a holiday, had required, since 2003, government buildings to fly their flags at half-mast—was staged with greater solemnity and touted by the government as "a national commemorative ceremony honouring all of Canada's First World War service men and women to pay tribute to their achievements and contributions" and "the end of an era." On the day, at an Ottawa ceremony in which both Prime Minister Stephen Harper and then Governor General Michaëlle Jean, the commander-in-chief of the Canadian Forces, were in attendance, it was the prime minister who was more bowed and measured in his comments. Canada, said Harper, was "the most peaceful, prosperous and generous nation the world has ever known." Freedom was Canada's "gift," and responsibility demanded that it be used "for great purposes." Canadians should not be "captive to the past," said Harper, clearly alluding to the sorrow of Vimy as much as its veterans' example of fearlessness in his solemn emploring to Canadians to, "always be tireless as they were to work for that which is right and good."

What the advocates of a state funeral for John Babcock knew was that the funeral marches of soldiers, the RCMP and other police officers have been integral to the reinforcement of the martial cult of the hero in the decade's epic story. Since 2001, such ceremonies have been attended in increasing numbers, typically bolstered by colleagues in uniform from out of province as well as from the United States. In 2004, at a ceremony remembering the death of RCMP corporal James Galloway in a standoff outside Spruce Grove, Alberta, along with five colleagues who died that same year, 4,000 colleagues were in attendance, and 8,000 after police officer Eric Czapnik was killed by a suspended RCMP officer in December 2009. The week after Toronto Police sergeant Ryan Russell was killed, on January 12, 2011, by a deranged man driving a stolen truck with a snowplow, hundreds lined up to pay their respects on each of the two days of visitation. On the day of the funeral, traffic was cut off in the city's downtown core for a procession that was attended by police from across Canada and the United States as more than 14,000 officers and civilians marched to the Metro Convention Centre, where the service was held, and filled it to bursting. Attendance massively eclipsed the hundreds who attended the memorial service for the six victims of the attempt to assassinate Arizona congresswoman Gabrielle Giffords, including nine-year-old Christina Green, held the week before in Tucson, Arizona. It was an unprecedented public service tantamount to the state funeral that John Babcock did not get. It drew 2,000 more than attended former prime minister Pierre Trudeau's funeral in 2000 and 4,000 more than came out that same year for French-Canadian hockey legend (and political hero) Maurice Richard.

On the day of the Russell funeral, the *Toronto Star* dedicated its front page as well as an editorial to the occasion and provided a map and the details of the funeral service. Toronto's television station CP24 asked, in its *In the Line of Duty* live broadcast, "How are you paying tribute to Sergeant Russell today?" CBC Radio reported from the procession descending University Avenue and from the Convention Centre for several hours, live, and made the sergeant's death the lead item of the local and national news and the theme of special shows all day long. The speeches of the service were broadcast in their entirety, and Russell was repeatedly remembered by police officers as "one of our own," this simple description serving to entrench the distinction between those who wear the uniform and the majority who do not—and at a time when the mishandling of Toronto's G20 Summit had made the police services the focus of a lot of attention they did not want. Gushed a CBC Radio reporter, "I saw two policemen shaking each other's hands and one saying, 'I'm sorry about your loss'—and they didn't know each other!" Tragedy, said the *Toronto Star's* editorial, had "made Russell a household name." On the next day, the entire front page was dedicated to reporting the funeral, and it was apparent just how much the language and rituals of the war had permeated civilian life. Cutlines spoke of Russell's "service, sacrifice and a life lived for others"; of "remembrance" and a "brave young father cut down in the line of duty." Toronto Police chief Bill Blair spoke of a hero determined to "make a difference" and of a "legacy of service and sacrifice that has been earned by generations of police officers who have gone before him." Construction workers on the job stopped work to doff their hard hats and clasp them to their chests in solemn poses familiar from the movies. Ardith Quanbury, the first civilian in line to attend the service, spoke of Sergeant Russell on his "worthy mission" having "paid the full price."

Did Sergeant Russell slip? Did the driver aim at him or not know he was there? Whose accounts of the incident were being depended on? These are spoilers' questions. What is being defended in such moments—whether in the Ontario Police Memorial's "Wall of Honour" dedicated to "the fallen," in the ramp ceremonies for dead soldiers or in the funeral marches of police forces—is the integrity and vitality of the epic narrative. To wonder about the circumstances of police sergent Ryan Russell's death and if these have any bearing on its "heroic" nature, or to what extent the massive numbers of officers in uniform in attendance at his funeral represented a public relations opportunity seized after the unnecessary and alienating police violence of the G20 Summit; to wonder about the *privilege* of being a police officer and the authority of a force that appears frequently to be persuaded that investigations of its actions are immoral and unnecessary is to challenge the whole mythic construction of the funeral demonstration—of police officers having the common purpose of fighting evil so that ordinary civilians are safe in their beds. In the city, as in the battlefields of Afghanistan, it is to challenge the idea of the war as just. Only the bold write, as one *Star* reader did the day after the funeral for Sergeant Russell (effectively answering CP24's poll), "There is a tangible way for the Metro Toronto Police to honour the memory of the late Sgt. Ryan Russell, in addition to gathering en masse to attend his funeral. Any who know the identities of fellow officers who inflicted unnecessary violence on members of the public during the G20 Summit should break the code of silence, come forward, and make the identities known to the authorities. I can't think of a better lasting tribute to Sgt. Russell than upholding the standards by which he apparently conducted himself."

Today, the meaning of the word *hero* has been stretched to absurd dilution. Numerous decently minded and honourable sites and archives exist (and are proliferating) that honour the service of Canadian veterans, and it is also possible to do "Hero" workouts at CrossFit gyms across the country in honour of Afghanistan war dead (a 400-metre run, 40 dead lifts, 40 box jumps, 40 wall balls and a second 400-metre run). A plethora of video games propound the shoot-'em-up epic narrative of good against evil; a kid can be a "Guitar Hero." During the 2009-10 NHL playoffs, billboards in Toronto displayed a picture of a Toronto Maple Leafs hockey player in his mask and the slogan, WHERE HEROES ARE MADE, which was stretching it given that the team had not won the Stanley Cup in over fifty years or made the playoffs in six.

In her lively challenge of the gender-discriminating myth-making behind the United States' wars in Iraq and Afghanistan, *The Terror Dream: Myth and Misogyny in an Insecure America*, American Pulitzer Prize-winning writer Susan Faludi paints a provocative picture of a country in which, its psyche defensive and besieged after 9/11, the heroic requirement provoked a revival of bigoted, knee-jerk male chauvinist feeling that, elsewhere, essayist William Deresiewicz has described as an expression of "desperate machismo." With consequences. "Now that the peaceful life can no longer be guaranteed," Faludi quotes U.S. military historian Martin van Creveld telling *Newsday*, "one of the principal losers is likely to be feminism, which is based partly on the false belief that the average woman is as able to defend herself as the average man." Van Creveld and the multitude of American politicians, pundits and hacks who thought like him evidently put little stock in Herodotus's account of the Amazons, antiquity's fierce women warriors of Asia Minor, who were said to cut off a breast to make shooting a bow easier; Tacitus's description of the Anglesey warrior Boudica, scourge of the Romans in first-century Britain; or the continuing phenomenon of women having played prominent roles in the terror movements of the last century and this one. (English journalist Eileen MacDonald's *Shoot the Women First*, a 1992 book about female guerillas, took its title from the phenomenon of West German anti-terrorist squads instructed to do just that.) Faludi's scathing indictment of a bewildered, insecure nation finding succour in its Daniel Boone mythology of frontier conquest reveals a country in which women are portrayed as helpless and ineffective and needing to be rescued and the men are brazen, rifle-wielding defenders of the family. She describes how the United States reverted, under the government of George W. Bush, to the "recurring trope" of "the white maiden taken against her will by dark 'savages,'" one descended from the mythology of the frontier dubiously recalling a time when male settlers repeatedly failed to protect their families from the sacking of their homes, and scalping. In the media coverage of the attacks on the World Trade Center, women and their actions do not figure. They are conspicuously absent from the recounting, in fact. The primitive singing of the heroic male country is entrenched during the war in Iraq, by the military and the media's utterly misleading reporting of the dramatic rescue by U.S. Marines of the captive Pfc. Jessica Lynch from a Baghdad hospital. (Lynch was being well attended to and certainly not imprisoned by the caring and surprised Iraqi doctors.)

War has long possessed its own institutionalized phallic imagery and lexicon—of "hard" versus "soft" power, of nuclear warheads and so on—so that even within the Canadian Forces, a military with a progressive sensibility, the gender-oriented undertones of what is traditionally a male-driven culture are in evidence. In *Afghanistan: The Other War*, a television documentary made for PBS's *Frontline* in 2007, British foreign correspondent Sam Kiley spent time with Canadian troops trying, and failing, to fix a village's water pumps. The development work is the woman officer's job. The men are indifferent and in their spare time play video war games. (Desmond Morton, McGill University's prolific professor emeritus of history and the author of *When Your Number's Up, The Canadian Soldier in the First World War* [1994], has remarked that the war in Afghanistan may well be "the first war in our experience in which feminists have often been in favour in the hope that somehow it will improve the status and prospects of Afghan women," the activist and writer Sally Armstrong one of the notable champions of this point of view.) But, in Canada, the period of first contact and the territory's European settlement did not take the bloody course that it did in frontier America so that there was neither the same atavistic fear nor a similarly delusional machismo-driven relapse to save the national sense of fortitude from embarrassment. And yet, since 9/11, an orthodox idea of the hero to reinforce the new order, and the simple gender stereotypes upon which the epic's clear-cut and unambiguous representation of a threatening world depends, have known a resurgence. These are patterns that started in mimicry—the country, as it does so often, looking to America for its cues—but that have gained a momentum and a discourse of their own with each Afghanistan fatality.

Over the course of the last decade, the notion of the "hero" as someone who is capable, in any quarter, of demonstrating extra-ordinary qualities has taken a back seat not only to the fact of wearing a uniform but also to the bearer being part of select and, by and large, manly forces. The heroes in today's story are, as Christie Blatchford put it, "indisputably men." They are "old-fashioned," "alpha males" and the "universally beautiful" young. They are the "guys wars can't be won without," whom the former *Globe and Mail* reporter loves "unabashedly" in "the *Boy's Own* world of war," serving in the last arena in which men are "left to their own devices, largely untouched by the most effete of modern cultural conventions." (In one of the stranger moments of her paean to the work of the Canadian Forces in Afghanistan, *Fifteen Days*, Blatchford writes of one killed soldier's mother who continues to send dirty magazines in her care packages to the son's platoon "because they like it.") They are, in the eye of Rosie DiManno of the *Toronto Star*, "combat virgins" returning as "ripened veterans." They are men "in the vigour of their manhood" and the "backbone" of the country, "doing what soldiers do" while the rest of us sit "idly by." Blatchford and DiManno's erotic fancies stand in a long line of hero-worship that started at least a couple of millennia earlier, the original Greek heroes having been admired by gods with a surfeit of sexual appetite—as too, they were by the good citizens of the poleis did. The soldiers of the Canadian Forces are sexualized by the candid pair just as, with more lyricism, young male soldiers of the First World War trenches were by a handful of enviably educated British officers finding an outlet for their attractions, catalyzed by the perils of the front, in the beautiful young bodies of their charges.

Such homoeroticism is, however, no matter how kindred, patently too unsettling for many of the champions of the warrior nation's primitive epic schema to contemplate. When it comes to the business of being a hero, fags and fancy dressers, men whose gifts are not derived from muscle, need not apply. (After Canada's exit from the war, Blatchford wrote in the *National Post* of being "mortified" and "appalled" upon her return to Toronto at the site of children hugging and men "in touch with their feminine side" and generally being alarmed at "how much in need the modern male of the species is of some toughening up.") Those who even dare to question the war or its morphing raisons d'être belong, it's very likely, to misguided factions on the left that actually think it is possible to be against the war and "support our troops"—or, for that matter, to entertain ambivalence of any kind. "Aggression," wrote Blatchford in September 2006, "is part of who soldiers are, as integral as boots and weapons, and was even when Canadians were posted in Cyprus"—that is, when Canadian soldiers acted as peacekeepers, and other Canadians were proud of these troops in their more cautious, negotiating, interpositionary and (dare it be said?) more feminine role.

True to this paradigm are other admonitions from on high, such as that which Andrew Cohen delivered in the *Ottawa Citizen* in

December 2009 concerning Amanda Lindhout, the unfortunate as-piring Canadian freelance journalist who he had attacked with such off-putting condescension. "Bless her," wrote Cohen, "she has landed the biggest story of all: herself. The irony is exquisite, an emblem of the vanity of our time." By comparison, when Tim Hetherington, the director of *Restrepo*, was killed in Libya in April 2011, he was remembered for his "bravery" and "camaraderie." Without question, the award-winning British photojournalist was more accomplished, though his remembrance was also conforming to more conventional, male ideas of heroism. Hetherington was one of the guys. Never was it implied that he was being, in any way, irresponsible. He was doing what becomes a *man*.

In a similarly chauvinist vein, *Globe and Mail* columnist Lysiane Gagnon wondered about the wisdom of a policy of embedding media that saw two "young women" travelling with troops. An in-depth report had appeared in the same newspaper the month before, concerning the deaths in December 2009 of Sgt. George Miok, Pte. Garrett Chidley, Cpl. Zachery McCormack, Sgt. Kirk Taylor and a reporter from the *Calgary Herald*, Michelle Lang, who was travelling with the unit. The thirty-four-year-old reporter was older than all four soldiers, and the twenty-five-year-old Ottawa policy analyst Bushra Saeed, who was injured but survived the roadside bomb attack, was older than two of them. The clear implication of the Gagnon article was that the two women were liabilities who needed to be protected and that their mingling with locals during the patrol may have made them a choice target and led to the ambush of the soldiers' convoy.

Lang became the first civilian to receive the same repatriation honours as soldiers killed in the line of duty. At the later ceremony, the prime minister spoke of a debt to the soldiers "that we can never repay" and took care to offer condolences to "the loved ones of journalist Michelle Lang, who courageously risked her life reporting from one of the world's most dangerous countries," but Gagnon's judgment struck a chauvinistic contrast, diminishing as it did the possibility that either of the women, though clearly risking bodily harm for their vocation and the public good, was acting "heroically." The modern definition of the hero has gathered in its embrace those who excel in a plethora of pursuits, and lately journalism has become one of the more perilous of these, but what Gagnon's column and myriad others have shown is that Canada, like the United States, has reverted in its state of war to a much narrower, more conservative idea of what constitutes heroic action.

The soldier, in the epic reduction, *acts* and *protects*. The armed forces, but also police officers and firefighters, have come to be incontrovertible symbols of a society, in this mode, relying on brute strength to protect itself—and this rather than "soft power" or any of the other more "effete" qualities of "intellectual elites," artists and the diverse and generally peaceful civilization on whose behalf the battle is at least ostensibly being fought. Today, the invocation of courage and its announcement in the uniform take precedence over the sort of illustrious achievement or nobility of purpose that may well be "heroic" but is also exemplified in a host of pursuits in which only civvies are required. Thus, on his last tour to Afghanistan as Canadian troops were withdrawing in July 2011, Minister of Defence Peter MacKay was able to tell soldiers, "You are the best citizens of our country." The rest of society, the un-heroic portion, prevaricates, discusses and debates. And in so doing, it *subverts*. (Alongside the history of war is the recurring story of the hero who returns to the blithe society he has suffered so much to protect. Shocked by the comforts and even gaiety he discovers, the soldier and his acolytes hold it in contempt, undeserving of the deaths and sacrifice he knows viscerally.) Supporters of the epic view, adamant in the conventional constructions of heroism and sacrifice that underpin it, hate the confusion, relativist ideas, culturally specific explanations and arguments from "root causes" that progressives draw from the novel's more tolerant, empathetic understanding of the world. The battle lines being drawn, doubters and equivocators of any kind cannot be tolerated—neither querulous liberals, nor artsy types with their unhelpful doubts and inquiries, nor the wounded and defeated. Hence, a full seven years after Canada's start to the war, the not so subtle damning of American war resisters finding refuge in Canada in the *Globe and Mail*'s 2009 Remembrance Day editorial, quoted earlier, extolling those "who could have hidden, or feigned an injury, or simply refused to fight." Or, in June 2011, after the Conservative Party of Canada was elected to its first parliamentary majority, Minister of Citizenship, Immigration and Multiculturalism Jason Kenney's spectacularly invidious put-down of liberals "focused on the obsessions of the chattering classes—like Taliban prisoners." Trudeaupian layabouts that they are, they "believe that Canada's history began in the Summer of Love," Kenney extolling instead "the brave soldiers, in every generation including our own, who have laid down their lives"—not for the country but (another throwback to bygone Canadian fealty) "the Dominion."

An alpha-male construction reflects neither the composition nor the ideal of the Canadian Forces, but it is the one that was championed during the period of 2001-06, the first period of the war, most ardently by newspaper columnists Christie Blatchford and Rosie DiManno and CBC hockey commentator Don Cherry. "A militarized culture," writes Chris Hedges in his 2010 polemic, *Death of the Liberal Class*, "attacks all that is culturally defined as the feminine, including love, gentleness, compassion, and acceptance of difference...It is a moral cancer that the liberal class once struggled against." The former foreign correspondent's analysis of the abandonment of progressive values by the very people who rose to power on the back of them goes some way to illuminating why, in Canada, the complete abandoning of peacekeeping and the refashioning of the country into a so-called "warrior nation," may have been an innately Conservative project but it was supported by the Liberal leader of the day, Michael Ignatieff. Such was the weight of consensus in Canada during the period of committing to the war that no opposition to the deployment of Canadian Forces was expressed by Ignatieff, one of a set of liberal thinkers with tremendous influence in the United States and Britain who, intensely interested in the Balkan Wars and other instances of UN-administered humanitarian intervention, were embarrassed by their setbacks into more hawkish military stridency. The Liberal Party leader chose not to resist the Conservative bolstering of the military even in the war's lesser details. When, in September 2009, Liberal MP Gerard Kennedy proposed a private member's bill protecting American war resisters whose actions were based on "sincere moral, political or religious objection," Ignatieff chose not to be present in the House when the bill was voted on and it did not pass.

Ignatieff's vote would have made no difference, except to Canadians desperate for some kind of meaningful opposition to the political tide. So great had the damage to the prior version of Canada already been that it had no able defenders in Ottawa outside of NDP leader Jack Layton, an ineffectual force in Parliament at the time. The Conservative military project demanded heroic language and imagery and acquired it. The desecration of the country's prior foundation myths, notably those of peacekeeping and of the country as a forgiving, safe haven, were consequences. Attacks on the arts and the country's "cultural elites," along with the elevation in social status of men and women in uniform and the promotion of the right of not just soldiers or RCMP to bear arms, were a few of the others. (In a sense, this has always been so, even Homer putting the boots to artists in his great work, *The Iliad*: in Ancient Greek times, heroes were well-rounded folk prone to delivering soliloquies on the battlefield and succumbing to other moments of skilled and also valued oratory. When, in *The Iliad*, Odysseus arrives at Achilles' and Patroklos's tent to beseech the greatest of heroes to fight, the warrior unsurpassed in ability is at the peak of his sulky indulgence and—an eminently useless activity in the Greek camp—playing the lyre.)

The growing strength of the military lobby and the impetus of the war in Afghanistan led, at home, to the zealous use of electric-charge-firing Taser guns by the RCMP and police services across the country, even postal workers wanting a chance at the new firearm toy for their dangerous rounds with unleashed pets. As disturbing a reflection of the flourishing of the same gun culture was the battle of Stephen Harper's Conservatives, bitterly fought, to dismantle the Gun Registry. Bill C-68, leading to the Firearms Act, had been the effort of the Liberal government under Jean Chrétien in 1993 to record all legitimately owned firearms in the country—legislation conceived, in part, as a response to the mass murder of fourteen female engineering students at l'Université de Montréal by twenty-five-year-old Marc Lépine in 1989. Ultimately the legislation was successful, the Conservative hatred of the original bill so intense that not only the registry but every single trace of it, the ownership records of every one of the more than 7.6 million guns registered in Canada by the end of 2010, needed to be destroyed—contrary to the wishes of the Canadian Association of the Chiefs of Police and others decrying the pointless destruction of its already gathered, valuable data, a campaign of legislative nihilism that finally became law in February, 2012. The drive to undo the contentious legislation pitted, in its Conservative fantasy of dread, morally upright members of an imagined working-class countryside against the decadent populations of well-to-do cities where where the arts, homosexuality, Internet peeping Toms and other deviant behaviours prosper.

Hence, at the inauguration of new Toronto mayor Rob Ford in December 2010, the ranting of Don Cherry, Canada's self-appointed professional imbecile, against "all the pinkos out there that ride bicycles and everything." The epic's view that certain members of society are less necessary than others—its artists, "intellectual elites," "left-wing pinkos" and the like—is a corollary of the culture of the uniform. Heroes, guns and police officers are good. Homosexuals, pinkos, bicycle riders and those who dare to believe that the mere registration of guns is a helpful measure are bad. The first bunch makes up the defenders of the Good Society, the second the ingrates and debilitated specimens that hardly warrant defending—they are the residue of the Summer of Love in which so much of Canada's rot was started by the quintessential nemesis of Canadian conservatives, Pierre Elliot Trudeau, along with subsequent Liberals whose premier transgression was to emasculate soldiers and paint their helmets blue. Doing the conventional task of the city clerk, the *Hockey Night in Canada* commentator put the chain of office around Ford's neck, the mayor then applauding his pal Don Cherry because "what you see is what you get." Later, there was more of the same. Entirely in line with this hunkered, regressive hedging of Conservative and police forces against the imagined degradation of civil society, Cherry pledged his idiosyncratic brand of windy, vociferous support to candidate Julian Fantino, the former OPP commissioner and before that the chief of the Toronto Police Services, in the latter's successful campaign to become the Conservative MP for Vaughan, Ontario. Epic storytelling depends upon the staunch division of good and bad and the fostering of vigilance to keep the imagined threat at bay, neccessarily turning its attention to home in order to sustain its closed view.

Ironically, the divisive tendency of epic thinking is the outcome of a society in which armed forces are less integrated than would be the ideal. The encouragement of an officer class of educated members drawn from the so-called "intellectual elites" and "left-wing pinkos" would dissolve a lot of the deliberately stoked rural-urban tension upon which the conservative view of the country depends, making the presence of soldiers in uniform in civil society altogether less remarkable — as it is in Britain, for instance, where some of the most entitled (and titled) Oxford and Cambridge graduates enlist if they have not served as cadets already. The enlisting, as a matter of course, of young members of the Royal Family is the acme of this idea, in which not just the selflessness of military service but its ordinariness is telegraphed at the same time that at least a symbolic unity of aristocracy and working classes is achieved. A number of Canadian Forces reserves attend university as students like anyone else but, in Canada, where a majority of its citizens suppose class tensions not to be an issue, such a course of study and professional development does not occur to nearly all of the country's most privileged citizens — this, through no particular fault of their own. The idea is simply not there. A cult rather than a sensible respect of the hero flourishes as a consequence and becomes the wedge of a point of view that pathologically elevates one portion of society while it holds another in contempt.

The Australian John Pilger, who established his career reporting during the American war in Vietnam, believes that in the present decade journalism has itself become "a weapon of war, a virulent censorship that goes unrecognized in the United States, Britain and other democracies; censorship by omission, whose power is such that, in war, it can mean the difference between life and death." In a speech Pilger delivered at Columbia University in 2006, the radical journalist went on to say:

> Language is perhaps the most crucial battleground. Noble words such as "democracy," "liberation," "freedom" and "reform" have been emptied of their true meaning and refilled by the enemies of those concepts. The counterfeits dominate the news, along with dishonest political labels, such as "left of centre," a favourite given to warlords such as Blair and Bill Clinton; it means the opposite. "War on terror" is a fake metaphor that insults our intelligence. We are not at war. Instead, our troops are fighting insurrections in countries where our invasions have caused mayhem and grief, the evidence and images of which are suppressed. How many people know that, in revenge for 3,000 innocent lives taken on 11 September 2001, up to 20,000 innocent people died in Afghanistan?

The "historic task" of war correspondents who accept the terms of government embedding, said Pilger, has been "to soften up the public for rapacious attacks on countries that are no threat to us" and to speak of "regime change" as if the country where it was being planned was "an abstraction, not a human society." To do so requires a particular kind of obfuscating language, one to whip the home crowds into patriotic compliance, if not fervour. To set the military juggernaut rolling, narratives of nations embarking upon military campaigns indulge in the use of terms that American writer Paul Fussell, a veteran of the Second World War, calls examples of "high diction." Since Homer's *The Iliad* and likely before, the paradox and the trick of heroic reporting has been to inure the civilian to ugly deaths through such enthralling language. The subsumption of terms to the epic cause is key.

In *The Great War in Modern Memory*, Fussell's classic and immensely readable study of the First World War in literature, the Wolrd War II U.S. Army veteran lists fifty words and phrases that, in use as the European conflagration started, he considered to be examples of a "raised, essentially feudal language" born out of the work of poets and novelists of Empire such as Alfred Lord Tennyson and Rider T. Haggard and the "pseudo-Mediaeval Romances" of William Morris. Its euphemistic terms would be replaced, in the wake of the gruesome experience of the First World War, by a truer and more graphic language at odds with the prevalent romanticism's false elevation of glorious, heroic notions. The sheen of confident, turn-of-the-century Empires would be swept aside and replaced by that of a more sombre, steely realism. Looking back decades later at the suddenly distant epoch before the First World War, Fussell finds the bygone literary scene "hard to imagine. There was no *Waste Land*, with its rats' alleys, dull canals, and dead men who have lost their bones: it would take four years of trench warfare to bring these to consciousness. There was no *Ulysses*, no *Mauberley*, no *Cantos*, no Kafka, no Proust, no Waugh, no Auden, no Huxley, no Cummings, no *Women in Love* or *Lady Chatterley's Lover*. There was no Valley of Ashes in *The Great Gatsby*. One read Hardy and Kipling and Conrad and frequented worlds of traditional moral action delineated in traditional moral language."

Among the traditional words and phrases prone to high diction that Fussell lists are:

Friend	*comrade*
Obedient	*brave*
Earnestly brave	*gallant*
Cheerfully brave	*plucky*
Bravery considered after the fact	*valour*
Unpretentiously enthusiastic	*keen*
Not to complain is to be	*manly*
A soldier is a	*warrior*
The legs and arms of young men are	*limbs*
The dead on the battlefield are the	*fallen*

The object of deliberate semantic confusion behind these turns of phrase is familiar to anyone who has followed the reporting on the wars in Iraq and Afghanistan. Such deftly evasive and ultimately propagandistic terms have only proliferated over the course of a century in which mass communications have been on the rise and the best fight back of government needing to dampen the emotive effect of war's bloody truths spreading via newspapers, then radio, television and the Internet, has been to control words and images and, to the extent that it is able, the media that proffer them. The first Gulf War and the earlier one in Vietnam added to the deflecting lexicon greatly, even before the conflicts in Iraq and Afghanistan. *Collateral damage*, a euphemism believed to have originated in the Vietnam War, is probably the most notorious of these terms. During the Vietnam War, the term was used to describe the killing of non-combatants and the destruction of their property. Now the term is an accepted part of U.S. Department of Defense literature that describes the destruction of property and fatalities, usually civilian, that may occur along with whatever is the intended military action, considered to be lawful so long as the harm is proportional—that is, "not excessive in light of the overall military advantage anticipated from the attack." Now the term is commonplace, used by military spokespeople and in the courts, but also in ordinary discourse where it performs its job of cloaking meaning even more expertly, so that the reader or listener of the term is vaulted over and away from the troublesome depths like a stone skipping over water. *Friendly fire* is another stellar euphemism (and one that has acquired a particular resonance in Canada) that describes the inadvertent shooting of one's own troops.

Many of the terms, propounded in television and film, are so established and commonplace that even a president may use them —Barack Obama having spoken in his CBS *60 Minutes* interview after the assassination of Osama bin Laden in May 2011 of "taking bin Laden out," rather than, say, "killing" him. Today, the repository of such terms is not the extraordinary body of Christian romantic literature to which the First World War put an end but the output of the media and the schlock of the entertainment industry. An appendix to Fussell's list, easily added to after a trawl of the Web, would include these and other terms accumulated over the course of the Vietnam, Gulf and Afghanistan wars:

Torture	*enhanced interrogation*
Torture by interrupted drowning	*waterboarding*
Bomb	*soften up*
Bombing	*air-campaign*
The use of preponderant force against an enemy interspersed with a civilian, usually rural, population	*asymmetric warfare*

Lethal precision bombing	*surgical strike*
Journalists who cover a conflict in the prescribed company of armed forces and according to strict rules of censorship	*embedded*
Sending terrorism suspects to states that practise torture	*extraordinary rendition*
Prisoners	*detainees*
Popular uprising	*insurgency*
Escalation of a war going badly	*mission creep*
Occupation	*liberation*
Kill	*neutralize or take out*
Government overthrow	*regime change*

The point of such doublespeak is to reinforce the "moral distance" that "killologist" Dave Grossman described. The terms are useful because they make devastating military actions that result in human fatalities and scorched earth sound inoffensive, even benign—and, at the box office, attractive. These terms can be exciting and compelling and serve a further purpose in a world where fiction and the virtual are indiscernible from "reality."

Some of the terms have a more cynical application, as they are legally misleading and exempt the perpetrator from the onus and penalty of international laws in wars fought by the *international community* (a phrase that is itself a euphemism for what was, at the height of Empire and immediately after it, the "Great" or "Western" Powers and is now, effectively, the caucus of states of the G8—Canada, France, Germany, Italy, Japan, Russia, the United Kingdom and the United States). *Enhanced interrogation* makes the process of acquiring information by methodically inflicting intolerable pain—a procedure more accurately described as *torture*—sound acceptable. It also makes it legal. An *unlawful enemy combatant* becomes a *detainee* and does not have the rights under the Geneva Convention that, conveniently for the U.S. Army prosecutors of Omar Khadr and their Canadian government supporters, a prisoner of war or a child soldier has. *Enemy combatants* in Afghanistan are *insurgents* rather than *rebels*, as they were in Libya during the Arab Spring of 2011. Calling a conflict a *counterinsurgency* or a *mission* rather than a *war* has allowed the Canadian military to argue as did, in 2006, Canadian lieutenant-general Michel Gauthier, then commander of Canadian Expeditionary Force Command (he retired from the post in 2011), that "the Geneva Conventions apply in an armed conflict between states, and what's happening in Afghanistan is not an armed conflict between states." Conveniently, this means that the enemy may be described as "unlawful" and that there is subsequently "no basis for making a determination of individuals being prisoners of war." This was the position voiced by the successive Conservative ministers of defence, Gordon O'Connor and Peter MacKay, too, though never to the point of declaring, no surprise, that Canadian soldiers had been sent into an arena where there was "no war to fight."

Fussell shows in his marvellous book, reprinted more than twenty times, how, after the First World War, ironic memory was the result of carnage on a scale not ever witnessed before. (Quantity theory, a version of the mythic view, would dispute this last point as, in a sense, beyond a certain point the statistics that rate a carnage do not matter: war can only be as devastating as the destruction of one's family, friends and community. Anything beyond this intimate domain of hurt is experience that can only be abstract and theoretical.) By the time the Second World War came around, said Fussell in a 1996 interview with Sheldon Hackney, then Chairman of the United States' National Endowment for the Humanities, "we didn't need to be told by people like Remarque and Siegfried Sassoon how nasty war was. We knew that already, and we just had to pursue it in a sort of controlled despair. It didn't have the ironic shock value of the Great War." What Fussell described in *The Great War and Modern Memory* as the "wet, cold, smelly and thoroughly squalid" reality of the industrially fought war had become, after 1915, starkly incompatible with its romanticization at home. Four years of trench fighting undertaken in circumstances that were previously unimaginable and horrific would put a permanent end, it seemed, to the possibility of the experiences of soldiers of either the "Great War" or any other bloody conflict after it being described in terms so empty of meaning. No longer could the military actions of one group over another be upheld as categorically heroic.

Except that the "war to end war" did neither that, nor change the way we speak of it. The lexicon of high diction survived, and has even thrived. The "ironic memory" that was supposed to have been the legacy of the "Great War" has ended up being one of the first casualties of the war in Afghanistan. Today, high diction is all-pervasive. Denial of the damage done by war abounds in the recounting of Canadian military history and, in particular, of the Battle of Vimy Ridge. It flourishes, too, in the sexualization of soldiers to be found in the profuse outpourings of Christie Blatchford and Rosie DiManno, though in other media too. Today, not just in histories but also in artistic representations of First World War trench fighting, the macabre is sanctified and not allowed to hinder the patriotic message. Fussell's "blood, terror, agony, madness, shit" are a part of the romantic script—as, to cite just a couple of examples, was the case in Paul Gross's 2008 film *Passchendaele*, but also in "Remembrance Dance," a piece of contemporary dance created by Andrea Nann and her Dreamwalker Company and performed at Toronto's Young Centre for the Arts in 2010. Inspired by Joseph Boyden's novel *Three Day Road*, the dance was set to Boyden's live narration of trench scenes from the First World War novel, Nann using the human body to honour exactly the sort of fighting that tears such beautiful limbs apart. Here was high diction of a balletic kind.

In succumbing to epic thinking, we excuse ourselves from the onerous implications of our common humanity and of having to imagine that we might think or behave as the enemy does. Instead, we describe the enemy as monsters and their actions as "unspeakable." We treat them as a breed apart and, in this way, are relieved of the responsibilities and obligations, but also the benefits, of human empathy. We do not have to consider, for instance, that prescription drugs just might have played a part in Col. Russell Williams's degeneracy; that Norwegian mass murderer Anders Behring Breivik's heinous and nauseating capacity for the murder of innocents may bear some relation, no matter how small, to less extreme manifestations of the same poisonous views that we tolerate in everyday political discussion and films. We do not have to consider that whistleblower Richard Colvin might have had a point to make. To imagine that an Afghan detainee, human as he is, deserves to be administered the H1N1 vaccine or why this demonstration of fairness matters; to ask if a Canadian Forces captain might be guilty of murder and not a "mercy" shooting; or to wonder if there might be substance in a diplomat's allegations of bad judgment concerning the transfer of detainees is to assail the whole military venture. So, in Canada, any opinion that even remotely hints at dissonance with what are imagined to be the moral dictates of the crowd, no matter how slight, must be prefaced by a pledge of support for the country's troops and an acknowledgement of their indubitable courage. To do otherwise is to treat heroes as fallible and their adversaries or merely their critics as possibly having a point to make.

The effect of the country's shift to an epic point of view was that the long-standing idea of Canada as a pacific nation was altered. And yet, the change that resulted from the first stage of the war may only have been superficial. An early indication of the tenuous nature of the shift in the Canadian outlook as Conservatives had worked so hard to see take root was indicated in the way that certain deaths, even ones in uniform, did not fit the ascendant "master narrative."

The first Canadian fatalities of the war had been due to "friendly fire," four soldiers of the 3rd Battalion of the Princess Patricia's Canadian Light Infantry (PPCLI) having been killed in April 2002 by an American pilot's errant bomb. The nation's upset was palpable. President George W. Bush, in requisite manner, called the four dead "heroes." But in this country, the incident led to a particularly Canadian rendition of events. an example of the kind of storytelling I have previously characterized as being true to the country's "myths of disappointment." According to this narrative paradigm, it's story of disappointment a reflection of the country's sense of meaningful political decisions about the nature and destiny of the country historically having been made elsewhere, good Canadians are let down by the distant authorities that should be their stewards. In the initial reporting of the "friendly fire" incident that led to the deaths of Sgt. Marc Leger, Cpl. Ainsworth Dyer, and Ptes. Richard Green and Nathan Smith, a time when Canadians were still struggling with how to come to terms with the nation's new military commitment, the Americans were the bosses who should have known better, who should have valued Canadian lives more but who, it turned out, were responsible for the deaths—and, worse, did not seem to care much. The now seminal story of Canadian soldiers fighting in the First World War *used* to fit into this model, when the controversial actions

of British field marshal Sir Douglas (sometimes called "Butcher") Haig
were emphasized, rather than the Canadian Sir Arthur William Currie's
brilliance, and the lives of this country's soldiers were perceived to have
been unnecessarily wasted by the officer corps of the very Empire they
were travelling selflessly to protect. The friendly fire deaths of April
2002 were an awkward Canadian beginning to the war very much in
this mould. They were "heroic" deaths of less clarity than would have
been the case had they resulted from a shootout or actual confrontation
with the enemy—and so, true to the prior, possibly less confident
version of Canada, the American F-16 pilot and the controllers of the
U.S. Air Force's Airborne Warning and Control System (AWACS) were
blamed and a modicum of furor aired out in public.

This was not simply a characteristic of the beginning of the war
and of the nation needing, with some sort of consensus, to commit to
it. As recently as July 2010, when a WikiLeaked U.S. military report
suggested that the deaths in 2006 of four other Canadian soldiers
were a result of friendly fire, the rebuttal by general Rick Hillier was
swift and vociferous. The leaked documents, declared Hillier to the
CBC, were "written by people, as first response, who don't know what
they're talking about and have the facts wrong." The DND denied the
deaths were the result of friendly fire, though it was the effrontery
of some news reporters, after the battle log was leaked, daring to
have raised issues surrounding the nature of these soldiers' deaths
at all, that led Christie Blatchford to bay "Shame on us" in her front-
section column in the *Globe and Mail*. "This mess," wrote Blatchford,
"is not a WikiLeaks problem, nor a Canadian military problem, nor
a Canadian government problem. It is a problem with the Canadian
media—Ottawa-centric, conspiracy-embracing, unquestioning
and unskeptical so long as the information seems damaging to the
government, too quick to publish and, of course, absolutely without
a shred of accountability."

The mythic narrative of a new confidence was in play, one that brought responsibility but also a perverse sense of grandiosity home. The war was making *somebody* of the Canadian, a soldier standing up and being noticed in a new capacity that not just the media was relishing. In *Fifteen Days*, Capt. Jon Hamilton of the PPCLI is apprised of a piece of jihadist propaganda that includes Canada in its warnings. "It was finally nice to be recognized by the enemy," Hamilton tells Blatchford. "We're big enough to be recognized by guys who hate us, powerful enough to be recognized by those who hate Western society." The deaths, when they occurred, brought home "the irony that our peaceful and democratic way of life must sometimes resort to the organized brutality of war as the ultimate means of our self-protection," as David Bercuson wrote. This new narrative, in which pride replaces disappointment because the Canadian was now a figure on the international stage making decisions for himself (true or not), allowed the introduction of a dialogue of "heroes" such as had existed more forcefully and easily in the United States since 9/11. It allowed the press to develop a heroic story that was repeated eleven more times before it was complicated, in May 2006, by the loss of Capt. Nichola Goddard, the first Canadian soldier since the Korean War to call in a fire mission against enemy combatants, and the country's first female Canadian Forces soldier to die in combat. Then, in July, Canadian major Paeta Hess-Von Kruedener died at a UN post in the Middle East. Like the deaths of the first four Canadian Afghan War casualties by "friendly fire," and the problematic passing of the last living First World War veteran, John Babcock, too, Goddard's and Hess-Von Kruedener's deaths did not quite fit the template.

Major Hess-Von Kruedener was killed at the UN Patrol Base Khiam located, in the soldier's words, "approximately 10 km from the nexus of the Israeli, Lebanese and Syrian borders," by an errant Israeli Air Force strike in July 2006, elsewhere the middle of the most difficult year of the deployment to Kandahar. "The nature of my job here is to be impartial and to report violations from both sides without bias. As an Unarmed Military Observer, this is my *raison d'être*," wrote the officer of the PPCLI in an email sent to CTV on July 18, just after the IAF bombing had started. "What I can tell you is this: we have on a daily basis had numerous occasions where our position has come under direct or indirect fire from both artillery and aerial bombing. The closest artillery has landed within two metres of our position and the closest 1000 lb aerial bomb has landed 100 metres from our patrol base. This has not been deliberate targeting, but has rather been due to tactical necessity. I thank you for the opportunity to provide you with some information from the front lines here in south Lebanon."

A week later, Hess-Von Kruedener was dead. Harper's dismissive reaction, excusing Israel, was to wonder why the post "remained manned during what was, more or less a war." Rather than being a hero, cool witted as he was, Hess-Von Kruedener likely was being painted as a bit of a dupe for being where he was.

The inconsistency was shocking, the guiding motivations of Hess-Von Kruedener likely no different from those of a fellow soldier, Nichola Goddard, whose death was treated entirely differently.

"I would like to think that Nichola died to protect our freedoms, not to restrict them," said Tim Goddard—who, at his daughter's funeral, criticized the Conservative policy of not broadcasting the repatriation of the fallen. Evidently, the father was not going to be easily conscripted into the sort of behaviour that at least the government would have preferred. But whereas the Hess-Von Kruedener story was more or less ignored, a peacekeeper being of little interest (or profit), the Goddard story needed to be attended to, and fixed—as it was, inevitably, by a couple of deft articles by Christie Blatchford and a chapter in *Fifteen Days* that tidily gathered the father and daughter back into the epic's heroic embrace. In the book, Blatchford quotes Nichola's sister, Victoria, a doctoral student of English at the University of Toronto, who tells the reporter that, "most of great literature is about the nobility of the warrior. We need people who will fight to the death for things. It's important." Except that most of great literature is not—novels certainly not—though *epic* stories certainly are. Tellingly, the bereaved sister claimed to be writing a fantasy (not a novel) in which "there's good and evil, and you can fight it." She tells Blatchford, "I think the military helps people do that." But the significant details of the story have not been important Blatchford's purpose. By the end of the reporter's newspaper articles, and the *Fifteen Days* chapter, Capt. Nichola Goddard had taken her rightful place among "the cream of our youth" with proprietary claims upon the lexicon of the hero and the word *tragedy*.

Wrote Blatchford in the *Globe and Mail* in May 2006:

> The overuse of that word—applied in the modern world with equal ease to the adult survivor of a hard childhood, the piteous toddler felled by cancer, the starving and the merely disenfranchised—does Captain Nichola Goddard a disservice. This was a young woman who lived with purpose and deliberation and made conscious and considered choices. Hers was not the unexamined life that Socrates decried as not worth living, but rather the carefully examined one.

Her death, wrote Blatchford, was "not a tragedy at all [but] an honourable death, a soldier's death, in the service of her country and of another, Afghanistan, she had come to admire and love." Two weeks later, emphatically laying to rest even the slightest possible perversion of the heroic story that the father's funeral comments may have constituted, inadvertently or not, Blatchford wrote:

204 | CHAPTER TWO

In this family of storytellers, it was plain that father and daughter had heated discussions. Just last Christmas, he said, they discussed the role of the military in places like Afghanistan, Iraq and Darfur. Capt. Goddard subscribed to the view that military force is required to permit the reconstruction of civil society; Dr. Goddard argued that education is the key to development for the poor and oppressed.

"Quick as a flash," he said, "she punctured my professorial balloon. 'You can't do that when the bad guys run things, Dad,' she said, 'they just shoot you. You have to have peace and good government in order for the rest to happen. I do what I do so you can do what you do.'

"As always," Dr. Goddard said with his enormous smile, so like his girl's, "she was right."

Truth does not matter much here, though the heroic agenda does a whole lot. In Valerie Fortney's sympathetic biography, *Sunray: The Death and Life of Nichola Goddard* (2010), a far more whole and complex picture emerges of two generations of a family dedicated to the same ends, albeit by different means, and of a father and daughter participating in much more of a debate than Blatchford's manipulative rendition allows. The very fact that the portrait was complicated runs against the grain of almost everything that Blatchford has ever written about the war, both in her writing for the *Globe and Mail* and in her bestselling *Fifteen Days*.

Epic stories brook no complication.

CHAPTER THREE

Building Schools for Girls

"Whoever fights monsters should see to it that in the process he does not become a monster. When you look into an abyss, the abyss also looks into you."
—Friedrich Nietzsche, *Beyond Good and Evil* (1886)

"Canadians believe in this mission," said Gen. Rick Hillier to the assembled Kandahar press corps in October 2006. "I think they believe that we have a responsibility as the rich and luxurious and caring nation that we are to help in other places around the world where the populations don't have any of those benefits or advantages or rights."

The year had been a hard one, and ultimately it would prove to be the toughest of the deployment. The Taliban's summer offensive had taken not only Hillier and the Americans by surprise, a resurgence that Bill Graham, Paul Martin's minister of foreign affairs and then national defence, would claim was foreseen by no one. Hillier would profess as much himself, but Canada was in it, the war in Afghanistan at its height, and staying on was the order of the day. In March, before the summer offensive's dreadful toll—twenty-seven Canadian soldiers killed by the end of September—Stephen Harper had made his first trip to Afghanistan as Canada's newly elected prime minister. Visiting troops in Kandahar, Harper had declared, "There will be some who want to cut and run, but cutting and running is not my way and it's not the Canadian way. We don't make a commitment and then run away at the first sign of trouble. We don't and we will not, as long as I'm leading this country." (In the summer of 2010, as the country's combat presence was ending, the soldiers withdrawing from Kandahar would sarcastically refer to their decamping as "Operation Cut and Run.")

It was in 2006 that plans were launched to dub the stretch of Highway 401 along which military fatalities of the war in Afghanistan have been transported from CFB Trenton to the forensic centre in Toronto the "Highway of Heroes." It was the year in which city councils considered whether to allow yellow ribbons to be affixed to police cruisers and firefighting vehicles, and in which Harper joined an Ottawa rally attended by thousands in support of Red Fridays—the campaign for Canadians to wear red "in support" of Canadian troops that was originally devised by Dianne Collier and other service wives to remind the country that soldiers also had families in distress. American "support our troops" drives had inspired both the Canadian yellow Ribbon and Red Fridays campaigns, the latter having had a particular impact in the country because red is also the colour of the ensign. Spearheaded by Hillier and public figures such as Don Cherry, the campaign was so successful that the Tim Hortons chain relented in the face of public outcry its over initial decision against it and permitted, in 2006, red clothing rather than its own uniforms to be worn on the day in question. Comedian Rick Mercer, who had first travelled to Afghanistan in 2003 with Damhnait Doyle, Tom Cochrane and other musicians for the CBC-TV special *Christmas in Kabul*, made the trip again in 2005, and visited for another Christmas show in 2006, this time with Mary Walsh and the Montreal pop band Jonas. Blue Rodeo, NHL players, and the *Hockey Night in Canada* "Coach's Corner" team of Don Cherry and Ron MacLean would be among those who, over the years, would follow.

Said Master Cpl. Andrew Forbes of Canada's Bravo 2 crew, patrolling in Kandahar Province as part of its Provincial Reconstruction Team there: "I think people back home don't really understand the concept here—we are at war." Certainly the CBC did—or at least its commissioners saw in the war dramatic, patriotic opportunity. In 2006, the CBC Radio drama series *Afghanada*, created by Greg Nelson, Adam Pettle, Andrew Moodie and Jason Sherman, premiered, its half-hour transmissions portraying the lives of Canadian soldiers in Kandahar province who "don't have the big picture; they're not interested in the policy. They're just trying to help the people, protect each other—and survive." Asked about the soldiers' deployment to the province of Kandahar on CBC Radio's *The House*, Stephen Harper said flatly, "The fact of the matter is we are fighting a war in Afghanistan. We need to beat the Taliban on the battlefield." By the end of the year, a total of thirty-six Canadian troops and one diplomat dead, *Maclean's* magazine selected the Canadian soldier as the newsmaker of the year, as did the Canadian Press and Broadcast News, the country's new warriors amassing more votes in that coast-to-coast poll of editors and journalists than Harper, who had brought a Conservative minority government to power in January, or Maher Arar, the Canadian deported to Syria and tortured there after RCMP complicity with U.S. officials. "For the first time in a generation Canadian soldiers are being recruited, trained and sent to a war zone," enthused Jim Poling, managing editor of the *Hamilton Spectator*. "This story is a new chapter in Canadian history and the implications are broad and dramatic." Wrote managing editor Bill Scriven of Woodstock, Ontario's,

Sentinel Review, "Canadians have made it clear that while they do not support the war in Afghanistan, they proudly support the efforts of the Canadian troops."

In the rhetoric of the first years of the "War on Terror," Canadian soldiers were travelling to Afghanistan to fight an enemy that, in accordance with the epic schema, was a vague, threatening presence at the margins of the territory. "Let there be no doubt," Gordon O'Connor, a former general, had remonstrated from the opposition benches in November 2005, short months after the Canadians had made their first commitment of 250 soldiers, diplomats, aid workers and civilians to the Kandahar Provincial Reconstruction Team, "this force will be involved in a combat role, not a peacekeeping role." The Canadian Forces were fighting monsters in faraway lands to keep the homeland safe, and until rising casualties showed no sign of abating, the politicians' and media's simple talk of good and evil had been sufficient to propel the cause of a new, more bullish Canada along. But in the unanticipated, deathly slog of the southern province, a shifting of explanations for the war was becoming apparent. As early as February 2006, not yet in government for a month, the new defence minister overseeing the commitment of a full brigade to Kandahar was vacillating, his wavering position on the war a tacit acknowledgement of the mixed feelings of the Canadian public vis-à-vis the Canadian Forces' new, evidently war-fighting role. The troops, said O'Connor, were in Afghanistan to provide "a security environment"—a statement, *pace* Granatstein and Col. Sean Henry et al., suggesting that at least the government regarded the work as being something other than a "synonym for war." "We're not in Afghanistan to conduct combat operations," said the minister. O'Connor's view, commented David Pugliese, was "news to those on the frontlines." As it was to a public that, contrary to the constant characterization of it being blithe to Afghanistan's reality, was very much aware that the country's soldiers were involved in combat operations. After five years of military action, surveys indicated that less than 50 percent of the Canadian public supported the war. A Decima Research poll stated that 59 percent of Canadians believed Canadian soldiers to be "dying for a war they cannot win." A poll by the Strategic Counsel conducted between July 13 and 15, 2006, suggested that 56 percent of Canadians, up twelve points from the month before, opposed the deployment of troops in Afghanistan, with 41 percent believing that the soldiers should be brought home immediately.

A part of the public's ambivalence was undoubtedly a consequence of the rising death toll. On September 18, the last day of polling for the surveys cited and the day on which four Canadian soldiers were killed by a suicide bomber riding a bicycle, the total of Canadian dead had climbed to twenty-nine, including the diplomat Glyn Berry. The year's end total of thirty-six killed soldiers eclipsed by far the single fatalities of the two previous years. The total included Nichola Goddard, the first female soldier to have died in combat in the Forces' history, and yet two more soldiers lost to "friendly fire."

Four Canadian soldiers had died in Afghanistan in 2002, two in 2003 and one in each of the years 2004 and 2005. So it was in 2006, the losses so much greater, Stephen Harper's Conservatives forbade the media to record the repatriation of dead Canadian soldiers and decreed, as well, that flags on government buildings would no longer be lowered to half-mast with each new death.

Mounting fatalities had accounted for some of the nation's ambivalence, but another cause, more irksome to the "warrior nation" lobby, was the simple refusal of the Pearsonian version of Canada to recede before the Kandahar dust. This obstinacy of the liberal character of the nation was a trait that Harper and his core of social conservatives were determined to do nothing less than obliterate.

And yet it proved to be a tendency capable of withstanding the most powerful pressure to conform even at the very height of the mission. A substantial constituency within the country evidently believed in fighting as a last resort and, when undertaken, that it be with honest, official explanation—not obfuscation. But this was not the style of the Harper government, the most secretive and bullying in all of Canadian history.

It was a confounding task, this task of public persuasion, one to be achieved in stealthy increments so that 2006, a watershed period in the military campaign, also became the year in which a change of messaging started to be in evidence.

What Canadians had emphatically been told from the war's beginning was that the Forces were in Afghanistan to rout al-Qaeda and the Taliban and, in so doing, to protect the trade relationship with the United States that had been damaged by Chrétien and other Liberals pursuing an independent course within North America rather than placid deference to Washington. Canada had dispatched its soldiers and the DND procured new gear for them in order to promote security at home, not in Afghanistan, and to show to the Americans that their northern neighbour was ready to play its part and do the "heavy lifting." What the public had also been told was that the country was explicitly not in Afghanistan for the building of girls' schools. The phrase "building schools for girls" became a pat one, the moniker of a kind of intervention work that a lot of Canada thought the country should be doing, but that Harper and his acolytes had never had it in their minds to undertake.

"The core mission of all armies is not to wear blue-helmets and 'peace keep,' but to fight wars and to prepare to fight wars," wrote David Bercuson in the *Toronto Star* in 2006. "The word 'peacekeeper' is not a synonym for 'soldier.'" Rudyard Griffiths, still leading the Dominion Institute, appeared on CBC Radio to berate the supporters of Canada's prior peacekeeping role and to roll out the perfunctory charge of the public's naïveté given the paucity of the country's soldiers actually wearing blue-helmets. Griffiths called for the government to appoint an Afghanistan Study Group to quash such "unrealistic expectations," echoing in Canada, as many pundits' comments did, U.S. secretary of state Condoleezza Rice's remark vis-à-vis the United States' own war in Iraq that "we don't need to have the 82nd Airborne escorting kids to kindergarten." The notion that the expedition of the Canadian Forces had "humanitarian, not political and military" aims, said Griffiths, was "misinformation" spread by advocates wanting to bring the troops home. "I've been to Afghanistan," wrote Griffiths in October, 2006, "and if we think opening girls schools is the yardstick for gauging success then we should give up now." Creating a more tolerant and democratic Afghan nation was "the work of generations, not of the Canadian military," said Griffiths, declaring unequivocally that "our goal is no more, and no less, than providing the Karzai government with a vestige of political oversight over the country's perennially rebellious south." In *Fifteen Days*, Errol Cushley, the father of Pte. William Cushley (killed in September 2006), tells Christie Blatchford that the war was never, for his son, about "little girls going to school," though still the father recounted how his son would say, "We got it good here. That's what they want the chance to have. If we can give it to them, I just want to make a difference."

Griffiths was far from alone in his view of the war as—well, a war. Building schools for girls was effeminate work associated with what peacekeepers did. It was definitely not the job of the "warriors" the new Canada had sent in. The idea of the Canadian soldier as warrior that found vigorous sustenance in the story of the Battle of Vimy Ridge, that quintessential creation myth explaining the country as it had become, was, through its stirring message of the valour and the sacrifice of the Canadian Expeditionary Force, providing the moral impetus for the struggle in Afghanistan almost a century afterwards. It was no coincidence that in the fateful year of 2006 the campaign to have John Babcock awarded a state funeral was also well underway. Increasingly the example of the First World War was being offered to Canadians as a beacon lighting the way for the new "warrior" nation. This was happening to the perverse extent that the high mortality rate of Canadian troops in Afghanistan—a rate, in 2006, that was higher per capita than any of the other contributors to the ISAF coalition and 2.6 times that of even the United States armies in Afghanistan and Iraq—was being brandished as a ratio in which to take pride. Canadian soldiers were "paying the ultimate price" for peace and stability in Afghanistan, the grim statistic allowing Defence Minister Peter MacKay, successive Governors General and the Calgary School pundits and their acolytes to argue, as would the prime minister (in words that might have been spoken by anyone on this list), that the Canadian Forces' deployment was "about demonstrating an international leadership role for our country.... you can't lead from the bleachers." Canada, in this distorted view, was "leading" because it was able to show just how dutifully it was able to follow, even as the number of deaths mounted.

Between 2001 and 2006, it could reasonably be argued that a lot of influential Canadians—soldiers, politicians and the press—were enjoying the fight and the panoply of new images and leitmotifs it provided. But eventually the excitement of the war's incomplete picture abated. And incomplete it was. Afghan civilians barely entered into it. To the nation's discredit, few Canadians were ever made aware that what is regarded to have been consistently the site of much of the worst fighting in Afghanistan was not Kandahar but the neighbouring province of Helmand, where the British and the Irish were fighting. But neither this aspect of the war, nor the stories of the civilian wounded and their inordinate number, were of much use to Canada's fighting mythology and the puffed-up sense of self its propagandistic exploitation encouraged. Myths distort the truth, not least through omission.

For as long as nation-building at home is the true task at hand, myth-telling rather than truth will persist: such is the nature of propaganda. Today, we are so used to such manipulation of information that a lot of what used to be called "propaganda" now goes by the more anodyne, less alarming title of "spin." We understand the process and have made a PR profession out of it, the historical term too heavy-handed for a population that, with so many means of spreading stories at its disposal—and so much storytelling *required* of the person—is savvier about the dissemination of information than it has ever been. But propaganda exists. Called such or not, it still thrives, and after the initial work of creating it is done, institutions and the population at large are the forces that do the propagating and carry the enabling messages on. The story of Vimy was far from the only one used to propel the war in Afghanistan, though its exploitation was certainly the most successful piece of propaganda to drive a war effort undertaken at home as well as on the battlefield.

To describe the Vimy story as "propaganda" is not to say that its various renditions are false, though many of the details of its popular rendition are either omitted or can be disputed, but that the manner in which the overarching narrative was seized upon by the media and by citizens coming forth with stories of relatives who had fought in the war, served the national purpose. Vimy as propaganda substituted for the labour of government in its job of animating the nation and justifying the war. Vimy was an effective story because the ordinary

Canadian sense of self was augmented in its easy, balmy light. As it was told, it did not require much contemplation beyond the simple and pleasing idea of winning.

The uncomplicated nature of this message being the reason why the advocating of the military and of sports teams are activities often closely linked, it is not at all coincidental that the language of committing to the war in Afghanistan had its corollary, for instance, in the concomitant alteration in the tone of athletes' statements as the country entered into Olympic competition. The slogan of the 2010 Olympic Winter Games, "Own the Podium," one viewed as uncharacteristically brash by nations not used to a Canada announcing itself so ambitiously (the United Kingdom, especially, taken aback by the upstart former colony), had its precursor in new tough talk about athletes' motives delivered by the confident, even hubristic Adam Van Koeverden, the "kayak ace," prior to the Beijing Summer Olympics of 2008. "Some people think it's bad to say, 'I want to win,'" said Van Koeverden then. "Winning isn't everything. But in the race, that's kind of the point." His brazenness was adored by the media, who held up his example as the face of the new Canada that the warrior nation had released, and by Canada's Olympic team management, which chose the kayak champion to lead the Canadian team into the Beijing opening ceremonies as its official flag-bearer. "It's like an ultra-Canadian perspective to think you are there just to be with the world's best and get a pat on the back when you come home no matter what," said Van Koeverden, his put-down of the prior version of Canada having its parallels in the way the peacekeeping nation had been spoken of. (Van Koeverden eventually finished eighth out of nine in the 1,000-metre race he was expected to win. To his credit, Van Koeverden was equally forthright in defeat: "I'm not exhausted, I've been getting enough sleep, I've been eating well," he said afterwards.

"I have no explanation for this. All I have is an apology—I'm sorry.") Later, the companionship of sport and the military was quite explicitly encouraged at the 2011 Grey Cup in Vancouver, where Harper and Jason Kenney watched the (by then "Royal" redux) Canadian Air Force CF-18 flyby, the cup itself having been brought to the city by a military helicopter. Only days earlier, the Canadian Forces had been honoured at a special commemoration ceremony in Ottawa, at which the Canadian in charge of the NATO operation in Libya, Lt.-Gen. Charles Bouchard, was awarded the Meritorious Service Cross, the military's exceptionally easy role already having been honoured at the year's Remembrance Day ceremony a couple of weeks prior.

The story of the First Special Service Force (FSSF)—or, as it came to be known, the Devil's Brigade—was another useful story with a powerful propagandistic element. The success of the joint U.S.-Canadian secret commando unit that, about 1,800 members strong, fought in the Second World War from 1942 to 1944 provided its equally clandestine modern counterpart, Joint Task Force Two (JTF2), with the irrefutable vindication of adventurous folk history, as would a gamut of later books recalling the bravery and excellence of Canadian soldiers at Anzio, in Sicily, at Juno Beach and in the liberation of the Netherlands. Exclusivity breeds a cult following that in turn boosts the stringent standards upon which the quality of an institution depends, no more so than in the regiments of armies inspired by their particular histories and colours, so that it should come as no surprise that the Canadian Special Operations Forces Command (CANSOFCOM), which includes JTF2 under its aegis, should have bonded with the FSSF at special celebrations at Camp Petawawa in 2007. A year afterwards, JTF2 instituted official ties to its predecessor by having the battle honours and legacy of the FSSF formally endorsed by the Canadian Special Operations Regiment (CSOR). The secret operations of JTF2 and the not-so-secret access to special weaponry that Col. David Barr, head of CANSOFCOM in 2008, described as "nifty stuff" and "part of the lure for the regular force guys" augmented this impression of the unit's exclusive nature. So did the barring of access to information concerning the disbanded Devil's Brigade, classified by the DND as top secret in October 2006 on security grounds. Suppressing historical information about the Devil's Brigade was a way of preventing, through stories in the news, discussion of specific operations by JTF2 but also, given the proliferation of books and movies about its predecessor, a force renowned for its commitment to what were often effectively suicide missions, something of a farce—what, that threatens to be subversive, is still to be known about the FSSF? The restricting of information concerning the Devil's Brigade may have had a practical element but was also a very effective way of elevating its mystique and attracting Canadians to its "legendary" story of undefeated engagement, dedication and stealth. The latter move was described as "idiotic" by Bill Story, a Canadian Devil's Brigade veteran and then the executive director emeritus of the FSSF Association, but to no avail. In actively proclaiming the rallying stories of Vimy and Passchendaele, the selflessness and tactical superiority of Canadian soldiers from the First World War through Afghanistan was implied and, conversely, in *not* talking about the Devil's Brigade, the special reputation of JTF2 and the general quality of Canadian troops was upheld. There was in the culture, wrote *Sun* columnist Peter Worthington in 2010, "a heck of a lot of 'wannabe' in secret commandos—and JTF2 members adapt to the colouring with gusto." If there was a problem, it was that the unit conducted itself as "a secret army within the army" in a manner that was "anathema to democracy." This issue of cultish, institutionalized unaccountability was brought to the attention of the public in 2010 when news broke that JTF2 had been undergoing investigation since

2008 for what may have been their part in the alleged abuse of Afghan detainees. "Canadian regimental soldiers in Afghanistan," wrote Worthington, "have mixed feeling about JTF2. For soldiers (and they are soldiers, despite not mixing with regimental units), they play the secrecy role, but hardly blend unnoticed into the surroundings. JTF2 (Joint Task Force 2—there is no JTF1) members are distinguished in camp, often by beards, wearing dark non-uniform clothes, sunglasses and ear pieces. Sort of *Men in Black* without the humour."

Humour, tellingly, has been in short supply in Canada for the entire duration of the Forces' participation in the war in Afghanistan, and was during its first two stages, especially. The censoriousness of a country ill at ease with its role after 9/11 was displayed, early on, by the utter failure even of the Liberals to have enjoyed the actually fairly anodyne comedy of MP Carolyn Parrish's doll-crushing appearance, in November 2004, on *This Hour Has 22 Minutes*. As the war proceeded, the humourlessness only got worse. When consensus evades a society in which there exists an oppressive drive to "support our troops," there is, when it comes to military matters, hardly room for irony, let alone a good laugh. Here was a mild Canadian demonstration of the idea that, in the wake of true calamity, whether it be the Holocaust or 9/11, no poetry is possible. Such a lack is not unusual for a couple of reasons, the first of these being the absence of the palliative distance from hurt that time, after a while, provides. It took more than fifteen years before Joseph Heller's tragicomic *Catch-22*, on its surface one of the funniest novels ever to have been written about war, made light of the Second World War's absurdities, and eight years would need to pass before Kurt Vonnegut's highly distressed and satirical rather than humorous response to the fire-bombing of Dresden, *Slaughterhouse-Five*, was written. In Canada, where there is traditionally a great deal of uncertainty about material that, in the face of multicultural aspirations, constitutes fair grounds for a joke, this self-ordained prohibition was extended during the Afghanistan campaign to any fun at all at the expense of the enemy, let alone ourselves. In previous Western wars (and plenty of contemporary conflicts), the enemy is the reasonable butt of all sorts of ridicule, mockery and vituperative satire—the better to support the war in question. In today's migratory world, however, and no more so than in Canada, the "enemy" is very likely not to be a separate and ethnically distinct people inhabiting the far side of the margins of the territory but, confusingly, just another stitch in the national tapestry. The enemy may well have originated in a community that is a part of the domestic fabric, indistinguishable from others without any other traits considered to be hostile, so that many worry, often unnecessarily, about the meanness of a joke and the discomfort it may cause to particular members of society—Muslims, in the present epoch.

The second reason Canadian humour about the war has been scarce is that the joke, a form of story that precedes the myth, is almost always a method of establishing at least a kind of mischievous dominion over a situation that is ostensibly beyond one's control. From the Anansi tale to nineteenth-century caricatures of, say, the long-nosed and greedy Jew, the joke at its most savage diminishes the person or the thing that is its object and, in so doing, elevates the narrator and his listeners and makes them feel better about themselves or the circumstances they cannot otherwise affect. Humour, however, does not only ridicule, or enforce hierarchies—that would just be mean and not funny at all. It also creates empathy across bridges, as English satirist Christopher Morris's comedy, *Four Lions*, demonstrates. The feature film, released in North America in 2010, shows its homegrown London *jihadist* terrorists to be hilariously incompetent but also to be sorry, distressed and *human* figures. But the drive to war demands the belief that the situation *can* be controlled—that

Canadians, here the Forces, are able to execute a national plan, even if no plan or no good one has been formed. To respond to volatile circumstances with humour rather than seriousness is to foster a form of anarchy and to belie the infallibility of the martial approach—to reveal it as one that is not *confident*. Humour is feared because it is subversive, though the idea that it may actually be so merits a laugh is the thing that is ridiculous. In more pedestrian, less offensive realms, the joke is an indication of confidence. It is the mark of the teller, and of those who listen, feeling sufficiently certain about their position to be able to brook the joke's challenging of it. Only with the insecure, does humour becomes an assault on the fragile and ardently defended construct of an ideology.

In the Canada of the twenty-first century's first decade, the commitment to the war in Afghanistan had all the tenets of an ideology and so was difficult territory for jokes. The war was no laughing matter. The country was one in which a more powerful military was perhaps the most important plank of a political party platform relying for its force upon bullying, intolerant and demagogically winning ideas about the military and law and order—a party that, even in eventual 2011 majority, remained so suspicious and insecure that the social mark of it has been a shocking meanness of spirit. Had the Conservative Party been more confident of anything other than its radical agenda, then it would have been able to tolerate argument—and humour. But it was not. Still is not. And so, for the duration of Canadian participation in the war in Afghanistan, there was a lot of place for insult though little for humour and its healthily unsettling lessons.

None of this is to pretend that either the war in Afghanistan or the greater "War on Terror"—or, indeed, any war—is inherently funny, though humour also provides a release, the opportunity to laugh when seriousness is, as much as anything else, practically and morally exhausting. When al-Qaeda needs to publicly refute one of their great allies, Iranian president Mahmoud Ahmadinejad, claiming that he is spouting nonsense when, in typical ranting fashion, he repeats the conspiracist theory that the World Trade Center's twin towers were brought down by Americans—when al-Qaeda needs to holler from the corner of the room that, in fact, *they* did it—there is a hilarious opportunity for satire at play. The dearth of humour about Afghanistan is a barometer of the difficulty, if not total absence, not just of confidence but of the sort of scrutiny of politicians, the media and of the war itself that would allow Canadians to brook the complicated questions brought on by fighting.

But the war, in Canada, is still too sensitive and politicized a subject for jokes.

So, instead of the brilliant *Flashman* series of historical comic novels by Scotsman George MacDonald Fraser, a veteran of the Border Regiment and its Burma campaign of 1942-45 (writing nearly a century after the Victorian campaigns that provided his settings), or Christopher Morris's *Four Lions* (2010), Canada has Paul Gross's *Passchendaele*, CBC Radio's *Afghanada* and the country's long-standing surfeit of valedictorian First World War poetry—examples, historical and current, of exactly the sort of high diction and myth-making that Fussell takes such pains to deconstruct. In *Afghanada*, the tense lives of soldiers and the dangers they face "outside the wire" take centre stage, though to the exclusion of any real inquiry as to why the war was started or what, if anything, was achieved by it. The reasons are accepted a priori, as they are in Global Television's 2011 series *Combat Hospital*, set in Kandahar Province in 2006, a good drama that, for want of American interest, lasted but one season, charting "the frantic lives of the hospital's resident doctors and nurses from Canada, America, the U.K. and other coalition countries" as they deliver "the best battlefield surgical care anywhere to wounded soldiers, civilians caught in the crossfire and even the enemy." These dramas' depictions of injury and death, remote occurrences to which we have effectively been inured, never pay more than perfunctory homage to war's cost or the contradictions that we put aside in order to be able to pay it—our heady, unquestioning elevation of the man in uniform as hero a prime example. The Fraser novels, a series of rollicking faux memoirs by Harry Flashman, disgraced Rugby School old boy and alumnus of the popular nineteenth century Thomas Hughes classic *Tom Brown's Schooldays*, offer a stark contrast. Flashman is a bully who has been expelled for drunkenness and other loutish transgressions but who, despite himself, becomes a hero of the Charge of the Light Brigade and other British Empire episodes, including Afghanistan. He is, the accidental hero himself confesses, "a scoundrel, a liar, a cheat, a thief, a coward—and oh yes, a toady," his officer's commission one purchased (as was the custom of the times) by his father. Fleeing combat in Afghanistan, Flashman inadvertently charges a Russian regiment, becoming with each such misadventure more decorated and admired. But he's not one to fool himself, whatever the lies he tells others and the patriotic hoopla that accrues to him. "This myth called bravery, which is half panic, half lunacy (in my case, all panic), pays for all," says Flashman. "In England, you can't be a hero and bad. There's practically a law against it."

Flashman, when it comes down to it, is not a bad fighter at all, so that what the novels do is prove, once again, that at least official morality infuses the heroic act after the fact. "The ideal time to be a hero is when the battle is over and the other fellows are dead," says Flashman. "God rest 'em, and you take the credit." Fraser's novels are adored by a fanatical legion of readers as much for the accuracy of their historical details as for their humour, though it is the author's ironic and entertaining evisceration of the idea of the hero that makes them exceptional and an example of the kind of writing that is entirely absent from fictional Canadian representations of war in Afghanistan. (Interestingly, Fraser himself was not a particularly tolerant man—having little time, for instance, for soldiers claiming stress disorders.) In the Canadian literary panoply, there can be no Flashman, nor any enduring underling to rank with the comic creation of Czech writer Jaroslav Hašek, *The Good Soldier Švejk* (1923), either. A Czech conscript in the Austro-Hungarian army, Švejk is little more than a good-natured incompetent in a story that starts with the assassination of the Archduke Ferdinand in Sarajevo and sees Švejk eventually being taken prisoner by his own army. Hašek fought in the First World War. He never finished the six parts of the story that he had planned, but the four that he did complete have survived to make immortal fun of military bureaucracy and incompetence. But contemporary Canada is a confused and hectored country so there can be no accommodation of a Flashman or a Švejk, or even for a *Dad's Army,* the hilarious British 1960s sitcom about the Home Guard during the Second World War. As if to prove the point, the former *Trailer Park Boys* director Mike Clattenburg's *Afghan Luke,* written by Doug Bell, Barrie Dunn and Patrick Graham and released in 2011, offered a disgruntled young Canadian journalist and an amusing Afghan fixer as part of its sideways entry into the conflict but was only diffidently received. Humour provides power and dignity to a player who would otherwise be a victim, and reveals a greater and more variegated truth to those who take it in. But humour challenges authority, cagey leadership and the propaganda such regimes generate. In Canada, the absence of humour proves that there has only been room for the ultra-seriousness of the myth-makers of the "warrior nation" and the more earnest opposition of those who, in the peacekeepers' camp, hang on to their own myths vying for contention. Histories and the digitized archives of soldiers' memories filtered only by their establishment curators must suffice. Until this is not true, there can be no bona fide claims to a vigorous contest of views in the country.

Staying on is a complicated matter, and up to the point of the Forces' exit there could be no joking.

In the absence of the sort of swift and decisive triumph that the ISAF had been expecting, the war in Afghanistan became, during its second phase, a contest of attrition, typical of the region's history, one that was considered, in the war's early years, traitorous and even idiotic to cite. When, as happens so often, the short war becomes long—when, in today's vocabulary, war "escalates" or the mission "creeps"—it is incumbent upon the combatants to avert being exhausted by the war for as long as possible on the front line but also at home. It is in this period of being dug in and needing to find a societally acceptable way to stay on that the call to "support our troops" becomes the dominant, clarion call.

Opposing Canadian voices striving to be heard during this period of forcefully imposed establishment sentiment were not many. Notably, in English Canada, Murray Brewster of the Canadian Press proved a thorough reporter of the old school, as did David Pugliese of the *Ottawa Citizen*, while the *Globe and Mail* columnists Jeffrey Simpson and Lawrence Martin consistently offered judicious and often dissenting opinion nationally, as Thomas Walkom and Haroon Siddiqui were also doing at a metropolitan level. Michael Byers, Noreen Golfman, Janice Kennedy, Paul Robinson and Steven Staples were among the few with-out a regular media platform who dared to do what, in a healthy Parliament, opposition MPs might have done. Certainly the Liberal opposition could not protest much as its leader, Michae Ignatieff, had before his ascension been a vocal supporter of the United States' war on Iraq and could only with difficulty be seen to be abandoning his prior position. Advocates of the war, wrote Kennedy in a September 2007 *Ottawa Citizen* piece, were wallowing in their own "meaningless clichés," but it was a wall erected by parliamentary consensus that she was up against. Said Kennedy, formerly a columnist with the *Ottawa Citizen*, of the Red Fridays and the "Support Our Troops" movement:

> We say things like, "they're putting their lives on the line
> for us." Or "they're fighting for Canada." Or, in the words of
> Ottawa councillor McRae (though they could be anybody's),
> our uniformed men and women are "willing to sacrifice
> their lives to make sure this country stays as great as it
> is." (Could someone please explain to me how any of the
> debacle in Afghanistan is a fight for Canada, Canadians or
> our national greatness? Please?)

When it came to narrating Canadian soldiers' participation not just in the war in Afghanistan, but Libya and the First World War and any subsequent episode of full combat (as opposed to the confusing non-combat of peace operations), nothing less than full praise of the military cause in the most heroic of terms was acceptable. The point of the war and the performance of the Canadian Forces were confused—deliberately—and to offer anything less than full, unqualified and simultaneous praise of each was to be unpatriotic. The result is that, acknowledged or not, a substantial part of the population prefers not to speak or does so uncomfortably when it addresses the conflict at all. For much of the duration of the campaign in Afghanistan, any critical commentary was viewed as an assault on the character of the nation and, in its hesitation before the idea of the vaunting of Canadian greatness, a compromise of our "national security." Utterly unjustified, the assumption by the military lobby was that anyone who was not about to come out and wholeheartedly "support the troops," that is, the war—anyone who might have preferred, instead, the more moderate and inquiring values behind the actions of Canada's previous peacekeeping incarnation — would, de facto, also be a proponent of not arming the forces. For the Right to accommodate these people would be to give in to a lax cartoon world as it is conceived in the dire fantasies of Bercuson, Blatchford, Granatstein, Col. Sean Henry et al. It would be for Canadians to take a step back into the 1990s, "nickel and diming ourselves into another 'decade of darkness,'" as wrote Mercedes Stephenson in the *National Post* in July 2011, gleefully declaring that "we've come a long way, baby, the Canadian Forces are back," and falsely implying that the stark choice the country faces is of having a military "prepared for anything" or, left to the naysayers, one prepared for nothing at all. The logical truth of it not being in any way oxymoronic for Canadians to be prepared to spend adequately on the military, though also to have a say in what they do, was beyond imagining — or simply not to be admitted as a possibility by supporters revelling, as Stephenson was doing, in Canada having "the best small army in the world," soldiers who were known for "holding their nerve in Kandahar, while other NATO allies cowered on heavily fortified bases munching lobster instead of fighting insurgents." Who is the arbiter is hard to say.

In such an atmosphere, bereft of any possibility of active dissent by the absence of conscription and the unanimity of Parliament at critical moments in the war's timeline, even the slightest criticism of Canadian military operations needed to be prefaced by the doubter's declaration that he or she "supports our troops" — and, for that matter, our police officers and our firefighters too. During the second testing period of staying on, the "you're with us or against us" paradigm came to dominate, this time-tested bit of sociological blackmail reinforced by influential gatekeepers of opinion such as Don Cherry or Christie Blatchford damning, as the *Globe and Mail* writer did, with vehemence, anyone who thought it possible to be "supportive of the troops while also being opposed to the mission"—a coexistence of views that need not be contradictory at all. So, after Jack Layton, her nemesis, spoke of New Democrats who "grieve with each family that loses a loved one in this and all conflicts, or that sees a loved one injured in the line of duty," Blatchford, unable to come to terms with the NDP's discomfort with the war, declared, "Their grief is dishonest." The charges were nonsense, designed to intimidate and laid on the back of the habitual, bullying demand to "support our troops" that the prime minister was also using to shut down opposition at any opportunity on the floor of Parliament. In the words of William Deresiewicz, whose 2009 address to the West Point military academy, "Solitude and Leadership," has been widely circulated and taught, the tactic was one of "bait and switch" that came to the fore during the Iraq War. The powerful "Support Our Troops" movement had its origins in "a justified collective desire to avoid repeating the mistake of the Vietnam era, when hatred of the conflict spilled over into hostility towards the people who were fighting it," said Deresiewicz. "Now the logic was inverted: supporting the troops, we were given to understand, meant that you had to support the war." The tactic has worked well for governments pushing their wars and for military administrations using them for their own institutional gains—the dynamic identical in Canada, vis-à-vis Afghanistan—and it allows the ordinary citizen to pay "lip service" to the fighting. After all, wrote Deresiewicz, "it's a lot easier to idealize the people who are fighting than it is to send your kid to join them."

The confluence of the "Support Our Troops" slogan and the cult of the uniform makes any soldier's character unassailable, and that of the outsider who challenges its meretricious blending of separate ideas, a villain—a traitor, even. This nasty method—so vindictively and cynically applied by numerous journalists and politicians that it most certainly may be described as a "method"—was illustrated viscerally when it came to questions that started to be raised on the floor of the House of Commons in early 2007 concerning the transfer of suspected Taliban combatants captured by the Canadian Forces to Afghan prisons. After it was alleged that the detainees were being abused, the prime minister indignantly declared that "the real problem" and "disgrace" was, to his calculated reckoning, the opposition's "willingness to believe, to repeat and to exaggerate any charge against the Canadian military as they fight these fanatics and killers that are called the Taliban!" And so on. The rhetorical ploy was outrageous but normal, the defence that the Conservative (and only the Conservative) supports the troops nonsensical but routine, its demagogic aim to exploit and rouse the anxieties and fears that Canadians entertain on behalf of men and women put into the dangerous theatre of war or, at home, onto the streets as police officers. This most venerable tactic of leaders and parties in authority twists these sentiments and makes of them an obstacle to any reasonable discussion, let alone challenging of any part of the work that those in uniform do. "Canadian soldiers go only where their government tells them to go, do only what their government asks them to do," wrote Blatchford sanctimoniously. "The soldiers should always be supported, because they only do the bidding of their political masters. If the political masters get it wrong, soldiers ought not to carry the can." Anyone who pretends to be "soldier-loving" (Blatchford's term) but does not support the war "is a fraud"; as Hillier had demanded back in 2003, nothing less than Canadians who "visibly support" the troops would do.

No Canadian wants the country's soldiers participating in conflicts of any kind with less than the best gear for the job, or without any of the appropriate resources that contribute to the Forces' capacity to perform excellently and—as much as can be expected of an inherently dangerous craft—in safety. But statements soliciting "visible" (i.e.

non-discerning) support of military endeavours as inherently unimpeachable acts, whatever their nature, need not be entertained. The dysfunction of doing so is illustrated by the numerous instances in which the likelihood of some kind of culpability on the part of the accuser invariably follows allegations made against the dissenter showing, in the very brazenness of his doubt, a failure to "support our troops." Two years after General Hillier's personal outrage at the mere possibility of *inadvertent* Canadian complicity in Afghan detainees' abuse, Chief of Defence Staff General Walter Natynczyk would admit to being aware of at least one instance that he, Harper and MacKay had vehemently, categorically denied. And, too, Hillier's show of being appalled on behalf of Ahmed Wali Karzai, the governor of Kandahar, "angry about allegations made about his government being accepted as straight fact," would equally be undone by the eventual *New York Times* exposé of the president's brother, the governor in question, as corrupt and a likely drug dealer on the payroll of the CIA.

Writes sixth-century BC general Sun Tzu in *The Art of War*: "In all history, there is no instance of a country having benefited from prolonged warfare. Only one who knows the disastrous effects of a long war can realize the supreme importance of rapidity in bringing it to a close."

About industry and the prolonged war, Sun Tzu might have said the contrary, but no matter. In war's first stage, it is the visceral urgency of conflict and the proclamation of a cause that carries the troops along. Later, as soldiers live away from their families for extended periods and others are repatriated dead, meaningful support of the troops is of the essence. The support, however, is not only a matter of yellow ribbon bumper stickers or public demonstrations of allegiance to the new war and its "stories of bravery, friendship, life and death in the new Canadian army" (the last, the subtitle of *Fifteen Days*), but also a matter of committing to the sizable sums of money that must be spent to reintegrate those who do return and to care for the wounded among their number. The onus moves from an epic domain, in which high diction and clichés rally citizens in the face of a battle that government has mandated the country to fight, into the more empathetic realm of the novel. Away, and then at home, the drawn-out war brings with it the burgeoning opportunity to identify with the wounded, with the fighting soldier and with the Afghan families in whose distant backyard the ISAF, al-Qaeda and the Taliban were fighting. During the first period of the war in Afghanistan, in which the right attacked the blue-beret version of the country with unrelenting fervour, Canadians were berated for being hopelessly unknowing about the dangers their soldiers in UN peace operations faced in geographically distant operations. In their unworldly innocence, was the charge, Canadians had been entertaining self-congratulatory fantasies about what could be done and about the virtues of peacekeeping and the nation's power, hard or soft. In the war's second stage, the same allegations could easily have been laid against those in awe of the new "warrior nation" and working hard to keep it in its place. Exactly the same phenomenon of distance from the combat arena is what allowed, during the ten years of Canadian involvement in the ISAF, a fostering of epic ideas about the war that were equally romantic, naive and unknowing.

During the First World War, the front had been so close to the seats of the major powers that even the soldiers were surprised at the short distance trains needed to travel to bring them to the trenches where the post and newspapers arrived dependably. It was a lack of mass telecommunicated media that made the fissure between the front lines and home life great. In the Second World War, as with the First, the fighting was undertaken in such numbers that it was impossible to avoid second-hand but still intimate experience of it, regardless of how it may have been reported in the news. In the ensuing cases of the duelling powers' Cold War "proxy" fighting of the second half of the last century, however, the theatres of conflict were remote and, as much a measure of Western societies' combat fatigue, in the case of the Korean War, the fighting was "secret" or even "forgotten"—a catchphrase, now, for wars or battles such as that in Croatia's Medak Pocket (or, in 1919, on the Siberian Front) that do not make the headlines. The war in Vietnam that saw Canadian arms manufacturers profit, some 30,000 Canadian volunteers fight and the government clandestinely participate in missions, weapons testing and arms production is also called "Canada's Secret War" sometimes. More recently, Sean Maloney has made the case that Canadian Forces carrying nuclear warheads for NATO during the Cold War were operating secretly too. Wars are often remembered as secret" because, at the time, they appear not to matter much at all, their overlooked aspect a reflection of none of these conflicts having been hugely important to Canada—of their not having been, in the traditional terminology, "wars of existence," but wars that Canadians have chosen to travel to find and that often governments need to justify in convoluted terms typically invoking democratic freedoms and the greater good. That was the case of the war in Afghanistan in its second phase, some of its battles surely destined to be described as "secret" someday. Certainly the war has not been so important that in 2011, the country's combat role ended, it continued to make the news as other than a font of self-congratulation, of a job well done, of NATO allies pleased. Had the campaign in Afghanistan truly been important to Canadians, in the sense that they would have found it impossible to imagine *not* fighting it, then the end of the war would have brought more than a befuddled sense of relief at the strangeness of the fight being over because Canadian leaders had decided they had done their bit, the country able to quit a war constantly being assessed in terms of the viability of the alliance fighting it, rather than as a matter of survival. How much did Afghanistan really matter to Canadians?

Hardly at all.

Television is said to have brought the war out of Vietnam and into the living rooms of America, though it is also the case that wars after it have not projected their brutality into the tender bubble of family anywhere near as much because of the draft lottery for nineteen-year-old men having been suspended in the United States and any form of conscription being non-existent in Canada. It is the prospect of national service that ensures a battle's affecting the greater population and not only the volunteers, hereditary soldiers' families sending the representative of another generation on, and the poor and disenfranchised typically making up the bulk of those who turn to the military for employment. Small wonder, then, that protests against the Vietnam war were so much more prevalent than was any kind of organized civil disobedience in Canada during its ISAF fight. The collective slide of countries into a state of edgy wariness accounts for some of this lack, but it is also true that in previous wars a much greater portion of the population had a stake. Telecommunicated images from the trenches of Vimy Ridge would likely have made the "Great War" intolerable and put a quicker end to its carnage, though what the conflagrations in the Balkans and Afghanistan have proven is that ultimately it is the threat of middle-class involvement, not reporting, that drives peace protests and the likelihood of mass objection. Kill the draft and you kill popular dissent and permit haughty talk about obligations, too. In Canada, support for American "war resisters" was negligible and easily ignored, and political leaders and opinion-makers such as Michael Ignatieff, leader of the Liberal Party in opposition at the time, but also Toronto's CBC Radio morning anchor, Andy Barrie, himself a former Vietnam War draft dodger, were able to reduce the issue of unwilling compliance in war to an issue of contract breaking by United States citizens who, we are told, joined the U.S. military of their own free will and with subsequent duties to perform. No matter that, in many cases, poverty offered its own duress or that a significant number of the war resisters were being recalled for further tours of duty under the United States' "stop-loss" policy allowing *government* to break its contract, arbitrarily overriding its own terms of employment in the name of national security. The unfortunate war resisters had a surfeit of enemies in Canada's government kowtowing to the United States and underperforming allies in a population with such a negligible stake. Gone, certainly, was the idea of Canada as a safe haven in which objection could possibly be conscientious or experience change a person's mind. The war resister was condemned to one category of classification only before a Liberal Party hopelessly, narcissistically distracted from the job of opposition and a vindictive government bent on making a humiliating example of dissenters: that of the coward.

With only a small civilian involvement, there has been in Canada almost no will to protest the war in Afghanistan in any manner whatsoever despite polls that, between 2002 and 2008, repeatedly suggested that half of the Canadian population was against the war, these including a Strategic Counsel poll showing 54 percent of Canadians to be against the war and a later Ipsos poll in 2011 indicating that about the same number was against the extension of the Canadian Forces' participation in the ISAF even as trainers "inside the wire." (Undertaken in November 2010, the commitment to the training mission was set to expire in 2014.) The practice of "embedding" reporters undermined resistance to the present war from the very beginning, most reporters not about to speak out against the authorities that make their work possible, and the sum effect has been that it was as easy for Canadians to live with the "warrior nation" thanks to myriad forms of self-deception and easy avoidance, as it was alleged that Canadians were doing during the period when peacekeeping was the national mantra. So the call to "support our troops" has been bolstered, in Canada, by proponents of the military able to take advantage of a public that is no closer to understanding the conditions of the wars they promote than the supporters of peacekeeping supposedly were, and by others who do not dare to create an argument or a fuss. This was true even in Parliament, where either a complete consensus reigned, rendering the House useless as a forum of debate, or (as Paul Robinson, a professor in the Graduate School of Public and International Affairs at the University of Ottawa, has suggested) parliamentary bills such as spring 2011's delivering soldiers to Libya with "wholehearted support to the men and women of the Canadian Forces" brook no resistance simply because members are worrying about their popularity rather than their conscience.

The fact of an only remote involvement with the war on the part of a majority of Canadians is what has allowed its accommodation by those who are only peripherally interested and what has permitted, in its more strident advocates, an invidious intolerance of anyone questioning it. In wars that are not immediately about survival—where the issue is not the actual defence of the territory but rather something as shape-shifting as a "Global War on Terror" ("We're making war on a noun," said Maine novelist Peter Behrens)—the factor of distance is, as Lt.-Col. Dave Grossman worked so hard to point out, critical. In the United States, distance was evaporated after the attacks of 9/11 by worry and by fear. In Canada, the country's natural kinship with the United States fostering genuine sympathy for the nation that is our best friend, distance was subsequently bridged by talk of necessity occasioned by our alliance and our trade relationship with our southern neighbour, and then by Bercuson's "higher principles of our national self-interest"—the latest reiteration of our service to the cause of "making the world safe for democracy" (as chaplain Capt. J.B. Paulin put it to the Empire Club in Toronto in 1918)—by talk of the "just war," in other words.

Studies of the viral spread of information have proven that the rate of dissemination of a story is greatly multiplied when adopting its tenets and repeating the information in question does not contradict one's extant beliefs. During the troubled period of 2006-09 and in Canada, with no draft and a media that was by and large compliant, it was far easier to "support our troops" by saying nothing than to wonder if their dedication, their willingness to put their lives on the line, might have had some other application. To do so was to risk the contemptuous wrath of Blatchford and company and to impede the soldier in his task. This faction's accusatory reasoning reached its contradictory zenith in relation to a series of military-related incidents that took place between 2005 and 2010, a couple of them far from the theatre of war. The first was the murder in Toronto's Moss Park of fifty-nine-year-old Paul Croutch, a homeless man, by two off-duty Canadian reservists in 2005, the second was the "mercy killing" of an injured Taliban fighter by Capt. Robert Semrau in October 2008 and the third an undignified argument between two public figures in the wake of the injury that Master Cpl. Paul Franklin, a medic and driver, had sustained in January 2006.

The 2008 trial of Jeff Hall and Brian Deganis, the two reservists who beat Paul Croutch to death in August 2005, was one that Christie Blatchford, then working for the *Globe and Mail*, did her best to portray sympathetically—not an easy job.

"Soldiers, even part-time ones like reservists, are not supposed to be wolves," wrote Blatchford. They are, instead, the "protective sheepdog." Her use of the terms *sheepdog* and *wolves* alluded to Grossman's *On Killing* (1995), in which the lieutenant-colonel postulates that society is made up of sheepdogs (soldiers and police) willing to use force in order to protect the sheep (ordinary citizens indisposed to or incapable of violence) and keep them from the wolves (villains who have no such compunction). "The sheepdog, paraphrases Blatchford, is "a warrior, someone who is walking the hero's path. Someone who can walk into the heart of darkness, into the universal human phobia, and walk out unscathed." The reservists Hall and Deganis—lousy sheepdogs, though apparently not wolves—showed their sympathetic witness, "with their tears and their shame," that they recognized "how gravely they breached the dearest tenets, and paid the only tribute they could to Mr. Croutch."

Wrote Blatchford:

> It is not often in the criminal courts that the guilty weep for what they have actually done, that they are suffused with palpable shame and regret.
>
> Usually, they cry for themselves and you can tell by the timing: The tears come at a moment of impact for them, not the victim, when they were caught, arrested, questioned by police or when they are being sentenced and remorse may be useful.

The timing of Corporal Hall being "convulsed with sobs," and of Private Deganis, who subsequently "burst into tears," is what, we were to understand, distinguished the reservists' grief from the "dishonest" kind that was, in another forum (Parliament, and not court), displayed by the apparently disingenuous Jack Layton commiserating with the families of the dead and the injured on behalf of the NDP. How could it be otherwise? Layton (like Clarkson, like the Liberals, like the Ottawa press corps) was *not a soldier*. Blatchford's delicate construction of an edifice of support for the two tearful murderers, vicious and drunk at the time but just happening to be soldiers, is at odds with the headier assessment she made in 2006 when she concluded that being a good soldier was entirely about the primary and defining quality of aggression. Then, unencumbered by the untidy matter of a lowly homeless civilian's death, Blatchford wrote proudly that "aggression is part of who soldiers are, as integral as boots and weapons, and was even when Canadians were posted in Cyprus. Aggression is not a bad thing or a character flaw; it is a prerequisite of those who wear what soldiers call the 'green suit,' the uniform." The difficult task of exonerating troops that the columnist regards as family demanded the most dexterous elicitation of public sympathy. Her nimble manoeuvring around the murder was reminiscent of her earlier tiptoe around Tim Goddard and a far cry from her repudiation of the tribute that was later paid to NDP leader Jack Layton after his death in August 2011. The memorial to the "vainglorious" party leader was a "thoroughly public" event, an "over-the-top" spectacle at which the emotion was as patently false as it had been at the sending off of Canadian ships at Halifax Harbour back in the autumn of 2001. Truly, "there is no escape from these people"—better the company of a couple of scared, regretful killers in uniform.

The second incident involved another killing by a soldier, but on the battlefield in circumstances almost impossible for the ordinary citizen to judge. Still, such incidents have long been a part of war's execution, and the tone of the debate to which the killing gave rise said something about a society off kilter, in which citizens who dared to raise the possibility of transgressions by the military or insist upon the maintenance of standards of decency in wartime found themselves assailed with the full force of angry blinkered patriotic sentiment. This happened, first of all, with the issue of the transfer of Afghan detainees and the excoriation of the diplomat Richard Colvin and was repeated with the "mercy killing" of a gravely wounded Taliban combatant by Capt. Robert Semrau in 2008, the Canadian soldier tried by a military tribunal in 2010. Semrau was found not guilty of murder but convicted of disgraceful conduct, demoted and dismissed from the Forces. The military judge, Lt.-Col. Jean-Guy Perron, told the thirty-six-year-old captain that he had failed in his role as a military leader and as an "ambassador of Canadian values," a judgment with which David Bercuson concurred, though others viewed the sentence, mitigated by a lack of evidence, as an affront to the "warrior" doing his job. If meddling, patsy Canadians had put peacekeepers in harm's way by providing them with guns that rules of engagement forbade them to shoot, here they were again, dictating from the comfort of their living rooms how soldiers in the heat of war should behave. How is the soldier to do his job if he is subject to the judgments of non-combatants and their utterly sentimental lack of experience? That was the acrimonious charge. Soldiers cannot be hindered by such constraints. They cannot be doing battle on *two* fronts, for killing is exactly the means of *restoring* the law and the orderly society in the name of which the war is being fought. And yet what are we defending, if not our civilized insistence on behaving as best we may, even and especially in moments of great distress? The soldier is not exempt but an example.

The third incident to show how specious can be the demand to "support our troops" came in the wake of talk between a wounded soldier, Master Cpl. Paul Franklin, and the CBC's Shelagh Rogers, that proved to be one of the most moving conversations of the war.

The year 2006 had started with the death of diplomat Glyn Berry, the director of the Kandahar Provincial Reconstruction Team, killed on the way to his headquarters in the attack by a suicide bomber's explosive-laden taxi. Berry's armour-plated car was being driven by Master Cpl. Paul Franklin, who, along with two other soldiers driving with them, was gravely injured. The blast also killed two children and wounded ten other Afghans, though this is rarely mentioned.

After twenty-six operations and the eventual amputation of both legs, Franklin took to Edmonton's Rice Theatre stage for a 2009 CBC Radio interview with the *Sounds Like Canada* host. Franklin, on home ground, was in high spirits. He spoke of having enlisted, aged thirty, after looking for a job with "pension, education and travel." He joked that only employment in government as a paramedic with the army could provide them. He described the unrelenting pain he had suffered since his injury with diffidence and candour. "It's part of the deal," said Franklin. "You have to shake hands with it." Of his new condition he ribbed, "I'm shorter," and then went on to display a worldliness and interest in the welfare of others, in his conversation, that is one of the most positive traits of the Canadian character. He talked of his belief in the mission, his love for Afghanistan and for its people wanting peace and "looking out for us." On the question of being a hero—a common response of soldiers who discover themselves being singled out for praise—Franklin was self-effacing. "I didn't do anything," he said. "I blew up. In fact, I failed in my mission. My mission was to protect the senior diplomat in southwest Asia and I didn't do that. That's why, for me, the whole idea of being a hero—you can throw that out the door. The guys that are heroes are the guys that won medals of valour for an action under combat. Those are the kinds of guys that are true heroes." The master corporal's wife, Audra, joined him on stage and spoke of hearing "stories from the guys" about how "they've opened another school or another village has fresh water and things like that and then you just think that's why we do this, that's why we go through all of this stuff." Franklin described himself as "someone who gives to the civil service for the greater good" and then, with affecting equanimity, spoke of the "blind justice" inherent in state decisions about the Forces' deployment to Afghanistan rather than, say, Sudan or the Congo, and explained, to repeated applause, that "we have to do it, we were asked by them and so we have to go." Then, mulling over whether or not the cause was just, Franklin spoke of the fog that prevents a fair assessment of a war by those who are actually fighting it.

Comparing the fight in Afghanistan to Canadians' fight in the Second World War, Franklin said:

> We'll have to look back, much like Dieppe, and you'll have to ask the guys, right after Dieppe, was this worth it? And the poor guys in Dieppe are going, "Well, yeah, I mean we've got to fight the cause." [But] I mean the Holocaust wasn't known, it was simply a German leader and maybe even some of the Canadian Forces were fascist, at the time that was sort of the trendy thing to be. And everybody treated the Jews bad back then. We had no concept of what was really going on and Canada's failing—it's failing in Norway, and it's failing in other places, and Britain's almost bombed to death and America hasn't joined the War, and all this other stuff. And so, at that point, you see complete failure but you have to stick to the cause. And then when you look back later, 1945, you go, "Yeah, it was righteous." And now as we look back further and we go, "Wow, that was the one great war, the one reason to be there." But you ask the

>people why they were there at the beginning, they were
>there for adventure, they were there for fun, they were there
>for excitement.

And then, a gifted storyteller playing the room, he provided a punch line while deflecting attention from his condition, again. The soldiers of "the Greatest Generation" had, as he had done, found jobs with "travel, education and a pension." His reflections on heroism and the humanitarian outlook he was advocating amounted to a far more self-deprecating and thoughtful message than had been bandied about by the media and then Chief of Defence Staff, general Rick Hillier, during the first five years of the war. And here it was being spoken by a man from the Forces for whom the cost of combat had been dreadful.

What unexpectedly ensued, however, were ugly remonstrations of popular television comedian Rick Mercer against Noreen Golfman, a fellow Newfoundlander and a professor of English at Memorial University in Newfoundland, that showed the divisive new rhetoric of the "warrior nation" to be in distressing evidence. Golfman had made the hardly egregious mistake of having referred to the injured Paul Franklin in a newspaper article as a "poor sod." Neither did Golfman use the injured soldier's name, a detail that becomes hugely important when injury renders a soldier's commonality undignified. Mercer, who would soon be appointed as an honorary colonel to 12 Wing Shearwater's 423 helicopter squadron for the favourable attention he brought to the Forces, had visited Afghanistan with the *Rick Mercer Report* a couple of times already and went off the rails. He wrote a nasty, bullying and savage response in a Newfoundland newspaper in January, 2007 that swiftly prompted all sorts of abuse and threats against Golfman over the Internet. Mercer's article and the tide of hateful, Web-posted insults to Golfman proved just how potentially abusive is the mechanism of the edict to "support our troops," smothering in its demand any possibility of reservation, let alone dissent. In an article marked by inadvertently poor, though not ill-intentioned phrasing, Golfman had dared to question why the country was in Afghanistan and just what the killing would achieve. Mercer, a friend of Franklin, wrote in his public letter:

> Personally I would have thought that as a professor of women's studies you would be somewhat supportive of the notion of a NATO presence in Afghanistan. After all, it is the NATO force that is keeping the Taliban from power. In case you missed it Noreen, the Taliban was a regime that systematically de-peopled women to the point where they had no human rights whatsoever. This was a country where until very recently it was illegal for a child to fly a kite or for a little girl to receive any education. To put it in terms you might understand Noreen, rest assured the Taliban would frown on your attending this year's opening night gala of the St. John's International Women's Film Festival. In fact, as a woman, a professor, a writer and (one supposes) an advocate of the concept that women are people, they would probably want to kill you three or four times over.

The letter's display of vindictiveness and its petty indictment of imagined cultural elitism was plain to see. (*Gala*, in the new Canada, was a keyword in the demagogic right-wing assault of liberals, arts and culture that Harper and his bully ministers, John Baird and Jason Kenney, routinely furthered.) But what Mercer's letter also showed, as Master Corporal Franklin's conversation with Shelagh Rogers had done before it in an altogether better light, is how the language that started after 2006 to be used in defence of Canada's cause in Afghanistan was taking on the humanitarian, developmental and peace-building character that, previously, had been so spitefully disparaged. Canadian aid, humanitarian work and soldiers' relationships with people in the villages were becoming, stealthily, more and more a part of the narrative. Immovable in his position, Jack Granatstein was writing, as late as 2007, in *Whose War Is It? How Canada Can Survive in the Post 9/11 World* of the so-called Canadian values of "equality, diversity, advocacy of human rights, the rule of law, gender equality and good governance," that

> Those are all worthy values to which other nations like the
> Dutch and the Scandinavians aspire, as do we (though to
> judge by our record in some of these areas, our aspirations
> do not reach very far), but it is patronizing in the extreme
> to suggest that we will carry those flaming ideals to the
> unenlightened and the downtrodden of the globe. That's
> a policy for missionaries preaching a twenty-first century
> gospel, not a policy for a nation that never even comes
> close to meeting its foreign-aid targets. And just as I resent
> missionaries selling the heathen another and better god,
> so I dislike nations or civilizations pronouncing their values
> the best and urging others to adopt them.

Forget about building schools for girls, in other words. Or how their construction and the foreign aid targets might have been met by a modest displacement of funds now invested in the military. The war was not about opening the realm of possibilities for a better and safer life for Afghans, it was not about a world without borders or being missionary in any way at all. The war was about defence and, its equivalent in the economic realm, the improvement of trade relations with the United States that would surely come about as a result of the "indissoluble bond" that ensues because of the young men and women of Canada and the United States having "fought and died in a common cause," nonsense proven again and most recently by Washington's reward to Canada of a "Buy America" program, tariffs for Canadian passengers at the border and the moratorium on the oil sands Keystone Pipeline project.

Except that Granatstein's grumpy intolerance of Canadians' talk of common values was no longer quite so advantageous to state. After five years of fighting and, by the end of 2006, the deaths of forty-four soldiers and one civilian, it was going to take a more persuasive story than the gung-ho record of the warrior nation to garner ongoing support for the war. Making it possible "for a child to fly a kite or for a little girl to receive an education"—in a phrase, all of those disparaged symbols of the stock of "unrealistic expectations" that were apparently "the work of generations, not of the Canadian military," measures that could not possibly constitute a "yardstick for gauging success"—was fast becoming the bulwark of the new narrative permitting the Forces to stay on. Doubtless, the humanitarian motive had always been there, the effect of the Canadian attribute of citizens knowing their exceptional good fortune and believing it incumbent upon the country to share it. And now here it was, percolating up no matter how the mission had initially been proposed and described.

The simple celebration of Canadian "war-fighting" that had carried the mission previously was proving inadequate to the task. Promotion of the government's "Three Ds" of defence, development and diplomacy, or the analogous military strategy of the "Three Block War," championed by general Rick Hillier, was tweaked to accommodate the public's recalcitrance. The Taliban were no longer

Hillier's "detestable murderers and scumbags" because they "detest Canadian freedoms, society and liberties" but because they detested Afghan schoolgirls, the prime emblem of a beleaguered people that, so went the argument, had invited us in. The very phrase *building schools for girls* that had been, in the opening five years of the war, shorthand for development work too liberal-minded and ineffectual for real soldiers to do was now becoming the job of the Forces through the partnership, in Afghnaistan, of Provincial Reconstruction Teams and the absorption of developmental projects into the militarily endorsed "Three Ds" and "Three Block" doctrines.

The Forces' performance of combat but also of developmental roles became a key part of the argument that peacekeeping, where it may plausibly be done, is just one of the many tasks an army performs and is a job best undertaken by soldiers. It certainly was not the work that Hillier and the military's backers initially wanted the Forces to do, and yet, by 2006, it was being heralded to emphasize the commitment of troops to the job of winning the "hearts and minds" of the people of Afghanistan. Soldiers, it was made known, were routinely making strategic forays of good will into villages, visiting and conferring with tribal elders as Capt. Trevor Greene was doing when, as part of a civil-military co-operation unit in March 2006, the reservist removed his helmet and a young Afghan struck his head with an axe. Greene was the war's "most famous casualty," wrote the *Toronto Star*'s Mitch Potter of the slowly recovering Vancouver resident who, in 2011, was returning to his civilian life as an author and journalist. "Older than most," wrote Potter, "he had not gone to make war. He had gone to make a difference."

This was a new kind of summation. The model of the "Three Block War" was versatile, serving on the home front to accommodate and nudge a public that was still reluctant, after five years of combat, to accept the army's new face or to attribute logic to the shifting presentation of the conflict and standards by which to judge it. So, in the second stage of the war, the work with tribal elders, of microfinance and "building schools for girls" superseded, in PR terms, the war's original and publicly stated aims of national security and ensuring the continued flourishing of the country's vital trade relationship with the United States. It served to show the reinvented Canadian Forces and their work in Afghanistan in an appropriate light—a military that by 2008 had become the premier foreign buyer of U.S. military equipment in the Americas. By then according to the Canadian Centre for Policy Alternatives, the country ranked sixth in military spending among the countries of the ISAF—behind the United States, Britain, France, Germany and Italy, all countries with significantly larger populations and economies. In terms of actual dollars spent, Canada ranked thirteenth in the world, this before the planned $9 billion purchase of sixty-five F-35 stealth fighter jets announced in 2010. (In 2011, the DND recalibrated this figure to $17 billion, by which time the handy deployment of Canadian F-16s in the skies over Libya pretty much stymied any opposition to the purchase outside of the work of Kevin Page, the parliamentary budget officer, whose office estimated that the purchase would end up costing $29 billion—more than three times the original government-stated sum.)

The Canadian Forces were, by 2007, the beneficiary of a budget greater than at any time since the Second World War, the country spending more money on its military than it had even in 1952-53, at the Cold War's height. In the same year of 2007, the country had plummeted to fiftieth rank in terms of its contributions to UN peace operations. By the end of 2009, Canada ranked sixty-third. Bill Robinson, the author of a report for the Canadian Centre for Policy Alternatives, described peacekeeping work as having been "abandoned," the battle against Pearsonian Canada apparently won. And yet no longer was it opportune for the government and the military lobby to disparage the conventional humanitarian expectations of Canadians. Thus, as early as October 2006, the minister of international co-operation and development, Josée Verner, announced two new projects "that focus on the role of women and girls in society"—one, Integrating Women into Markets, that encouraged popular and enabling microfinance programs and another, the Girls' Education Project, promising to "establish up to 4,000 community-based schools, after-school learning programs and provide training for 4,000 new female schoolteachers" and that "about 120,000 schoolchildren in eleven provinces (including Kandahar) will benefit, 85 percent of them girls." (By June 2010, halfway through the three-year "signature project" to build fifty schools, only nineteen had been built.) Concomitantly, prominent members of the media were making adjustments to the tone of their commentary. Suddenly Christie Blatchford was writing of Taliban notes warning Afghans not to go to school and, cloyingly, of the country's "gorgeous darting children" and Canadian soldiers' efforts to protect them. From Blatchford we learned that one young captain just returned from weeks of combat "described entering the smouldering ruin of an elementary school the Taliban had occupied and gutted, burning everything—children's desks, little pictures of the students, drawings on the wall." The *Toronto Star*'s Martin Regg Cohn, criticizing the NDP for wanting troops out, made the case for staying on because of

> Afghan women like Nilab Zareen. The Taliban threw her
> out of the country's medical school....She led me—a
> journalist—down Kabul's winding alleyways where she
> had defiantly set up a room out of public view for girls the
> Taliban had banned from school. When I think of the NDP's

previous demands that we pull out our troops immediately,
I think of Zareen's struggle, and the girls who are no longer
illiterate.

Even David Bercuson, pointing to the Taliban destroying schools and
their subsequent reconstruction as a vital part of counterinsurgency
strategy, was suddenly describing the loss of four soldiers who had
left "their vehicles after trying to help little kids" as "the best reason
to stay."

In 2007, in the face of the Canadian Forces expiring mandate in
Afghanistan, the Conservative government had appointed Derek
Burney, Jake Epp, John Manley, Paul Tellier and Pamela Wallin to
report on Canadian participation in the ISAF and whether or not
and on what terms it should continue. Rudyard Griffiths, still at the
Dominion Institute and prescient in a number of ways, had made his
call for a study group a couple of months earlier, modelling his vision of
a commission upon the United States' Iraq Study Group. But whereas
the American study group was initiated by President George W. Bush
though its members were not appointed by him, Harper handpicked
the five members constituting the Independent Panel on Canada's
Future Role in Afghanistan, subsequently known as the Manley
Report, himself. According to Michael Byers, a respected expert on
international law who has written extensively about Canadian foreign
policy and was asked to appear before the commission but refused,
the panel was highly problematic. All of the panel members, writes
Byers, had ties to big business that would have made the priority of
the trade relationship with the United States a determining factor.
Three had close ties to the Conservative Party and two to the defence
industry. Manley, formerly the Liberal deputy prime minister and one
of the first to scamper away from the party rather than have to toil

in opposition, had already publicly stated his support of the mission prior to his appointment. Manley and his team did their duty, visiting Afghanistan and submitting a report in January 2008 that recalled the Afghanistan Compact entitled "Building on Success" that had been drafted in London in 2006. The Manley Report spelled out "priorities for Afghanistan's development and for aid donors to Afghanistan," identifying the "three critical areas of activity as security; governance (including rule of law and human rights); and economic and social development" just as the Compact, a manifesto of instructions for the newly installed Karzai government, had done. The report invoked the UN resolution, immediately after 9/11, "to bring to justice the perpetrators, organizers and sponsors of these terrorist attacks." Then it resorted to the sleight of hand persistently used by supporters of the war wanting to silence Canadian multilateralists more inclined to the country's prior, peacekeeping role. It pointed out that the "ISAF forces are in Afghanistan at the request, and with the approval, of Afghanistan's own elected government."

The president, Hamid Karzai, had been installed by the "invited" forces in 2004, three years after the United States-led coalition of Operation Enduring Freedom and then the UN-sanctioned ISAF started operating in the country. The assembly that provided "the consent of the Afghan government and the support of the Afghan people" was not elected until 2005, rendering the "request" and "approval" akin to smashing down the door of a house, thrusting a pal inside, telling him the place is his and then having him say, "Come on over." But no matter, the doctrine of occupation as freedom is one, as military historian and professor of strategic studies at Johns Hopkins University Eliot A. Cohen has pointed out, with a long pedigree. It was initially tried by the thirteen colonies in their attempt during the American Revolutionary War of 1775 to wrest the province of Quebec away from British Canada, the prospective attack preceded by a pamphlet explaining to the Quebeckers that they would be "conquered into liberty." (Henry Middleton, the president of the delegates of the united revolutionary colonies and author of the 1774 Letter to the Inhabitants of the Province of Quebec, might as easily have drafted a pamphlet for President George W. Bush's 2001 invasion of Afghanistan. The Afghans, like the French Canadians of two centuries earlier, were "a small people, compared to those who with open arms invite you into fellowship" for whom "a moment's reflection should convince you which will be most for your interest and happiness, to have all the rest of North-America your unalterable friends, or your inveterate enemies.") By 2007, the task of smashing the Taliban had become one of aiding a "democratic" government, the entreaties of which could not be refused. The "terrorists" had become "insurgents" and the task of the invading force was transformed into one of altruistic purpose. Afghan public opinion, the Manley Report noted, "remains overwhelmingly hostile to any return of Taliban rule [and to] that important extent, the insurgency is a failure." And yet, said the report, "As many Afghans told the Panel, the weakness of the existing elected Afghan government compounds the threat of a Taliban return." The report praised Canadians who, their presence clearly a necessity, "don't need any lessons in sacrifice," the military deployment one in which Canada's "3Ds (defense, diplomacy and development assistance) are all pointed at the same problem, and officials from three departments are beginning to work together."

The Manley Report was a neat public relations exercise. It provided the Conservative government the mandate it wanted and needed to be able to continue the war, while at the same time travelling what used to be called the "high road"—stating what has been obvious, since the end of the Second World War, to just about any decent

Canadian: "Canada is a wealthy G8 country," wrote the report's authors. "Our good fortune and standing impose on us both authority and obligations in global affairs."

Here was the reviled Canada seeping up again: Canadians knowing their good fortune and wanting to share it. Contra Granatstein, Griffiths et al., during the war's second stage Canadian soldiers, aid workers and diplomats were, there was no doubting, in Afghanistan to "building girls' schools"—or at least to be able to illustrate to the country that this good work was being done.

Following the report's recommendations, the Canadian ISAF mandate was extended beyond 2009 to July 2011 with the unilateral approval of Parliament. That happened in February 2008, the same year in which the Canadian government made the building of fifty schools in Afghanistan a "signature project." In 2010, the leaking of some of the Conservative government's use of Message Event Proposals (MEP)—the controversial memoranda of government bureaucrats seeking permission from the Prime Minister's Office to be able to speak on just about any subject to the national media—showed the high priority behind this new communications strategy controlled by a public relations staff unprecedented in its power, number and reach. At least as early as February 2008, the month in which the campaign was extended, officials of the Canadian International Development Agency (CIDA) had been preaching that "more children—most notably girls—are going to school." The stringently permitted key message, carefully produced, was of tremendous value to a PMO wanting to paint the mission in a more humanitarian light so that when, for instance, the Canadian ambassador to Afghanistan, Arif Lalani, returned home in June 2010 to undertake a publicity tour to garner support for a war in which, by that time, eighty-three Canadian soldiers had died, an MEP prepared by the Privy Council Office strove to reiterate the government's new "Desired Soundbite"—namely that "Canada's mission in Afghanistan is refocusing its mission towards development, reconstruction and diplomatic efforts."

The realignment of the government's approach to the ongoing war showed how humanitarian aspirations that had previously been disparaged had never lost resonance in the country. Social worker Deborah Ellis, the multi-award-winning author of the Parvana trilogy of books about a young Afghan girl who dresses as a boy to become *The Breadwinner* of her family, has donated the more than half a million dollars in royalties her writing has earned her since 2001 to Afghanistan women's charities. Ellis's work or, for example, the missionary activity of the Presbyterian Church in Canada, have typified the way in which ordinary Canadians' "unrealistic expectations" were not only unchanged but being adopted by the higher powers conforming to the church promise to online visitors that "you can make a difference and bring hope to young girls" like Mastura, "ten years old and who had never been to school." Proclaimed the church, "In a country where the female literacy rate is under 18%, the chance for girls like Mastura to receive an education, get a job and overcome poverty feels impossible. Without assistance these girls could find themselves trapped in a crippling cycle of poverty that will continue for yet another generation." A quiet measure of suppressed North American feeling, American authors Greg Mortenson and David Oliver Relin's *Three Cups of Tea*, about "One Man's Mission to Promote Peace...One School at a Time," became a runaway Canadian bestseller—whatever the truth of its claims that another popular American author, Jon Krakauer, would, in 2011, dispute. (Often, stories are affirming because we want to hear what they have to say and so we seek them out: the truth is bent to our ends.) Even on Toronto's CFRB Talk Radio, a forum for right-wing "talk-jocks" in which, previously, any Canadian who dared to raise questions about the war risked being vilified as much as the Taliban was, the message was altered to accommodate the humanitarian revision. The Taliban were still scumbags, only now it was the odious fact that they were picking on little girls on their way to school and throwing acid in their faces that was the provocation.

The public's ambition for Canada to be "building girls' schools" had turned from being grounds for yet another attack on liberal naïveté to being the "yardstick" of soldiers' selflessness and evidence of the country's goodness in the field, the assault with an axe of reservist Capt. Trevor Greene during his meeting with Afghan tribal villagers the tragic symbol of this decent and innate Canadian tendency. The rate at which Canadian soldiers were being killed in Afghanistan had not waned, but the emphasis regarding the country's reasons for being there was changing and no longer was General Hillier's brand of jocular tough talk particularly winning. The debate had moved from being about why and on what terms we were committing troops to do battle in the country, to what to do now that we were in it—and bound to be so for a few more years yet. To that end, a way of staying on was being provided in exactly the humanizing aspects of the war that its major public proponents—Bercuson, Blatchford, Cooper, DiManno, Granatstein, Griffiths, Hillier and the Conservative Party—had worked so hard to undermine, and that regulation such as the barring of the broadcast of returning coffins, in 2006, had been designed to defeat. Coincident with the Taliban resurgence—a fight back that even General Hillier later claimed was completely unexpected (an overweening confidence, more than on-the-ground intelligence, being the habit of Western powers in the Hindu Kush)—a consensus needed to be found and the elevation of the humanitarian aspect of the war proved the best way of achieving it. The security of Western nations had provided grounds for committing but "Canadian interests and values," providing much of the tenor of the Manley Report, had graduated to being the mission's credible reasons for remaining. This was the war's second remarkable turnaround, the very phrase *Canadian values* having been enough to send the most strident proponents of a stronger, more proactive military into apoplexy during the first half of the decade and for years before it.

By 2009, the new message—or at least the benefits of articulating it—had seeped up all the way to former Chief of Defence Staff Rick Hillier, now returned to civilian life and writing about leadership. In Edmonton promoting his book *A Soldier First*, the retired General Hillier was asked about former minister of defence Gordon O'Connor's remark that "retribution" had been the reason Canadian soldiers were in Afghanistan. "We don't have the luxury of retribution," said Hillier. "All we have the luxury of is justice and bringing peace and stability to places that desperately need some help from the chaos they're in." This was a considerably modified stance from his own often quoted statements demonizing the Taliban or his curt insistence that the Canadian Forces were not in the service of the Canadian public. Even Jack Granatstein eventually, if only for a moment, conceded a bit of ground before, inevitably, putting the cudgel to the peacekeeping version of Canada again. The most vocal of the detractors of the prior version of Canada and its humanitarian aims, Granatstein acknowledged in the *Globe and Mail* in September 2009 that "Canadians want to help build a more peaceful Afghanistan"and wrote, hard as it must have been, of the country's desire "to create a better life for a people who clearly want their daughters to be able to go to school." The justification of the war on grounds of "national security" alone had never been entirely convincing. Employing the rhetoric of "building girls' schools" was the means of rendering the war "just" in a manner more meaningful to many; a development that would not have been necessary had the Canadian popular will not required it. What allowed the government to continue its campaign in Afghanistan coincided with a truth understood by so many Canadians, which is that if Canada was *not "building girls' schools," then* all it was doing was protecting, through the lexicon of security and its epic stance, the surplus of its nequitable economic position and the war could only problematically be described as "just." An act of appeasement was also the rediscovery of Canadian purpose, but the promise that troops would come home when, in the words of the Manley Report, the ISAF had put in place "a better governed, stable and developing Afghanistan whose government can protect the security of the country and its people" would soon become problematic in its own right. The shifting narrative permitting the war in Afghanistan would have to change once again.

CHAPTER FOUR

The War Becomes a Mission (Impossible)

"I got past enjoying a civilian's recoil
  from things military, brutal, conformist, and took
   a peek at what my soldier was so engrossed in—

   Thoreau's *Walden*—imagine him, rubbing oil
  into a Sten gun's springed bolts, working through
his chances at a life away from men"
  —Ken Babstock, "The Essentialist" (2006)

"*Canada's military was at war,*" and it was at war in ways the whole country could see and feel," write Janice Gross Stein and Eugene Lang in *The Unexpected War.*

During the first phase of the war, the Canadian military was the entity being rebuilt "from the ground up." During the second, the failed state of Afghanistan was, though the rehabilitation of the distant, troubled state was not the only objective of the Canadian Forces' deployment and it had never been the first. The "nation-building" that was an enormous and likely insurmountable job in Afghanistan was working concomitantly in Canada, where the effect of the country being "at war in ways the whole country could see and feel" was having altogether better results.

Foreign policy has always been an extension of domestic politics, the alternating current running between them one that influences in both directions. The refashioning of the nation that was the adjunct effect of the restoration of the Canadian Armed Forces was a critical component of the Conservative drive to reconfigure the Canadian polity in a manner that would eventually secure the ruling party an unassailable majority and was proving a grand success. The events of 9/11 determined that a war needed to be undertaken in Afghanistan and the legacy of fighting it, bequeathed to the Conservatives in 2006, provided the government of Stephen Harper with effective means of disassembling an atrophied liberal society caught off guard and replacing its more nuanced approach to global conflict (who doubts that Harper would have sent Canadian troops into Iraq, in 2003, had he been in power?) with a schema for a simpler, more conventionally patriotic nation. Policies of "war-fighting" rather than peace operations; of smaller alliances with like-minded states rather than entangling ones under the aegis of the UN oriented toward some vague, quasi-utopian future; of tighter immigration and greater demands made of newcomers seeking Canadian citizenship than those made by the gatekeepers of the previous, more open society in which merely alighting in Canada was enough, became in less than a decade the underpinnings of a more monolithic version of the country.

"You won't recognize Canada when I'm through with it," warned Harper in 2006, the harbinger of his boast the elevation of the role of the Canadian Forces. The binding mortar of the new country that replaced the old was provided by its cult of the hero and a larger and more prominent military, and a discipline that extended to a terse

intolerance of dissent voiced by unruly parts at home. If, as Christie
Blatchford notes in *Fifteen Days*, it had once been the case that troops
were instructed not to create controversy by wearing their uniforms
in public, now the opposite was true. Uniforms were a source of pride.
The commemorations and rituals that invoked the role of the Forces
and ordinary citizens' debt to them were conducted with panache,
Remembrance Day most of all, and soon the presence of a soldier
would be made formally a mainstay at the oath-taking ceremonies
of new citizens. At the commencement of the fight in Afghanistan,
the valour of the CEF in the First World War had been the standard
invoked. But inevitably time rolls on and, after John Babcock's death,
the extraordinary feats and selflessness of the "Greatest Generation"
fighting the Second World War was becoming it. Rather than wait for
D-Day's John Babcock—the veteran was 109 when he died, 18 when
the First World War ended, so conceivably it could be 2036 before
that particular day—forward planning meant that, along with the
Canadians who had fought in the Second World War, veterans of the
Korean War were being stop-lossed into a further, now requisite tour
of duty, this time in service of the nation's myth-making requirement.
In July 2011, at the same time as he forewarned of cuts to the CBC
and arts organizations supported by his department, the minister of
heritage and official languages, James Moore, announced the funding
of an oral archive of Korean veterans' experiences, work zealously
taken up by the Historica-Dominion Institute in the extension of its
existing Memory Project

Prior episodes of combat provide a romantic link to the country
as it is imagined to have been, though not necessarily as it was. The
correlation of Canadian wars promotes, through remembrance of
various kinds, a nostalgic and highly politicized view of the country
in which "knowledge" of our history functions as the literary romance

does. The romance, the precursor of the novel, is the yearning of a society for a version of itself that it knows is no longer viable and is on the wane. It is the last look back, the protest and lament of a portion of society aware that the world is relentlessly moving forward and, in effect, forgetting it. The link between the war in Afghanistan and prior Canadian wars as the Conservative lobby maintains it is both mired in nostalgia for a Canada that is long past (the government's obsession with things Royal another symptom of this) and a foot in the sand against the tide of an ineluctable future rolling in. The Conservative stance is epic in its wariness, bigoted in its aspiration and fictive in its details. Take, for instance, the eager claim of Stein and Lang's that "Canada's military was at war, and it was at war in ways the whole country could see and feel," seemingly buttressed by much vaunted phenomena such as the naming of the Highway of Heroes and its being lined by Canadians wanting to pay tribute to the war dead. To suggest that the war was keenly felt in Canada—or even that it would be in the event, say, of a terrorist bombing such as occurred in London in July 2005, in Mumbai, India, twice since 9/11 or as backfired in Stockholm, Sweden, in December 2010—is disingenuous, a misrepresentation of the peaceful reality of the country and of its heterogeneous nature, the suppression of both these traits having allowed the epic version of the country to persist.

It is also an assessment that is belied by numbers.

The Canadian Forces suffered, through 2010, the highest casualty and fatality ratio among member states of the ISAF coalition, and yet it simply has not been the case that the "whole country" was seeing and feeling the war. The 55,173 Canadian soldiers who, by July 2011, had served in Afghanistan, their families, loved ones and the greater circle in their acquaintance and a minority for whom the war has struck a jarring or patriotic chord were affected directly. But the more dramatic assertion, while it may be a fair reflection of anxiety about just how far the conflict might have escalated, is a self-aggrandizing fantasy that has relied on the comparison with previous wars to portray the country in a flattering light. A simple numerical analysis of the portion of the population that can claim to be legitimately affected by each of the conflicts shows the extent of the lie that we are living when we pretend that the "whole country" sees and feels the war. The lie operates very usefully on a variety of levels: it has allowed Canadian politicians and civic leaders to make grandiose statements about the country's international standing, it has facilitated a reorganization of the domestic social order along the hierarchical lines that epic thinking encourages and requires and it has permitted innumerable Canadians to believe that we "support our troops" because, on the public face of it, we have easily been able to convince ourselves that we are in fact involved.

But the notion of our involvement is an illusion, as any glance about the streets and restaurants of Canadian cities over the last ten years will have shown. Beyond that immediate circle of the 55,173 and of the 157 military and four civilians who lost their lives in Afghanistan prior to the exit of combat forces in July 2011 (and one more soldier who, by time of writing, died during the Canadian Forces' subsequent training role in Kabul); beyond the CFB bases and their bedroom communities; beyond the faithful watching over the Highway of Heroes and others who have demonstrated their concern by withholding unequivocal support, the war has not even slightly been felt by Canadians other than as that flattering, self-aggrandizing idea.

During the First World War, 644,636 Canadians put on the uniform—a number that amounted to just under eight percent of the population of 8,148,000. Some 418,000 served overseas, more than 65,000 were killed and 172,950 were wounded. During the

Second World War, 1,081,865 Canadians—just under 9 percent of the population of 12,072,000 in 1945—put on the uniform, 545,000 served overseas, more than 47,000 were killed and 54,414 were wounded. In the ten years of the war in Afghanistan and its tapering denouement, approximately 65,000 Canadians and 25,000 in the reserves wore the uniform, of which a little more than 55,000 served overseas. The number of enlisted works out to fractionally more than a quarter of 1 percent of an estimated population, in 2011, of 34,278,400. If we assume that the life of a soldier touches another, then just a bit more than one half of one percent can claim to have been intimately affected by the war in Afghanistan, versus approximately 18 percent in the World Wars. If, however, we assume that the life of a soldier is intertwined with four others—two parents, a spouse and a child or a friend, say—then the portion of the population intimately affected by the war in Afghanistan is still only fractionally above 1 percent versus just under *half* of the population during the Second World War and 40 percent of it in the First. This overwhelming disparity does not even take into account either the length of the wars being compared (the First and Second World Wars involved not only a much greater number, but a greater number over roughly half the time, proportionately augmenting those conflicts' intensities) or the multiplying effect of each era's patterns of migration. Family and community ties will have meant that the general Canadian population far more intimately related to the people in the European countries that constituted the actual theatre of war in 1914-18, when half the CEF was British-born, and 1939-45, than is the present one with Afghans and Iraqis, diminishing the claim that the "whole country" sees and feels the war yet again. (In 1966, three-quarters of Canadian immigrants were European-born versus less than 7 percent from all of Asia. As late as 2006, more than three-quarters of Canadians claimed to Statistics Canada to be of European origin versus an Afghan-Canadian quotient of approximately 25,000, or less than one-thousandth of 1 percent of that year's population of almost 33 million.)

In Canada, the upholding of the fiction of our being a nation at war (fighting the war may mean that the whole nation risks becoming a target, but that is not the same thing) has allowed the Canadian government to pretend, as previous ones have done for more than a century, that the country will be the recipient of special consideration and favours from its partners in alliance and empire. It has done so with little effect, when plotting a genuinely independent course, one that might well have been alternate, is likely to have garnered as much notice and respect. Every bona fide war effort requires its older men fighting the war in their heads and hollering, "Charge!" from the safety of the back, and in Canada and the war in Afghanistan, the situation has been no different. The lie has allowed a particularly strident part of the establishment to argue that death and injury are the "price" to be paid for "freedom," for "security," that catch-all word, and that the war (when it is called a war) is "just." It is not only an example of the good fight that Canadians historically embrace, but of combat as *the* defining national characteristic that supersedes all others. This constant misrepresentation of the polity is evident in the numerous accounts of "lessons drawn from Afghanistan"—by Bercuson, Granatstein, Hillier and their acolytes—in which the assertion of Canadians having acquitted themselves as formidable soldiers, as worthy partners in the ISAF alliance, takes precedence over any more contrary information about the war. The heroic story is sufficient. It completes itself.

And yet, if the subversion of the peacekeeping myth by the war-fighting one has been able to take place, it is exactly because the war has *not* been more generally felt. The small number of casualties and deaths, no less traumatic to the affected because of their relative paucity, is one reason the war is one that most Canadians do not "see and feel" much more than as an experience of free theatre in which, knowing no harm, the play's resolution is more or less guaranteed to be a happy one. The absence of any form of conscription, the most obvious antidote to the country's generally negligible involvement, is a much bigger reason. Said Deresiewicz to West Point, "Now, instead of sharing the burden, we sentimentalize it." Virtually is how, in the privileged remove of the West, almost all emotional phenomena now occur, and in the absence of being one or two people away from the trauma of battle, the way most Canadians see and feel the war was always bound to be second-hand and received from the movies, television and radio shows such as *Combat Hospital* and *Afghanada,* and video and "news" games. The narcissistic entertainments of modern communications substitute for actual involvement, the length and breadth of society. Outside of the real experience of the approximately 90,000 members of the Canadian Forces and their families, the war was never much more, in Canada, than a received idea depending upon a stock of clichéd emotions routinely relied upon by government and commercially exploited by purveyors of mass-market media. Eviscerated of meaning, the pretense of our involvement in the war prompts a collection of reactions that are cued like clockwork: support, honour, shock, remembrance, regret et cetera.

By November 2010, this sentimentalization had become an issue even for one of the war's greatest boosters. "Remembrance Day," wrote Blatchford, is "one of those times, as with all great ceremonial occasions, when it is permissible to be seen crying." She urged Canadians to relish every moment in a country that was itself the peaceful legacy of previous generations' sacrifice—including her RCAF pilot father's. "I love the day, truth be told," opined Blatchford, then. "I love it for its memories, both grand and historical and small and personal; I love it for its sense of common purpose; I love it for the bagpipes, the bugler, and the grand old hymns."

The prodigiously writing reporter was in a sullen mood. As a result of her tours to Afghanistan, Blatchford had gained an intimate experience of soldiers in the field that a majority of the public lacks, and with clannish hauteur she complained in her *Globe and Mail* column, posted under the headline "BEST WE FORGET THE OPRAH-IZATION OF REMEMBRANCE DAY," about the commemorative advertisements of the iconic Canadian coffee and doughnut company Tim Hortons and their "wretched, syrupy music"; of television talk show host Regis Philbin (of *Regis and Kelly*) instructing that "everyone should thank a veteran today"; and about a corporate-sponsored True Patriot Love dinner at Toronto's City Hall at which "plonking down $750 a plate, or plonking down not a sou but being the happy recipient of corporate largesse and being invited to sit at your company's table, as I was, qualifies as heroic." The currency, Blatchford decided, was "cheapened." The reporter concluded, "I cannot help but imagine that as glad as [the soldiers] might be for civilian Canada's current devotion to 'supporting the troops'—if only because it is far less unpleasant than the dark days of the Canadian Forces when soldiers occasionally would be spit upon—they would have little stomach for the witless sappiness that has been in the air all week."

Her cantankerous objections were a departure from the wistful pleasures she had experienced during the Remembrance Day ceremonies that had taken place in Toronto five years before. Then Blatchford had accepted Canada's open society and the myth of rescue—the whole package that she had disparaged at the beginning of the war on the Halifax docks—loving every word that David Miller, then Toronto's mayor, used in his lauding of the national idyll. "We live in a city that shows what 'Never again' looks like," said Miller. "People come here from warring countries, and they become colleagues, neighbours, friends and lovers. They shop at the same stores, and listen to the same radio stations. Their children play and study together. Our city isn't perfect, but it does bring out the best in its residents."

But inevitably such days run the gauntlet of populist sentiment and come out feeling altogether less real. The most well-intentioned tributes eventually become inuring, whether Don Cherry's homages to the war dead on *Hockey Night in Canada* or various artists' attempts to give specific expression to Canadian casualties through individual portraits of each—as in the style of *The New York Times* honouring the 9/11 dead, Kinsman Dave Sopha's eighteen-wheeler Portraits of Honour tour, "bringing together Canadians to remember, honour and celebrate our Canadian Forces," or painter Joanne Tod's series, *The Fallen*. When, as Toronto Maple Leafs hockey player Luke Schenn started to do during home games of the team's 2009 season at the Air Canada Centre, members of the Canadian Forces are provided free tickets to the games, the words LUKE'S TROOPS are flashed across the electronic scoreboards and 20,000 fans rise to applaud. Promptly they turn their attention back to the game, or to playing various apps on their iPhones, and it is hard not to feel discomfort at the quality of support for the nation's military on display—that the clapping for the soldier's decision to put his or her life on the line is a perfunctory and empty gesture, the thing that films and government and the media say we should do. The applause is, to a disturbing degree, narcissistic—as the lining of the Highway of Heroes can also be.

More than honouring the valour of the soldiers, these gestures say, "Look what a good and proud nation we are" and "See how good and proud I am," without having to incur any cost or real exploration of whatever it is that we are defending, what it is we are "standing guard" against.

One of the many ironical effects that technology has had upon the reporting of war is that today's listener, now viewer, very much wants to be affected by the narrative of battle, but on his own terms, ones typically defined by watching movies or playing video games. The effect of the camera and of its swift dissemination of images has been not just the disappointment of making so little difference that major networks can no longer easily commit to the expense of keeping substantial crews in today's theatres of war, but that the concurrent mimicking of the news in Hollywood movies and television drama has helped to push the bloody horror of battle into a realm far beyond the "pornography of war" that novelist John Rae decried years ago. Ever since the Vietnam War, when television was supposed to have brought the horror of war into the living rooms of America and, in so doing, to have contributed to the end of the country's role in that fight, another phenomenon played its part that is also attributable to the power of the camera.

Filmmakers, today, compete to make the old new. The primary mechanism that they use—of revealing what used to be taboo—has robbed the gritty reality of war of much of its ability to shock. Kathryn Bigelow's 2008 Academy Award-winning film of a U.S. Army bomb disposal squad operating in Iraq, *The Hurt Locker*, was mostly remarked upon because a woman directed it (with nothing to suggest that its point of view was the result of one or the other gender). While the movie's swift disposal of its box-office stars in cameo roles, communicating the arbitrariness of death in the battlefield, was quite ingenious, its message of the alienated soldier unable to adapt to civilian life and so returning for a further tour of duty was already familiar. Enough so that today's soldiers, true to that odd wheel of life imitating art imitating life, repeat the message readily: thirty-one-year-old Sgt. Ed Wadleigh, who, returned home, finds himself "longing for the stark simplicity of life at a combat outpost," who finds "normal, everyday life to be boring, mundane, insignificant and dull, particularly when compared to the rush and thrill and terror of combat"; twenty-six-year-old Bruce Legree, at home in Manitoba, who, reported the *Globe and Mail* in 2011, "can't begin to tell you how much it hurts to not be a soldier any more," and complains of living a "vagabond experience, where you just kind of wander around trying to figure out where you fit in."

Once again, Fussell's observations about the reporting of the First World War are illuminating.

Writes Fussell in *The Great War in Modern Memory*:

> Logically, there is no reason why the English language could not perfectly well render the actuality of trench warfare: it is rich in terms like *blood, terror, agony, madness, shit, cruelty, murder, sell-out, pain* and *hoax*, as well as phrases like *legs blown off, intestines gushing out over his hands, screaming all night, bleeding to death from the rectum*, and the like [but] soldiers have discovered that no one is very interested in the bad news they have to report. What listener wants to be torn and shaken when he does not have to be? We have made *unspeakable* mean *indescribable*: it really means *nasty*."

War's story of wasted limbs and lives is mostly extraneous to the narrative. It is mostly extraneous because the majority of legs blown off, screaming all night, madness, shit, cruelty and murder is suffered not by the ISAF but by ordinary Afghans while the alliance's own wounded are few and relayed to the public in entertainment, most of all. In Michael Cimino's distressing movie of 1978, *The Deer Hunter*, John Savage plays Steven, one of a trio of Pittsburgh pals profoundly damaged by their experience of the Vietnam War. Steven comes home to Pennsylvania in a wheelchair after having had both legs and an arm amputated. Dreading his return, he reacts to his broken body as a something other, a symbol of what cannot be reconciled, and says, "I don't fit." In the 1989 film *Born on the Fourth of July*, American director Oliver Stone put Tom Cruise in a wheelchair in a dramatization of the life of paraplegic Vietnam veteran Ron Kovic, who manages to rise out of his morass to become something of an activist champion. In these two laudable films, the visual information was alarming and trenchant—and new. In subsequent ones, the same scenes have been repeated so often that they have become a staple and cliché. Portrayals of battlefield carnage have followed a similar arc. In 1998, Steven Spielberg's movie *Saving Private Ryan* opened with an unprecedented and technologically masterful recreation of the D-Day landing, on June 6, 1944, on Normandy's Omaha Beach. The extraordinary, quasi-documentary footage featured, among other grisly moments, the sight of blood spurting from the shoulder of a soldier whose arm had been blown away, walking in a daze—raising the bar, again, when it comes to graphic images. Certainly the language of film is "rich in terms like *blood, terror, agony, madness, shit*," in phrases like *"legs blown off, intestines gushing out over his hands, screaming all night, bleeding to death from the rectum*," and so on. Except that literal images of the violence of war have become such an integral part of art and reportage that most renderings of war have lost any real capacity to alarm. Who is surprised? The "blue films of war...titillating our senses with the imagination of great deeds, the masturbation of war," were always going to be subject to the same laws that govern pornography of the more pedestrian, sexual kind—pornography, by its very nature, demanding a constant vaulting of the limits that precedents have set for it. So, as with sex, a more graphic rendering of war is not just permissible but necessary for it to achieve the same effect that was reached before, short moments ago, our nerves were desensitized to yesterday's shocking portrayals of the "unspeakable."

And yet, in competition with reality, the violence as pornography has failed in offering anything close to a portrayal of war that may be considered "true"—just as, in its analogous realm of paying entertainment, virtual experiences of the sexual kind create instead the appetite for even more extreme experience and a very profitable industry relying on its pursuit. The pornography of war cannot do otherwise. In effect, war's reporting has reached a fork in the road in which the path of gritty hyper-realism has ended in a cul-de-sac of its own making and, second only to actual experience, art is more likely to provide the navigable avenue to understanding war's nature. The film *Restrepo*, nominated for an Academy Award in 2011, months before one of its makers, Tim Hetherington, was killed while on the job in Libya, eschews narration and analysis in its attempt to show something of war's reality. On the surface, the documentary rejects art as a means of filtering or reconstructing what is "nasty" and "unspeakable" about war. Instead it relies on fairly unmediated camera work to describe the soldiers' experiences though there is artifice, of course, in the choices, segues and edits that the production team makes. Fiction, today, has a much better chance of conveying war's vicissitudes than the news does, though the challenge remains just as profound for those grappling with the real in art. Contemplating this modern paradox in relation to the Holocaust is what led Canadian writer Yann Martel to contend with the challenge of conjuring up appropriate feeling in himself and in his readers in the wake of such a monstrous happening and testing, in his 2010 novel, *Beatrice & Virgil*, the limits of fiction and non-fiction in the struggle to remember it truthfully. How does one make stories, told so often, fresh and new? How is the descent into cliché's realm of unreflective, automatic feeling avoided in reportage or in art?

What were once thought to be "indescribable" and "unspeakable" events of wartime are, today, entirely visible pieces of information uploaded to YouTube and social networks—whether beheadings or Libyan dictator Muammar Gaddafi's bloody, bullet-riddled body (the execution of Romanian autocrat Nicolae Ceaușescu in 1989 and the torture and death of Liberian dictator Samuel K. Doe in 1990, both precedents)—that television networks competing with Tweets are compelled to mount in turn and that Hollywood features and television dramas then recreate and seek, for effect, to surpass. The time we take to pay dues to war's brutality and senselessness, typically in the safe confines of the home or cinema (but also from the side of the road or in the hockey rink), constitute an ersatz moral act that excuses actually having to do anything more proactive about a subject that is innately horrific. An understanding of the lexicon is sufficient—whether the image of the shell-shocked soldier captured in the famous Don McCullin photograph of a gaunt U.S. Marine gripping the barrel of his rifle at Hue in Vietnam to, today, the torment of the officer who must deliver to a family a soldier's notice of death (see, for instance, Oren Moverman's 2009 film, *The Messenger*), the well-meaning combatant who has inadvertently killed his friend and colleague in the crucible of battle with "friendly fire" (see, most recently, 2011's *Combat Hospital*, Season One, Episode Two, "It's My Party") or the broken soldier returning home and ultimately killing himself (see Ryan Redford's 2010 film, *Oliver Sherman*, based on the Rachel Ingalls short story, "Veterans").

What moral repugnance might once reasonably have been thought to be the result of such representations in both art and the news is inevitably tamed by the inuring process so that ultimately we clock the whole gamut of tropes and signifiers of war with ephemeral feeling and then indifference. What is "nasty" about war is, in the graphic domain, easily and even compulsorily described. All that remains "indescribable" is, as it was in Fussell's day, only so because we'd rather not be "torn and shaken" when we do not have to be and because, despite all of the bellicose messaging, as a society distant from the fight and only peripherally at war, there is little pressure to acknowledge that which we are very easily able to ignore.

The banal reduction of these received experiences of war are by no means restricted to film, television and radio drama but there in the grandiose posturing of hockey commentator Don Cherry and the work and grave faces of reporters and dour television anchors, too. (When bulletins demand sixty- and ninety-second soundbites, perhaps the few minutes of a "feature" if the reporter is having a good day, how can journalists do other than use a set of reiterated phrases that act and are intended to act as mnemonics for the collective Canadian psyche?) Authentic feeling is individual, it is antithetical to the monolithic sentiment of the mobilized society in the grip of a "war effort" because, as is the case with a well-functioning army, the demagogic consensus of the general population depends upon a limited set of uncomplicated ideas and the group behaving as one. In the rhetorical climate of the last decade, one that is ongoing, it takes a strong person indeed to be able to maintain individual feeling and to ask what it means to "support our troops" when merely to raise questions about the war, as Noreen Golfman did, or to contravene ritual and wonder about the point of a daughter's ended life, as Nichola Goddard's father, Tim, did, is to risk being vilified by a crowd egging its members on with bullying, hateful vitriol. Christie Blatchford's deft gathering of Tim Goddard back into the fold was nefarious because it was doing the crowd's work: silencing him with its oppressive, disingenuous love.

The sad truth of Canada's small war being fought is that now even a father's ambivalence, outrage and anger are a part of the script. Not just the ramp ceremony and the funeral procession, but all moments of the lives of soldiers and their war, narratives including their families' and the general population's demonstrations of grief after combat deaths, have succumbed to the inuring syndrome of being utterly familiar and public.

If, as many writers have described, soldiers frequently returned from the battlefield not just displaced and alienated, sometimes with PTSD and on other occasions with anger and with hatred, it was because they tended to discover—and often, in their traumatized state, to misconstrue—just how high the home fires had been burning while they'd been away risking their lives. During the First World War, they came home to theatres and, during the war in Vietnam, to a country of sit-ins and "free love." This difficult adjustment of soldiers has been a characteristic of wars since the wily Odysseus, home from Troy after a long decade, discovered, but for his loyal wife, Penelope, nothing but mirth and merry suitors in Ithaca, his home, subsequently slaying the whole reckless bunch. Penelope's suffering is of a kind the soldier does not see, or that witnesses of the moment are often not keen to represent. It is less dramatically interesting. The misfit, for instance of Sgt. 1st Class William James, the explosives disposal expert whom Jeremy Renner plays in *The Hurt Locker*, is a romanticization of his (mad) heroic qualities more than it is an indictment of the violence to which he has become addicted. It is certainly not an indictment of the society failing to reabsorb the soldier into its midst. No attention at all is paid to that issue.

French Canadian Jean-Jules Richard, the author of *Neuf jours de haine* ("Nine days of hate"), fought in the Second World War and took part in the D-Day landings in Normandy. Richard, a social activist his whole life, was a former communist who came of age during the Great Depression, riding the rails and joining the hunger march that met Prime Minister R.B. Bennett in 1935 to protest the treatment of youth in relief camps. *Neuf jours de haine*, published in 1948, captures the violence, delusions and depravity of war remarkably. In its tense episodic narrative, in which a variety of characters represent a broad panoply of Canadian diversity and hopes, discipline on the battlefield counts for everything and "personal opinion has no weight." The rules of ordinary civil society no longer apply, and the soldier who kills because doing so is his job quickly forgets his humanity and is able to examine the man whose life he has ended with clinical indifference.

> Turn him over on all sides to find the place where the bullet
> hole was made. No need to flee. On the contrary. Your
> chums gather around to congratulate you.
> —Bravo, old pal! I couldn't have done better myself!
> You become a hero. A hero because you kill.

Soldiers, but also civilians, are implicated. In Canada, the readers of the newspapers that report from the front lines sit comfortably in their homes and "win the war in their slippers." And in France, when Richard's motley group of Canadian soldiers enters, in 1944, a liberated French village, they come across a crowd gathering to watch a young woman being publicly humiliated as punishment for her wartime romance with a German. A barber's chair is rolled out before the Hôtel de Ville, where her head will be shaved, and the woman's breast is exposed. The scene is one of barbarism, bloodlust and revenge, and the prop of a civic monument to "the war to end war" emphasizes the cycles we do not break, the history we repeat.

The people in the crowd shoved one another to get a better
view. Heads craned and stretched like the necks of giraffes.
A bunch of kids climbed on top of the memorial to the
dead of 1914-18. The balconies and roofs around the square
were filled with people. Men climbed the clock tower. They
screamed at those in front to widen the circle so that more
people could see.

A fight breaks out as the woman is tied to the chair and roughly subdued, the moment ugly and assiduously observed. As is the agony of a
comrade burned by a flame-thrower, the incendiary glue sticking to his
twitching body before one of his friends must shoot him, prompting
one soldier to reflect on war's horrors: "We have to pay. *Somebody* must
pay. For as long as death has not had its fill of atrocities, it will extend
a life." Shades of Robert Semrau, the dying man is killed.

How much do Canadians really know about Afghanistan? Next to
nothing, really, the theatres of war and peace existing as territories
apart, bridged by the few who are enlisted (a number, as we have seen,
that does not compare with those who provided a link between the
home front and battlefield in either of the two World Wars) and by
the communications of the media.

But the war comes home for real, certainly and problematically,
with the arrival of the wounded. The wounded are visible reminders
of the "nasty" not sanctified with the ritual of a ramp ceremony and
a funeral; casualties of the war who do not always engage with the
public that dispatched them with the dignity and exonerating good
humour of soldiers such as Master Cpl. Paul Franklin. The wounded
can be ignored. Indeed, the wounded veteran generally *is* ignored, and
compelled through tight-fisted bureaucracies to have to fight for what
should be his due: fair recompense, a good job; the right to remain
with the Forces, should he wish.

The trouble is that when it comes to dealing with the wounded, the epic view and its heroic lexicon that helps to launch a country into a new war becomes an impediment. Even the commonality of the uniform that, by design, renders the soldier an integral but unremarkable part of a collective, becomes, to the individually wounded, a disservice by denying the individual nature of his injury. What is demanded, if the wounded soldier's reintegration into society is to be meaningfully achieved, is an imaginative leap on the part of the public (and, most of all, by the military administration and by government) that recognizes the challenges and ongoing nature of the wounded soldier's condition. This imaginative leap runs against the grain of the epic requirement and its sorting of the members of society into distinct categories—into the protected and the "best of the best," into sheepdogs and wolves, into heroes and villains. Instead of the hierarchies and divisions of a society at war, in which even empathy is a failing that encourages the assumption that we are all alike, the presence of the wounded veteran demands that we ask what it means to be in another's shoes—or shoe, or wheelchair—and to include the soldier in our very human embrace. The wounded soldier's sacrifice tests the simple category of "ultimate." The soldier is still a hero—more so, even, but a problematic one. No longer is he a breed apart. The challenges he faces, whether of the body or of the mind, have reduced him to being like the rest of us. In the construct of the hero, he is no longer superior in kind—and empathy, that marvellous human characteristic of the novel, not the epic, is society's appropriate response.

Not just empathy is demanded, but cash. The new realm is a monetized one in which the existential dangers that soldiers face have been transformed into deaths, mutilations and traumas that come with costs and "benefits" to the soldier that can be measured. More than wearing red on Fridays, or lining the banks and the bridges of a Highway of Heroes, our commitment to the injured shows how, as a country, we "support our troops." But the unpalatable truth of the matter is that on this plane that is both symbolic and practical, we "support our troops" hardly at all. Wounded soldiers have never been a leading part of the heroic dialogue. In fact, the very opposite is true. The disfigured body of a veteran, of an amputee with prostheses, on crutches or in a wheelchair, the trauma of a soldier with mental health issues, communicate a problematic message that has constituted rich material for novelists and filmmakers but that is of little use at all to army administrators and citizen propagandists. Wounded soldiers are, at best, a complicated emblem of the heroic qualities of brave young soldiers unlikely to be portrayed as "universally beautiful" "in the vigour of their manhood," as "alpha males" and "guys wars can't be won without." They are no longer men and women whom reporters such as Blatchford and DiManno may trivially sexualize. They are no longer men and women who serve the nation at the front of a war behind which it is easy to rally. Rather, the wounded soldier becomes the symbol of dire consequences of war to be lamented, worse for our having known these existed. That war is not even specific anymore, but war in the abstract. No matter how proud and capable, the warrior who travelled to the front lines as a hero—whether to combat the particular threat to our security called al-Qaeda, to protect our trade relationship with the United States or to build schools for girls—returns as a casualty of war and as the evidence of a grim, eternal verity. He becomes the cruel embodiment of a sacrifice that the vague thing called "the nation" was ready to make, the "price" of which has evidently been absorbed by someone else. He is the "bill" that Ignatieff and Manley would have us pay. And he is someone who, unlike the "Unknown Soldier," is identifiable should we choose to look. He becomes, in his altered state, the symbol of something beyond heroism: of a life compromised; of the stoicism of an injured man and the family that must now stand by him; of a wager against the odds that the enlisted soldier, a calculation in the leadership's algorithm, lost.

Just how much greater are the odds of being maimed than killed is why not just the Canadian government, but all regimes, are loath to share statistics and information concerning the injured as they do with the dead. Of the 172,950 Canadians who were wounded in action during the First World War, some 75,000 returned permanently disabled, approximately 10,000 more than died in the war, the ratio of injured to the killed approaching three to one. The sum of Canadians injured in the Second World War exceeded the approximately 47,000 dead by about 7,000. Thirty percent of the U.S. troops that returned from Iraq before January 2011 had serious mental health problems, and the figure of more than 32,000 wounded exceeded, by far, that of the 4,757 dead, and the figure of 615 Canadian soldiers who suffered injuries directly related to combat in Afghanistan is four times the 154 who died during the same period. DND categories, however, can be misleading. From 2002 to 2010 in Afghanistan, the last year for which DND statistics were available — figures are released at the end of each calendar year — twelve times as many troops were reported to have been injured, though only a third of this group were considered "wounded in action." Soldiers who have died in traffic accidents are counted among the dead and make the hallowed journey home along the Highway of Heroes from CFB Trenton to the Toronto coroner's office. Those who are merely *wounded* in traffic accidents, however, are considered to have suffered "non-battle injuries" and therefore not to have been "wounded in action." The lesson appears to be that death makes a soldier, de facto, a "hero," but that soldiers who are injured are an inconvenient something else. Through paeans made to handicapped veterans that are mostly kept offstage and out of view, or more impassioned ones such as the *Toronto Star* made for a front-page week in autumn 2010, the public does acknowledge that war is a fatally risky venture that can carry a terrible price, and facing these odds and enlisting is why the valour of young men heading off to "make a difference" is sung in the first place. But it is the story that the bodies of the wounded tell that prompts the greatest and the most commonplace of war's necessary denials. The story that the actual presence of men without legs or arms or nerves tells in the flesh is too gruesome and deterring a sight to be efficiently a part of the same mythic narrative. It is DND policy, according to Capt. Christian Courtemanche, a spokesperson for the military's Strategic Joint Staff, to "basically limit the information available."

Denial of the damage suffered by soldiers in war occurs in a variety of ways, the most excruciating of these being the chronic forgetting of the public at large and the willful omission by government of the story of the maimed that permits it. In a sense, the behaviour of the nation can be analogous to that of the injured soldier who is the object of this calculated forgetting. In Liane Faulder's sympathetic chronicle of Master Cpl. Paul Franklin's recovery from the blast that took his legs, *The Long Way Home* (2007), the author describes how Franklin, traumatized and in hospital, would recount that, "in the moments after the explosion," the prostrate soldier

> saw the glistening white bone extending from his left thigh
> [and] pulled out his tourniquet from his pants pocket.
> Despite the chaos surrounding him, he had the presence
> of mind to use his medical training to save his own life,
> yanking the black band tight around his thigh, choking

the artery and staunching the gush of blood. To Paul, this
represented a triumph of sorts. Proud of his skills as a
medic, he felt he had drawn on his training when it counted.
As the black smoke billowed from the burning G-wagon
and soldiers scurried around the blast site, Paul did what
he had to do.

Franklin told his wife, Audra, this version of events in his telephone
call home from the hospital at Kandahar Airfield, and repeated it
to his surgeon and to journalists. Except that, as Faulder writes,
"The problem was that the story was not true." Franklin was not
lying, but had suffered an injury to the brain leading to a medical
condition known as confabulation, the false memory "as real to Paul
as everything that had happened since." The memory amounted to
a measure the brain needed to take to preserve the health of the
greater body. Franklin, however, had the remarkable courage to
revise the story of Action Man heroism that he had unwittingly spread
about himself, releasing a statement to the media and facing the
less palatable truth about his own helplessness in the moments after
the IED attack. The disseminators of our national "confabulation,"
can claim no such fortitude, the country's habits of omission and
oversight existing in the chronic forgetting of the public at large,
and in the obfuscation by the DND and Veterans Affairs concerning
not just the toll of injuries, but the fifteen suicides of active-duty
soldiers that took place at an average in 2008 and 2009. The rate of
suicide is ostensibly lower than that of the Canadian population at
large, though it is hard to know just how accurate this actually is. The
circumstances of suicides are revealed only when family members
force an investigation, and lethargically at that.

The suicide of Cpl. Stuart Langridge is, in Canada, the most blatant example of this deliberate tendency. Langridge killed himself at CFB Edmonton in 2008 but is not enumerated among the Canadian Afghanistan war dead. However, Capt. Frank Paul, who died on home leave in Newfoundland of natural causes, is. "Though his death came suddenly while on leave from his deployment in Afghanistan, he was still on duty and considered part of the mission," said Chief of Defence Staff General Walter Natynczyk. "Therefore his death is no less important than any other CF member who served and died while in Afghanistan. It is important that his name be added to the list of fallen." The heroic nature of Paul's "ultimate sacrifice" was reiterated by Prime Minister Stephen Harper, who said in his condolences that, "though he died on Canadian soil, Capt. Paul was still an integral part of our mission in Afghanistan and had worked diligently to help bring safety and stability to the people of Afghanistan. For that, he deserves to be recognized with his colleagues who have given their lives for this mission." All of these arguments could equally have been applied to the case of Cpl. Stuart Langridge, but his mother, Sheila Fynes, was compelled to engage in a long battle with the Department of National Defence to acquire any information at all about his suicide, suffering these further indignities after the loss of her soldier son.

The problem to the proponents of the war, any war, is that the evidence of physical injuries and mental ones such as post-traumatic stress disorder (PTSD) and suicides cannot be contradicted. And the ones who do not serve — especially those who, in power, are responsible for the deployment — are the players who are implicated in their awfulness. So the figures are not released in the way that the roll call of the "fallen" is, and no government, historical institute or fundraising body has been bold or decent enough to erect a monument to the wounded of any of the last century's Canadian wars. Such a monument is possible. In Toronto's Victoria Memorial Park, as part of

Frank Darling's monument to the War of 1812, a soldier with an empty sleeve where his left arm would have been, clasping his braided hat to his chest, gazes into the distance sorrowfully. An early work by renowned turn-of-the-twentieth-century Canadian sculptor Walter Seymour Allward—whose name would subsequently forever be associated with the Vimy Memorial—Old Soldier is a sombre figure cut in a classical nineteenth-century mould whose sorry countenance speaks volumes of the loss incurred by war. And in Thunder Bay, Ontario, a striking monument to Terry Fox was erected at the place where, in 1980, the cancer-ridden amputee civilian ended his Marathon of Hope, but nowhere in Canada does there exist a monument to the heroism of soldiers that mounts on a pedestal the bronze figure of a handicapped soldier on crutches, or in a wheelchair.

In the face of political uncertainty, of the conflicted feelings that emanate from a war that strikes too many, at some base level, as at best only dubiously necessary, the war must be commemorated in less challenging ways. The handicapping and physical debilitation of soldiers cannot be remembered in bronze or even in paintings because the message that would be conveyed is one of barbarism, rather than of the "heroic" qualities that do not exist in any lesser quantity because the soldier has not died. The hero, originally a demigod greater in his essence than ordinary men, is allowed only a wound that is fatal. Thetis, the mother of Achilles, did not explain to her son, the greatest hero of them all, that the existential choice before him was between the long, unremarkable life, the heroic one, or returning home from Troy on a plank of wood with his legs amputated below the knee and a child to pull him, helpless, through the streets as his wife, deciding the old warrior is far too much work, leaves him. This was never an option—neither for the hero, nor for the gods. (Only one lame god existed in the pantheon, and that was Hephaïstos, a master blacksmith and hero of technology and the trades. Hephaïstos was married to Aphrodite, the goddess of Love. She cuckolded him and slept with Ares, the god of War, instead.)

Today, wounded veterans and their families continue to have to fight for benefits and also the right to continue to serve. These demands are hardly unreasonable, even in the face of the Forces' insistence on the "universality of service"—the stipulation that anyone in the military is physically able to fight—given the plethora of desk jobs that a physically challenged person can perform. It is hard not to conclude that the culture of the military, in the face of these modern demands, is obstinate, and that the presence of the demoralizing wounded is the thing of which it is afraid. The random aspect of war's violence is underscored by the presence of the wounded. No matter the acts of bravery and courage that put him there, the injured soldier becomes the irrefutable picture of physical human frailty, of a body that can be broken. The myth-makers cannot afford to have the battle they have engaged with on a symbolic plane undone by the very powerful image of an injured soldier—an image that lingers for an inconveniently long time after a war is ended. The hurt and mauling and desecration of human bodies visibly amount to a cost that is messier than the loss of a soldier's life. Rather than a flag and a salute, or a grave ceremony attended by hundreds or even thousands that in the short passage of time ends, the existence of a soldier with a prosthetic limb, in a wheelchair, with a disfigured face or who is suffering PTSD is a living and breathing manifestation of war that says to the politicians who put him into the field: "This was my sacrifice, not yours." In a war that would be outrageous and fallacious to pretend that the whole nation was fighting, any real threat of harm was consigned by the civilian population to a lottery that the injured man has lost. The wounded soldier becomes the symbol of universal fallibility, too, for the first and biggest tragedy of war is that it should be necessary, that it should be an institution, and we are all to blame for that. Even when honoured with medals, maimed veterans tend to recede from public view and to have to fight, often with an outrageous loss of dignity, for exactly the sort of regard implied by the high diction that saw them off to war in the first place.

Without the immediately palpable threats to our society that are the traditional hallmark of wars of existence, and without much evidence at home that a war is being fought, the conflict in Afghanistan has remained a mostly political, almost theoretical affair operating far outside the deeply emotive, controversial realm of conflicts that authentically reach home. The war has been a display (as usual) of fealty to a greater alliance, the pursuit of kudos and a pat on the back rather than an ensuring of survival; good news for Canadian oil companies; an argument about military "readiness" and an opportunity to discuss, with the benefit of field work, what is an appropriate role for Canadian troops. Thus most of the commentary, more than debate, has been about how well (they can only do well) Canadian soldiers have been performing. The actual reasons for their deployment have become a secondary consideration to the primary ones of the troops being busy and distinguishing themselves.

But here's another ironic truth: the charges that were levelled so nastily against the supporters of peace operations can be laid with as much substance against those who cheer today's "war-fighters" on. Those hockey crowds standing for a moment's swift applause, the crowds lining the Highway of Heroes, the pundits in the papers and think-tank champions of the new "warrior nation" are indulging in the "feel-goodism" and the "hollow façade" of a "myth-making exercise" just as much as Maloney and Bercuson and Steyn and Granatstein thought the liberal "hippy-dippy" generation was, only now all that "unbridled love and unsecured trust" is invested in camouflage and a packet of stories that say how good war is. Critics who lambasted the supporters of peacekeeping operations for putting soldiers "in harm's way" are the same ones who uphold the sending of tens of thousands of soldiers up over the trenches and to near certain slaughter as a historical episode to vaunt. The detractors of peace operations who have classified the UN and its 1990s missions as failures are often the same ones who explain the un-ended job in Afghanistan as a failure but a *noble* one, by saying simply that "we did what we could."

These were the decade's lesser circularities. The greater one was that where, in 2001, peacekeeping became "war-fighting," nine years later at least the motives for combat were starting to resemble those of peace operations again, enough so that the realization of the omission of Canadians who served in peacekeeping missions was striking home. "As we attend Remembrance Day services," wrote Tim Dunne, a military affairs analyst with Dalhousie University's Centre for Foreign Policy Studies in the *Chronicle Herald* in 2011, "we should remember not only those who served and died on the battlefields of the two World Wars, Korea and Afghanistan, but also those who have served and died in other missions and deployments." Noted Dunne of the 114 Canadian peacekeepers who had died in service, "There was no ramp ceremony either on departure from the theatre of operations or on arrival in Canada; there was no official reception party, and there was no convoy along the equivalent of Ontario's Highway of Heroes." One Canadian peacekeeper, who had died in Bosnia-Herzegovina in 1995, had been shipped home as air freight. The tone of the dialogue that had greased the cogs of Canada's entry into Afghanistan and was then altered to help the country stay on had started to be modified a

second time in late 2009. Late that year, on December 23, Lt. Andrew
Richard Nuttall had become the 134th Canadian soldier killed in
Afghanistan and although a week later the *Globe and Mail* praised, in
its New Year's Day editorial, the Forces "continuing to face danger,
and to fight for the same worthwhile aims as when they started," it
was no longer stated what these aims were as they may have been
less straightforward even to the paper. Then, on December 30, four
soldiers as well as Michelle Lang, the *Calgary Herald* correspondent
who had reported on Nuttall's death the previous week, also died. It
was a bleak month, a terrible end to the year. In compliance with the
extension to the war that Parliament had unilaterally decided upon
in February 2008, Canada was having to come to terms with an exit
from Afghanistan that would happen for cogent reasons or not, in
2011. The critical matter of the end of a conflict complicated by the
post-Cold War phenomenon of liberal democracies announcing, in the
face of the mounting human and capital costs of wars, dates of exit
that have little to do with the situation on the ground and everything
to do with the government and the country needing a new story to
narrate its way out.

By the time of the funeral that was held for Lieutenant Nuttall in
the first week of 2010's New Year, the language that was being used to
describe the "mission" was showing more signs of having come full
circle. Nuttall, in his obituaries, was described as a young man dedicated
to helping Afghans. "Andrew did not die in vain," said the family's notice
on the website of the McCall Bros. funeral home of Victoria, British
Columbia, alluding to the John Lennon song "Imagine," hardly the sort
of rallying war cry that Granatstein and his CDFAI confrères would have
chosen. The army that Hillier had described as deploying "disciplined
managed violence" to fight a long and difficult war in which the Taliban
were "detestable murderers and scumbags" was returning to one in

which Canadian soldiers were acting as the promoters of peace and interests other than their own—of, dare it be said, "Canadian values." Nuttall, said the *National Post*, was "someone determined to *make a difference* in the world." The family's memorial notice described him as a windsurfing, spirited and charitable young man and suggested, in lieu of flowers, that donations be made to the dead soldier's favourite charities, International Plan Canada and the For the Love of Africa Society among them.

Thirty-year-old Andrew, said the notice,

> did not die in vain. He was protecting the most vulnerable
> of the world. He, along with a tough, educated, well trained
> group of men and women, were reaching out every hour, in
> everything they did, to make a positive change in this small
> global village of ours; to open the realm of possibilities for
> a safe and better life for everyone. He made the ultimate
> sacrifice to demonstrate these Canadian values—his values.
> *"Imagine there's no borders."* He imagined a better world, and
> walked out into life to make a change, no matter how small
> or large, whether with friends around a table in Canada or
> in full fatigues working with an Afghan villager.

Within six months, friends would remember the lieutenant with his own "Hero's Workout" at the Vancouver branch of the CrossFit gym, where, in 2006, he had worked as a trainer and met the soldiers who inspired him to join the military. These tributes to the soldier as *kouros* aside, the "Canadian values" Nuttall apparently brought to the Forces and the condolences attached to his obituaries sounded entirely like those that had compelled young Canadians to sign up for the military during the fifty years in which the country was actively contributing

to peacekeeping missions. Their articulation of the commitment—
to "trying to make this a better world for all of us," to "protecting
the most vulnerable" and "making a positive change in this small
global village of ours" are sentiments to be found, too, in the several
peace-oriented scholarships and monuments dedicated to Captain
Nichola Goddard's memory—amount to an expression of ambition
superseding arguments concerning *national* or continental security
and the better trade relationship with the United States aired to push
Canada into the war in 2001. Narrow and, ultimately, isolationist,
these latter arguments for the war use words such as *interoperability*
and *regional security* to justify Canada's enthusiasm for being a part of
the greater alliance, rushing into a position of American subservience
as once it joined the RALLY TO THE EMPIRE—ANSWERING THE CALL
OF THE MOTHERLAND. It does not have to, but it does, this tendency
having culminated, in 2011, in a call by the war's most ardent
supporters for participation in leagues even smaller than NATO, the
country's fundamental alliance being the one it has with the United
States, entrenched against a world it imagines to be ever more hostile.

But it is difficult, in Canada, to maintain the ferocity and the
chauvinism of such epic views. The nation wants and needs a well-
functioning, logistically supported, versatile and able military of
which it can be proud. It wants, and needs, a military that can stand
in defence of the country. It wants and needs the sort of armed forces
that, in various configurations, are able not only to defend the nation,
but to implement the higher ideals to which the fortunate country
aspires. In this last idea, one to which the country almost ineluctably
comes around, is the tendency that undoes the epic view—namely, the
habit that Canadians have of asking of themselves what it means to be
in another's shoes. This, already explained, is an effect of the land and
those who have settled it, and of the circumstances in which they did

and new Canadians continue to do so. It is the effect of communities of diverse origins needing to work out an accord in the new territory in the umbrage of the First Nations and their reaching this accord through negotiation rather than force of arms. Inevitably, this tendency finds its expression in the international theatre. Having suffered, as yet, no grave assaults on our borders (though a Canadian army should also be prepared for this, in the North especially, even if that dispute is progressing neatly toward a UN-brokered resolution), our abiding "mission" remains one of helping our fellow man and making what change we can in "this small global village of ours."

Foundation myths, in Canada, really are slow to budge.

By 2006, something else was at work to undermine the simple epic view seditiously, and that was the realization that the enemy did not exist solely at the margins of the secure homeland—an enemy unlike us and to be kept out—but also within our borders and sharing the territory. If—as had been the case in the July 7, 2005, London tube bombings—this was so, then the arrest in 2006 of the "Toronto 18" that revealed an aspirant jihadist terrorist cell whose members were disgruntled citizens of Canada made it clear that the "enemy" could be one of us, could be *like* us. The new questions of the middle period of the war were already beginning to turn, however controversially, to root causes. These are anathema to Conservative governments—whether David Cameron's British one, faced with the London riots of 2011, or Stephen Harper's fiercely intent on altering the character of Canada, from 2006, and doing whatever it was able to entrench its epic view. Harper's three successive governments have played along in the patriotically advantageous trial for murder of the teenaged Omar Khadr, captured in Afghanistan in 2002 after a firefight with U.S. Marines. A former child soldier, Khadr languished for years behind bars in Guantanamo Bay (where, like a character out of an Alexandre Dumas novel, he studied Shakespeare), despite the Supreme Court having ruled that the constitutional rights of the boy, now young man, had been violated. The demonization of the "other" and the multiplying of threats serve the government well. So the Conservatives have challenged the rights of dual citizens caught in the crossfire of Israelis and Hezbollah in Lebanon, and stoked good old-fashioned xenophobia to make human trafficking obscure the fact of immigration, as if the internment of Japanese during the last World War has not already taught Canadians that each ethnic group, even when it is vilified at first, becomes, in time, a vital part of the national fabric.

A measure of caution vis-à-vis new Canadians and what role they may play in the stability of the country is in order. But so is the sort of reaching out that ensures the viability of the greater community called "Canada," one that cannot be legislated into existence but is realized through the constant example of spiritually generous acts. The epic view's politics of segregation and of demonization are not these. They are the politics of fear, and of insecurity. They are not the values by which Canadians abide, already fully aware of the "good fortune and standing" that the Manley Report described. The moral "authority and obligations" that Canadians feel as a consequence of this are also practised, first and foremost, at home. The automatic response of a substantial number of Canadians, even in the face of the trial of the "Toronto 18," or of the "honour killing" of sixteen-year-old Mississauga student Aqsa Parvez and then, in June 2009, the murder of three daughters and the second wife of the Muslim Montreal Afghan patriarch Mohammad Shafia by drowning in the so-called "Kingston Killings," was to ask what would make a Canadian or recently landed immigrant here hold such murderous resentments? What are the processes of society that convert these intolerable, chauvinistic views into acceptable Canadian ones and why did they not kick into play?

If this job was hard at home, how much harder was it going to be in Afghanistan? And what were the rest of us doing, or *not* doing, that these events should come to pass?

And yet, here was not a sign of weakness in civil society, but confidence, the liberal worldview being one that is rooted not in bullish certainty but in intelligent, inquiring doubt. Here was yet more evidence of the open society that Canada, at its best, has always been, and that is currently under threat. Ten years of global political disturbance have closed many minds but, on the other hand, proven the benefits to society of the sort of curiosity and concern and generosity of spirit that are integral to the basically liberal Canadian character. There may have been, since 9/11, too much cultural relativism for many. There may have been, concerning Islam in particular, too much accommodation of narrow-minded arguments and too much entertainment of religious-based reasoning in public fora when explaining how the Bible or the Torah teaches this or that is not acceptable in comparable debates. There may not have been, within the Canadian Islamic community, the sprouting of moderate views that many Canadians wish had transpired (though the Mohammad Shafia filicides did, in February 2012, prompt a fatwa of the Islamic Supreme Council of Canada against "honour killings"). On the other hand, the net result of the decade of disturbance has been that a multitude of ordinary Canadians are now aware of the Koran, of Ramadan, of differences between the burka and the niqab and the hijab and debates concerning sharia law about which they had no idea, previously. Music and food provide the first inroads a newly arrived culture makes, the first bridges that are its means of integration with the greater host, and these expressions, but also greater knowledge of the Muslim world, were becoming in short years increasingly a part of ordinary Canadian life.

This is not a show of multiculturalism as a belittling idea, portrayed by its critics as a movement that reduces different cultures and ethnicities to baubles, costumes and table delicacies—and, in so doing, patronizes them. Not at all. It is a remarking of first steps that may not seem great, but auspicious and proof of the good sense of living inclusively and doing whatever is possible to promote the open society's healthy curiosity—and so to be less scared. These are the same first steps toward full participation in the Canadian panoply that have been taken by every other ethnic or religious group which mainstream Canadians have tended, for an incubating period, to be scared and wary of Jews with their strange hats and curls, Africadians, Japanese Canadians, Chinese Canadians and of course First Nations ("Indians") have all had to endure prejudice and internment in either camps, reserves or ghettoes before (at least in principle) being fully included in the fabric of a nation that defers, rather than to any particular ethnic or religious view, to the secular judgments of the Charter. Epic thinking may be useful, in the short term, to governments and constituencies wanting to take the sort of shortcut to nationhood that a sports team mentality offers, but the social divisions promoted by such an approach constitute enormous impediments to the building of the true democracy that liberal, multicultural Canada has always aspired to be.

Many Canadians know this, which is why the invasion of Afghanistan to assist it was a troubling but accepted venture for a country ill at ease with its new "war-fighting" role and not sure or able to remember what, in the confusion that descended on 9/11, its army and the nation stood for previously.

But then, in early 2010, as Canada was launched into the the third and final stage of the war, that of getting out, something extraordinary and unexpected happened—something that threw fresh light upon the country's "authority and obligations."

The earthquake that struck Haiti on January 12, 2010, did so with devastating force. According to the U.S. Geological Survey, the earthquake was the strongest to hit the island since 1770. It had a magnitude of 7.0 on the Richter scale with aftershocks that measured between 4.2 and 5.9. Of the 3 million Haitians who were affected, 2 million were displaced, 1.6 million were moved to temporary settlements, as many as 300,000 were injured and at least 250,000 were estimated to have died. In Canada, the disaster did something else that was both unexpected—and revelatory. It allowed Canadians to behave as they had always previously done, and to do so simply and without hesitation. Within ten days, Canadians had pledged more than $130 million to Haiti Relief, and by February, the country's donated total of $3.90 per capita was almost double that of Norway ($2.20) and nearly eight times as much as the $0.50 per capita pledged in the United States or Britain. Canadians were not helping Haiti to make themselves feel good but certainly felt right doing it. Suddenly they had been presented with a mission in which the idea of "assistance" was straightforward and unambiguous. Assistance meant extracting people from rubble and mending their limbs and providing them shelter and rebuilding hospitals and schools and distributing food and finding homes for orphaned children. In Afghanistan, the endeavour to help Afghans and to make their country better demanded the extraction of positive meaning from complicated and divisive arguments about patriotism, security and nation-building intertwined with the fact of killing people, of bombing and unmanned drones. Given the level of insecurity in that country, it was overwhelmingly difficult merely to be *useful*. Help in Haiti simply meant that we were needed, that we were able to supply goods and benefits that a beleaguered people wanted. Even the occasional bit of unlikely comedy helped to make the point—as when the *Toronto Star* featured, in its extensive coverage, a photograph of a bevy of soldiers trotting through a Port-au-Prince slum, armed and in formation, as if they were in Afghanistan. (In fact, the soldiers had been preparing for deployment and would end up being the last Canadian combat group on the ground there.) Canadians, whether they articulated as much to themselves or not, were relieved by the nature of the new mission. They were called to action by its urgency even if some members of the press were indifferent, even disappointed—a different country, a different issue and, once again, a different beat but one that was not quite as exciting this time. Hence, a churlish Christie Blatchford column in the *Globe and Mail* accused the public, with the earthquake, of turning its gaze and interest elsewhere. Wrote Blatchford, "Afghanistan's time in the sun of the world's attention was over the second that earthquake hit a country even poorer and more miserable and photogenic than it." Anyway, Blatchford went on, the moment had been coming for some time. And then, unable to resist, she repeated the old charge of Canadian complacency, even if it was not such a good fit this time. "Citizens of soldier-contributing countries such as Canada," wrote Blatchford, are "weary of the price in blood and treasure, as those who have given neither always like to call it." Haiti, wrote Blatchford, was a "feel-good opportunity" because the Canadians weren't there "to war-fight." No matter that in July 2009 an EKOS opinion poll confirmed the remarkable consistency of the general population's attitudes toward the war (with 59 percent of Canadians opposed to it and the much lesser number of 34 percent in support), the possibility that the mission in Haiti was consistent not just with the work that many Canadian soldiers had performed in peace operations for five decades but also with the values of at least some of the soldiers in Afghanistan—in other words, that Canadian citizens had not been shirkers for all that time but were, in fact, being true to themselves—did not come into it.

The aftermath of the earthquake also cast a sobering and implicating light on the selective application, in Canada, of the title of "hero."

Included in the horrifying toll were two RCMP officers, working as peacekeepers, who died in the rubble of the UN's headquarters in the Haitian capital, Port-au-Prince. They were men in uniform who had made career decisions that were inherently selfless, noble and—given the island republic's unruly nature even before the earthquake—courageous. They were, to use the former Ontario premier Ernie Eves's words from several years before, "putting their lives on the line for you and I and society" as much as any police officer on the beat or soldier in the line of duty. And yet, when the coffins of Sgt. Mark Gallagher and Chief Supt. Douglas Coates arrived home on January 22, 2010, there was only a small cortège of RCMP in red serge dress and a mere 100 onlookers outside CFB Trenton's chain-link fence. No one in the national media was applauding them as "heroes" and CBC *Hockey Night in Canada*'s Don Cherry was not paying dues on "Coach's Corner" or calling either, as he had done police officer Sgt. Ryan Russell, "beautiful." The RCMP issued a press release but police unions from across the country and the United States did not facilitate attendance at the funeral by their members as they had done for Sergeant Russell's last rites. Two Moncton RCMP officers, Sgt. Terry Kennedy and Const. Peter Korotkov, travelled from New Brunswick to Toronto to pay their respects, but there were nothing like the more sizable crowds and front-page newspaper articles and photographs, above the fold, that had accompanied the commemoration of Ottawa police officer Eric Czapnik's death earlier in the month or would Sergeant Russell's funeral a year afterwards.

The problem was that Coates and Gallagher were *peacekeepers*.

They were wearing a uniform, but the wrong one. They were wearing blue berets. They were representatives of the prior myth of Canada and as such were an embarrassment to the architects of the combative new one, the title of "hero" revealed once again to be shallow and arbitrary. (It will be interesting to see what twist in the mythology the proponents of Canada, the "warrior nation," will manage when Canadian peacekeeping work is the duty to be remembered and the last living veterans are ones that wore the UN's blue headgear.)

That supporters of the "warrior nation" would rather that the peacekeeping work of Canadian soldiers or police and RCMP officers such as Coates and Gallagher drew no notice had been in evidence, earlier, with Maj. Paeta Hess-Von Kruedener's death in July 2006 at the UN Patrol Base Khaim. The lack of tribute after Coates's and Gallagher's deaths indicated more of the same indifference. The possibility that the tiniest portion of Vimy's mythic legacy of valour might have doled out to Canadian peacekeepers was just not going to fly, especially if those in blue-helmets were merely *observing* or *training*. This attitude was evident not just in these serious slights but in the near tantrum that Jack Granatstein had in January 2011 when, discussing Canada's impending withdrawal from Afghanistan, Liberal MP Dominic LeBlanc (briefly a contender for the party leadership in 2009) had the temerity to suggest that the option of leaving Canadian Forces "inside the wire" to train Afghan National Police was true to the spirit of peace operations that, for half a century, Canada had specialized in. Occasionally Granatstein had made small overtures to peace operations, but his response to LeBlanc's characterization of the work Canadian Forces might remain to do, posted in a January 2011 blog entry on the CDFAI website called "The Peacekeeping Mythology Never Dies," was that of a scorned, petulant child:

Blah, blah, blah. This is straight-out pandering to the soft-hearted Canadian belief that all we should ever do is keep the peace, preferably with a blue beret firmly fixed on our soldiers' heads.

But is training equal to peacekeeping? No, it most certainly is not. In the first place, Afghanistan is a state at war, and there is no peace to keep. Then, Canadian soldiers will be training one side in that war, the ANA and ANP, how best to fight the other side, the Taliban.

On no peacekeeping mission that Canadians took part in have our soldiers trained troops. We did not train Israelis or Syrians; we did not train Iraqis or Iranians; we did not train Greek or Turkish Cypriots. We have done military training missions in Africa in the past, but no one ever called that role peacekeeping. So let's get our terms straight: military training in Afghanistan is a new Canadian role (not all that new as we've been doing mentoring for at least four years) in a long-running war. It is not peacekeeping, and no one should pretend it is.

This is what passes for think-tank work in Canada, which is remarkable but what we have to put up with until others speak up. And it is another example of the profound and disturbing contradictions heaped upon by the country a lobby that is now the establishment and simply cannot be trusted to have an equitable view. In the conflict's first stage, Canadian soldiers were fighting a war that was also apparently not one on behalf of national security and trade. Then, in its middle stage, the Canadian public was repeatedly told that Canadian Forces were in Afghanistan to secure a stable society for Afghans. The ISAF was training the Afghan National Army and National Police Force to do the job so that when these forces were capable of maintaining order it would be fair and justifiable for Canada to make its exit. If this is not a peace operation, then what is? And if indeed the campaign in Afghanistan is part of a long-running war and there is still "no peace to keep" (that limiting Chapter VI paradigm again), then why, in its third stage, were Canadian troops leaving and why were the campaign's leaders pretending, to soldiers as much as to the citizenry back home, that the "mission" was not about combat anymore?

And what happened to the girls?

The declaration that Canadian "peacekeepers" had never been involved in the training of police or military is simply not true. Training is exactly what Chief Superintendent Coates and Sergeant Gallagher had been doing in Haiti, and at the very moment that Granatstein made the charge, Canadian Forces and police officers operating as peacekeepers were "working with the South Sudan Police Service to increase their capacity and promote the rule of law" in that troubled nation, as they had been doing prior to the referendum of January 2011 and would for another six months afterwards. A bulletin on the government's RCMP website, current in 2011 under the headline "INTERNATIONAL PEACEKEEPING—THE WORLD IS WAITING, ARE YOU READY?", notes that its services are often requested and actively solicits members to support its "peacekeeping and peace support missions in partnership with over 25 municipal, regional and provincial police departments." It sets out the terms of contracts and specifies, among the obligations of the peacekeeper, not only the duties of "encouraging a neutral political environment free from intimidation during elections," "overseeing the security and human rights of returned refugees and displaced persons" and "investigating human rights violations" but also "monitoring and advising local police" and "training, reforming, professionalizing and democratizing police organizations." It notes that the Canadian police officers of its International Peace Operations Branch are deployed in "Sierra Leone, Iraq, Jordan, Côte d'Ivoire, the Democratic Republic of the Congo, Afghanistan and Haiti," that participants may be eligible for the Canadian Peacekeeping Service Medal and that "Canadian police officers are legendary for their humanitarian efforts. From the rehabilitation of playgrounds and community centres to securing free and democratic elections, Canadian police peacekeepers are often at the forefront of humanitarian efforts." The police in the photographs mounted on the site are seen training local police officers and wearing blue berets, just as the Canadian Forces taking part in Sudan's Operation Safari had been doing. Granatstein's remark, of African blue-beret work, that "no one ever called that role peacekeeping" is illuminating: is it the nature of the task at hand or what people choose to call it that defines its nature? Canada has its War Museum now, generously funded and the site of many activities. Why does the use of the word *peace* rather than *war* continue to be so enraging?

When Granatstein and company show such explicit disdain for peace operations in the past, present or even any possible future, or when they fail to honour peacekeepers such as Chief Superintendent Coates and Sergeant Gallagher in the way that is de rigeur with other uniformed officers, they are disclaiming these Canadians as "one of our own." They are showing callous, arrogant contempt not just for the work but also for the people doing it. They are displaying just how politicized the accolade of "hero" can be and circumventing an obvious truth of the Canadian character — which is that the motivation of the men and women who joined the Canadian Forces and participated in UN peacekeeping missions for fifty years is essentially no different from the contemporary motivation of soldiers or the spirit of the country presently. Peacekeeping, in its Chapter VI formulation, may, at least for the time being, be a thing of the past. What is not is Canadians' allegiance to the multilateral, pacific, policing ideas behind such actions.

The thing that Granatstein and the camp for a stronger "war-fighting" military appears to find inflammatory is simply the pursuit of peace and the creation of a space, by Canadians, in which such actions are promoted at home and abroad and by a variety of means. In the imaginations of Granatstein et al., the adulation of peace is a weakness, the sappy evidence of a constituency that is hopelessly ignorant of Canadian history and unprepared for the possibility of wars of existence. War, in this conception, is a noble opportunity rather than a deplorable show of human and societal failure. Theirs is a disdain for an unquestionably civilized idea, namely that *not* killing people is the preferable and more humane outcome so that war, when it is necessary, should be undertaken solemnly and as a last resort. Their point of view is shared by politicians, academics and journalists seeking to discredit the basically decent morality behind the Canadian popular support of peace operations, now seemingly crushed, but that could well win the day again so that the military lobby remains ever vigilant. So, in "Peacekeeping and Public Opinion," a 2005 essay by "communications adviser" (read "spinner") Lane Anker that appears on the DND website, hardly a non-partisan forum, the PR flak wonders why there is a lag behind "public perception" and his and the department's view of the "reality" of peacekeeping, which is that it has evolved so far away from its Pearsonian roots that it is neither the thing that Canadian soldiers do anymore, nor even practised anymore. (Comic in its transparent, cynical inconsistency, the only time in the last ten years that anyone in the Conservative lobby has elected to promote the idea of peace operations in any

way at all was when the nascent pro-tar sands website EthicalOil.
org, its founder Alykhan Velshi subsequently employed by the PMO,
posted a picture of the iconic peacekeeper on the Ottawa *Reconciliation*
monument with the caption FUNDS PEACEKEEPING next to an image
of a Saudi sheikh before a pumping oil well and the words FUNDS
TERRORISM.) Nine out of ten Canadians, wrote Anker, desire that the
country's top foreign policy priority should be to promote world peace
and yet, inevitably, the public and not the DND is blamed for being
out of sync with the zeitgeist. The military is "not a public service," of
course the DND should call the shots! In order to explain the persistent
identification, in poll after poll, of Canadians with peacekeeping rather
than "war-fighting" values, the charge that the peace operations lobby
is undereducated and "squeamish" at the thought of war is repeated.
It is always the public that is out of step. It is always the public that
does not see that peace operations are sure to lead to "a corollary
downgrading of the Canadian Forces." The extravagant and pointless
gestures of peace operations are, in the words of the retired Col. Sean
Henry, "akin to placing a band-aid on a festering boil. For a time the
infection is masked, but eventually it bursts forth again."

Bandages, compresses and slings work a lot of the time, which
is why doctors and hospitals stock them, but no matter. Here is the
old mechanism of attacking the Canadian predilection for peace
operations at work again, one that holds the performance and results
of "war-fighting" and peace operations to incompatible standards
and denies the evolution of the latter approach by classifying it
out of existence. Crucially, these allegations discount the desire of
Canadians for some more thoughtful approach to conflict resolution,
one that does not belligerently and complacently rely upon the force
of weapons, and demean the contribution of soldiers who fought in
such operations. Is a soldier's willingness to put his life on the line in

wars that are not about the nation's existence, as Hess-Von Kruedener and Coates and Gallagher chose to do, "squeamish"? Is a soldier, with the same family and friends and loved ones back home, *less* (and not more) heroic because he is ready to operate in circumstances in which there are strictures upon his rules of engagement? Does the view of Gen. Sir David Richards, then the British Commander-in-Chief of Land Forces and previously the commander of the ISAF in southern Afghanistan, that climate change and social inequality between states are legitimate causes of strife that Western nations must address, constitute a "lag" in public perception, or is the discrepancy between will and action attributable to the government and the DND?

Peace operations were born out of a determination not to forget the horror and anguish of two World Wars and out of the light of realizations about moral imperatives and the inevitability of a new, international order. These developments demanded an appropriately binding social contract, one that imagined universal and inalienable human rights and that folded into its vision, too, a recognition of the nihilistic dangers of "total war," of which the nuclear bomb was the supreme emblem—and the necessity of planning to avoid such an Armageddon. The other tendency, the one that says (Granatstein's words) that "peacemaking or peace enforcement... are just synonyms for war," comes out of a much older, more conservative attitude to combat that is altogether different in nature because, a measure of the times, it fundamentally refuses to accept the possibility that armies can be practically deployed in anything other than what are traditionally called "wars of existence." Even disinterested and "proxy" wars are these. Thus the hypocrisy of the powerful, orthodox faction that Granatstein's tirades represent, for while Granatstein has exerted considerable energy insisting that peace operations are what the army does better than "peacekeepers," he is in fact not interested in peace operations at all. War, to his mind, is what armies are trained for; war is what freely enlisted soldiers like. Though the same armed forces serving a state's narrow geopolitical ends may, in down time, be deployed in peace operations, the fundamentally different motives, habits and expectations driving "peacekeeping" and "war-fighting" remain the incontrovertible reasons why the two tasks cannot ever, in the militarist's mind, be equivalent. If there is, as Anker so disingenuously argues, a "lag" of understanding, it does not lie with naive Canadians forgetting that the country has previously fought wars but with a military lobby still struggling, following its decade in Afghanistan (after Hillier's "decade of darkness," would the one just ended be a "decade of light?"), to find ways to reconcile its views with the honourable, not "squeamish," position of a majority of Canadians who believe war-fighting is a primitive and barbaric path for a democracy to take when, tragically but reluctantly, it must.

Here's how the two sides line up: on the one hand, the pro-army lobby believes that *all* foreign policy engagements, military and not, should support the state. Peace operations, in the present political climate, are undertaken for two reasons: either to keep soldiers in fighting shape outside of war's arena (hence the Congo was briefly, but only very briefly, mooted as a possible mission after Afghanistan but dropped when it was decided the deployment would be too dangerous and under-resourced) or to act as a charade covering up a blatant choosing of sides, as NATO could be said to have done in the Libyan case, where the record of the new republic's supposedly democratic Transitional National Council was quickly marred by so many cases of torture that the NGO Medecins Sans Frontières suspended its work in prisons there in January 2012. War's causes and conflicts are derived from its alliances, the most important of Canada's being with the United States and, bolstered by monarchic nostalgia, with the

United Kingdom. The unbridled end of the militarist lobby hates the United Nations not just because of its sometimes outrageous failures and growing pains, but because it is the harbinger of a global world that stands starkly at odds with its narrow, unilateral construction of Canadian ambitions and identity. As a faction essentially uninterested in associations that are not immediately pragmatic, it envies its more powerful partners and has trouble accepting that Canada has a lesser place in the world because it is—well, *lesser.* This lobby wll not do anything to offend the Pentagon, including accepting war resisters as refugees because whatever may be their arguments come second to foreign policy requirements. Despite the argument that a stronger military allows Canada to "lead," the country follows. Misguidedly, it seeks to build itself in the image of its more powerful allies, the United States and the United Kingdom, having abandoned Pearsonian ambitions and having no idea how the country might wield its own, idiosyncratic, perfectly credible and effective version of power. This faction wants the country to be something that it cannot be. It enjoys the basic, atavistic appeal of war and how, as sports do (especially with teams that win), fighting builds national identity and reinvigorates the war machine in turn.

The peace operations lobby, contrary to all the manifold charges of naïveté, understands that armies must exist to defend national sovereignty, but it sees, too, that a narrow view of citizenship in an increasingly interrelated global world is less and less defensible. It understands that human rights, insofar as they have been extended to Canadians, are essentially, though not yet practically, the inalienable attribute of all peoples. It knows that internationalism is already here—as proven by the forces of migration and repercussions of fiscal policies and the economic performance of countries that are in no meaningful way isolated; by fast-travelling actual viruses such as H1N1 or SARS, or other virtual ones over the Internet that have borrowed biology's language and have no respect for borders; by worldwide criminal activity and, of course, "terror" and, most of all, by the need to contain the revived threat of atomic weaponry being used. It imagines greater international co-operation and the proliferation of multilateral bodies to contend with and police these issues. It sees such activity not only as inevitable but *desirable*. It knows that the UN is a flawed organization but also that it is the portent of an ineluctable future. So it wants to improve it and would prefer to be a member and to figure out how to deal with its shortcomings from within. It remembers Pearson for what he said and not what, ex post facto, we have decided that he said. It understands that a majority of Canadians are not afraid of multiculturalism because they see how the Canadian version was, at least until the war in Afghanistan, different. It does not construe its humanitarian multilateralism as an argument for not participating in wars that are either "just" or vital to national security or summoned to fight a particular "evil" villain but has the vision to see that war makes enemies and is likely to create as many, if not more, problems than it addresses, and that even Canada's exceptional good fortune can be undone by unjust involvements. It grapples with how to perpetuate the fair, multicultural version of Canada and understands that the primary question posed by the very fabric and plurality of the country is how it should operate honourably as a global citizen. It believes that war and peace are two separate pursuits, though in some cases that the former may be the only guarantor of the latter, and that it is incumbent upon Canadians to develop or discover a way of being in the world that is appropriate to the country's population, size, power and political beliefs. It knows that when this means expressing a point of view that is different from the United States', that it is merely being responsible in its position and not anti-American. It views the forcing of young men and women to kill others when they are morally unable to do so as uncivilized and barbaric, and so it sees no contradiction between accepting American war resisters and the maintenance of good relations with that country. It recognizes the sorrow and the struggle of economic migrants desperate to share the good fortune of Canadians. Above all, it believes we have an obligation to share.

In the founding vision of Dag Hammarskjøld—the UN Secretary-General when, in 1956, UNEF was created—the idea of a force for conflict resolution under the banner of the United Nations was imagined as a neutral one, respecting the sovereignty of the combating nations. But all ideas evolve away from their starting position and a lot of the time usefully, so that by the time the first UN peacekeepers were deployed they did so bound by a charter that foresaw all kinds of engagement. But there is one way in which the originating vision of UN peace operations really has been consistent over time, with the result that Granatstein's desultory view is apt: Canada, whatever its stated motives may be, cannot now possibly be a "traditional" peacekeeping power in Afghanistan for the simple reason that, in the perception of a vast majority of Afghans, it arrived as part of an invading and not a neutral force. It is conceivable that one day a blue-helmeted UN force might conduct proper peace operations in that country and be positioned (as peacekeepers' detractors find unimaginable) between two rival forces of approximately equal strength in that state's struggle toward some sort of equilibrium. It might even evolve into a peace operation of the Chapter VI kind, but Canada will not be that force. Canada is an independently minded, mediating power no longer. The effect of having fought in Afghanistan for almost a decade is that the Canadian Forces are perceived, like American and British soldiers, to be occupiers, so that they will have disqualified themselves from bona fide peace operations there and in any other predominantly Islamic country. Having been one of the combatant countries, Canada must leave that job to some other nation.

"I do what I do so you can do what you do," Christie Blatchford reports Nichola Goddard as having said to her father, Tim, a man who had been "making a difference," though through development work, for most of his life.

In the year 2006, development work in Afghanistan was at its peak, though it had started to regress as staff at the Canadian International Development Agency (CIDA), the main channel of Canadian government aid, were withdrawn following the blast that had killed Glyn Berry and maimed Master Cpl. Paul Franklin. Goddard died in May, by which time a measure of "mission fatigue" had already set in and at least one Canadian politician was suggesting alternate approaches to the war. In April 2006, Christie Blatchford wrote, contemptuously as usual, of federal NDP leader Jack Layton's demanding a "comprehensive peace process" at which all major combatants would be present. "You don't accomplish peace if those who are fighting are not involved in the peace-based discussion," said Layton, prompting Blatchford to wonder how "Taliban Jack" "might actually swing it, were he the PM and that process was starting today. Would he chide the 'combatants' ('Bad Taliban!') even as he welcomed them to the peace talks? Would he pull out the chairs for their representatives? Would he pour the tea for those who have killed 23 Canadian soldiers this year?" The NDP, carped Blatchford, did not like "the 'aggressive' nature of the mission; they don't like that it's a counterinsurgency; they don't like the 'combat' thrust of it." In September of the following year, Foreign Affairs Minister Maxime Bernier delivered the familiar government line: "We do not negotiate with terrorists for any reason," he said (though it would on behalf of diplomats Robert Fowler and Louis Guay, kidnapped by al-Qaeda operatives in the Saharan Maghreb in December 2008). "Such negotiations, even if unsuccessful, only lead to further acts of terrorism."

And yet, covertly, the Western powers were already busy trying to find ways to negotiate with the Taliban after a year in which the intensity of the fighting had taken the ISAF by surprise. "We are not going to ever defeat the insurgency," said Stephen Harper in a March 2009 interview with CNN's Fareed Zakaria. History—not of Vimy but of someone else's trenches—was suddenly handy. "Afghanistan has probably had—my reading of Afghanistan history—it's probably had an insurgency forever, of some kind." Canada, Minister of Foreign Affairs Lawrence Cannon would later say, had been looking to a "reconciliation process" since 2008, having "stated consistently that success in Afghanistan will never be achieved through military means alone." The work of the first "D," of defence (and aggression), is primary and the other two "Ds," of development and diplomacy, are but alternate means to the same end, so it should not be surprising that the latter two come into play most significantly when the gains of the first have been exhausted. Nichola Goddard might as plausibly have said to her father, "You do what you do when the point of what I do has lost focus."

Insult, escalation, exhaustion: Afghanistan was never a "war of existence" and was "just" only for as long as Canada, with little to lose, did not lose interest. In November 2009, the government started to. The revelation before Parliament of high-ranking Kabul-based diplomat Richard Colvin that Canadian officials and the PMO knew of the military's anxiety concerning the transfer of "detainees" to the brutal Afghan National Police exhausted the Harper administration's

will to fight a little further. Colvin was meanly excoriated by Minister of
National Defence Peter McKay as "a suspect source" and, in December,
Parliament was prorogued, inhibiting any further public discussion of
a mission that could only contentiously be claimed was going well.
It was evident that the direction of the war was changing. And then,
in January 2010, the London Conference on Afghanistan took place,
at the end of the same month that saw Lieutenant Nuttall and four
other soldiers and a journalist buried, another Canadian killed by
an IED, Canada send a portion of her Armed Forces to Haiti and the
country's Governor General, who had been born there, Michaëlle Jean,
reduced to helpless tears. Canada, said Cannon, had "always supported
a national reconciliation process that is based on the acceptance by all
groups within Afghan society"—which was news to many. The idea of
peace negotiations that included seats for members of the Taliban at
the table was mooted and passed by a majority of coalition members
weary of the expense and of the task of the war and looking for a way
out. That any losses might have occurred "in vain," or that Canada was
not a nation to "end the job before it was done," was being offered as
an argument to extend the war less and less.

By this time, the conflict in Afghanistan was hardly ever referred
to as a "war." It had become a "mission," a change in the lexicon that
enhanced the possibility of a dignified withdrawal of Canadian Forces
from an Afghanistan war that was far from won. Said Brig.-Gen. Dean
Milner, as the last combat troops arrived home in July 2011 following
the transfer of the Kandahar base to the U.S. Army: Canada's victory
lay in the achievement of "our goal to set up the Americans for
success" or, according to the country's top general, Chief of Defence
Staff General Walter Natynczyk, "the transformation of an al-Qaeda
training site in Kandahar, the Tarnak Farms, into an experimental
farm, [and] the re-opening of 41 schools in the province's Dand

district." Referring to the fight as a "mission," as politicians and the press had been doing almost categorically since 2009, presented a clever way around the shortcoming of having fought a match without result. War demands victory, or it concedes a loss, but a "mission" is something else—determined, as it was in this instance, mostly by its duration. Nine years of the Canadian Forces in Afghanistan did not need to provide "victory," as that was neither the objective nor the "yardstick of success" anymore. "We did what we could."

The rhetoric of the first five years of the war was put aside and, too, the commitment to the women of Afghanistan. In its third phase, the fight became about various duties fulfilled—not even for the people of Canada but for the "mission" and for the new reputation of the Canadian Forces. The transformation of the war into a mission allowed the political leaders of the country and their supporters, even in the face of a war that Granatstein so vehemently insisted was ongoing, to appear consistent and irreprehensible in their claim that Canada does not "cut and run."

The evolution of the war into a mission was not the sole alteration in the rhetorical presentation of the conflict that served to facilitate the Canadian Forces' exit. Another lay in a recalibration of the framing of friends and foe. As the final year of Parliament's commitment to Afghanistan was looming and the business of disassembling camps and deciding what gear to keep and what to leave was starting, the demonizing of the enemy that has always been essential to the public relations of a military cause found a new target, the assailing of whom would help to vindicate moral arguments for the troops' departure despite what were essentially unaltered conditions in the country. That target was the country's installed president, Hamid Karzai.

From early 2010, grumblings about rampant corruption in Karzai's government started to circulate. Corruption had been endemic for the life of the new government as it had been for decades before it, but in 2010 the *noticing* of it brought a particular opportunity to the troubled allies of the ISAF. It was the year following the installed regime's second presidential election, one that had ended up rife with charges of intimidation and ballot stuffing. After the first round of the presidential elections of August 2009, Prime Minister Harper stated—an apology of sorts—that "while the first round of elections was not without controversy, it is important to remember how far Afghanistan has come since the fall of the Taliban regime." Six months afterwards, the prime minister but also the Canadian media were taking a different tack. In the spring of 2010, the allegations of corruption against Karzai gained wider currency. They became, during this period of the allies' waning of interest, catalysts on the moral stage for a revision of the West's commitment that did not, conveniently, impugn the countries and armies of the ISAF by casting them in a wavering light. It was Karzai who was characterized as erratic, possibly bipolar and impossible to work with. A revelation to the general public, he was suddenly portrayed, as he was by Campbell Clark in the *Globe and Mail* in 2010, as someone who had "long been viewed as a leader who suffers mood swings and changes positions dramatically from one week to the next." His government was portrayed as systemically and intolerably corrupt so that the coalition's unease and impatience with his regime was understandable. "It was not hard," wrote the CBC's Afghanistan correspondent in March 2010, "to put an individual's name to the malaise: Afghan President Hamid Karzai." The president, according to an April editorial in the *Globe and Mail,* was "rash." The very viability of the coalition was clearly going to be "impossible if Mr. Karzai acts and speaks recklessly"—as he was alleged to have done the week before, when his threat to join the Taliban "resistance" in the face of Western pressure at a behind-closed-doors legislators' meeting was widely reported though denied by his office. A couple of days later, the *Globe and Mail* reported that "the United States and Britain will find it harder to argue that Canada must re-up its NATO commitment as the doubts of allies deepen," and that "for almost two years, Mr. Harper has harboured deep doubts about the Afghan mission. He worries that extending it would mean throwing good money after bad, and, more importantly, lives with it. After years in which progress has been elusive, he doubts the impact Canada can have."

Of the bad money, there had been plenty, sums that throw an alternate light on what can be said to constitute the ISAF operation's success. The median figure of the government and Rideau Institute estimates for the cost of the war by December 2011 amounts to $24 billion, a figure that works out to approximately $800 that might have been awarded to each of the country's approximately 30 million citizens by Canada or some $10,000 by the ISAF if the total military expenditure of approximately $300 billion is taken into account. Given that the al-Qaeda debacle can be attributed at least in part to the United States' Central Intelligence Agency having chosen to fund the wrong mullah in Afghanistan several years prior (one called "Osama"), it appears astounding that the Western powers should have been disappointed quite so quickly, again, in their choice of local puppet.

The allegations of recklessness and unreliability ebbed almost as quickly as they had mounted but served their purpose as a cornerstone of the new narration of the war as either a finished job or one that was impossible to pursue. Tellingly, the discussion of political corruption in Afghanistan has always been highly selective. Little was said about the president's brother, Ahmed Wali Karzai, who was governor in Kandahar where Canadian troops were stationed. At home, the irrepressible Vancouver activist and rabble.ca columnist Derrick O'Keefe (the co-writer of the Afghan feminist politician Malalai

Joya's memoir, *A Woman Among Warlords* in 2009) wrote, in 2010, that the country's soldiers were "killing and dying to prop up Kandahar's Al Capone." The governor, who would be assassinated in July 2011, was notoriously corrupt and a known drug trafficker. He had also been creating enormous headaches for development workers at the Dahla Dam (a "signature" irrigation project) with his "security" firm. In October 2009, *The New York Times* had exposed Ahmed Karzai as likely being on the CIA payroll (shades, once more, of bin Laden before 9/11), but as such he was useful to the ISAF and his transgressions were effectively ignored. Nevertheless, by 2010 Canada had passed that fork in the road at which it was either to dig in its heels and entrench or negotiate a way out of Afghanistan. The latter was the path that had been taken and so a new form of narration had begun. At the special ceremony, on April 9, 2010, remembering the passing of the generation that had fought at the Battle of Vimy Ridge, Harper actually sounded less hawkish than Governor General Michaëlle Jean as he spoke of how Canadian soldiers in the Great War had fought "not to expand our borders or for old hostilities but risked their lives so that others could live in the same freedom that existed in Canada." It was a very different tone than that which Harper had been using previously, this new one embodying a conception of the country and the role of its military that was more subdued and altogether less inimical to the packet of liberal tendencies that lay at the root of the peacekeeping version of Canada that Conservatives and militarists had found so obnoxious in the war's first stages. By the time Harper was addressing the troops in Libya, in September 2011, following the so-called Arab Spring, his tempering of the jingoistic talk that had been used in the period of Canada's commitment to the war was even more obvious. The role that Canada played in the NATO operation was, said Harper, "in the best of Canada's military tradition." Continued the prime minister,

"We are not a country that makes war for gain or for territory. We do not fight for glory, and if we covet honour, it is only a reputation for doing the right thing in a good cause. That is all, that is enough."

In April 2010, at the same time that Hamid Karzai was enduring this sudden escalation of doubts of his regime, a Canadian peacekeeping role in the Congo was proposed for a surplus of soldiers imminently needing new deployment. The pronouncements that were being made by the country's top generals—and being noticed by the press—were markedly more deferential to the Canadian public than they had been at any time during Gen. Rick Hillier's tenure as the country's "top soldier," and the gung-ho character of the Canadian Forces was the thing that was acclaimed. The issue of appropriate work for a revitalized army soon to be out of a job was taking precedence over any of the moral causes that had been touted for the preceding few years as justifications for the Forces' deployment in Afghanistan. No longer was there much talk of "building schools for girls," at any rate—or, at least, not until the autumn of that year, when there was pressure in both Canada and the United States to extend Canadian participation in the war again, this time to 2014, and a picture of eighteen-year-old Bibi Ayesha duly appeared on the cover of *Time* magazine, her nose and ears cut off, with the headline, WHAT HAPPENS IF WE LEAVE AFGHANISTAN? (Later it was reported that the young woman had been mutilated by her family, and not the Taliban.)

By 2011, when the Royal newlyweds Prince William and Catherine, Duchess of Cambridge, visited the country and were in Ottawa for Canada Day, the "Harper Government" (the moniker by which the PMO, in February 2011, decreed that the Canadian government should subsequently be referred) seized the opportunity to emphasize the performance of the military and its work building schools for girls, though the plaudits were strategic, a bit of PR spin and not for a job being fulfilled in an ongoing way.

But with the July 2011 deadline for the withdrawal of combat troops fast approaching, the message that was being communicated *sotto voce* was of armed forces that were tired, with good reason, after work exemplarily done but that it was now incumbent upon the Americans to perform. Six months down the road, only Canadian trainers left *in situ*, reporters who initially had travelled freely from apartments in Kandahar City and who were later very restricted on the few occasions they did travel "outside the wire" would take issue with the necessary suggestion by the war's backers that the Canadian Forces were leaving behind a more secure province. In 2001, wrote Mitch Potter of the *Toronto Star*, Kandahar City was "a place where foreign journalists could tread unhindered, even after nightfall. One encountered grinning Pashtun tribesmen everywhere, not only delighted to be free of austere Taliban rule but anticipating their lives were about to be transformed for the better by these welcome outsiders." What Nic Lee, the director of the Afghan NGO Safety Office, a security service that advises NGOs, calls "ambient violence" has increased in Afghanistan by 119 percent since June 2009, making the country much more dangerous for aid workers and journalists and Afghan civilians, most of all.

Regardless, the "mission" was ending and generally described by its Canadian contingent as a success. Concerns graduated from the streets of Kandahar to a consideration of what to do next. Lt.-Gen. Andrew Leslie, Chief of the Land Staff of the Canadian Armed Forces and soon to be charged with the tough job of the military's restructuring, told *Maclean's* magazine in April 2010: "I would never want the Canadian army to stay somewhere that the Canadian people didn't want us to be. We go where the government sends us, we fight the good fight or whatever else the role requires us to do, we come home when

Parliament sends us home." Even the boosters seemed tired, Jack Granatstein among them and appearing uncharacteristically subdued as a peace operation in the Congo was mooted. "There seems no doubt that the Canadian public continues to believe that Canada is uniquely gifted in peacekeeping. Lester Pearson's Nobel Peace Prize, the 60-year-long record of service in UN missions, and the popular sense that doing good is what the Canadian Forces should be doing make UN service hugely popular," wrote Granatstein on the CDFAI website. "What better way to re-establish the national *bona fides* than by taking over a UN peacekeeping force?" With the caveat of a firm mandate and the support of the UN, previously an organization that was habitually the object of so much contempt, Granatstein concluded there was a peacekeeping role that the Canadian Forces could play—though it needed to be "in a suitable arena."

Given the acrimonious rhetoric that had dominated since 2001, this was an extraordinary concession. For nine years of war, Canada had been rallied around epic thinking and its vaunting of the hero and, the necessary principle of both, the implication that some citizens are more necessary than others to the survival of the community that is being defended—a community defined in narrow, *nationalist* terms. But after the devastation of Haiti and the inadvertent light that nation's plight threw on the seemingly endless, possibly wasted military effort in Afghanistan, the country had started to veer away from its new swagger and to return, again, to being a country cogitating along more internationalist lines. The country was feeling not just exhausted by the war but more secure as a result of leaving it. The unanswered question hanging over the country's future, however, was that should it suffer threats to its well-being at home, would it abandon the fairer and more humanizing ideas about community that, after nine years, Canadians and their military had again arrived at, or would it more permanently revert to the simpler but ultimately self-defeating strictures of epic belief that led it into the war in the first place? After 158 soldiers' and five civilians' lives lost and more than ten times as many wounded, it is surely incumbent upon every Canadian to ask if these really are competing paths, and if the way the war was fought in Afghanistan is an example of the best Canada can do.

CHAPTER FIVE

What Is to Be Done?

"Canadians, like their historians, have spent too much time
remembering conflicts, crises, and failures. They forgot the
great, quiet continuity of life in a vast and generous land.
A cautious people learns from its past; a sensible people
can face its future. Canadians, on the whole, are both."
   —Desmond Morton, *A Short History of Canada* (2006)

Epic behaviour is the easiest kind. It's a primal way of being that we
practise in the schoolyard and revert to on the battlefield. The epic's
reduction of the world to a dichotomy of black and white, of a world
peopled by heroes and villains in which good and evil are absolutes,
is, along with everything that supports its uncomplicated view, a
necessary condition of our talking ourselves into war in the first place.
Its mainstay, the larger-than-life figure of the hero, has survived the
ages because it suits the political ends and social habits of societies
that in their day-to-day conduct do not see the world as mysterious
and surprising but as entirely known and presenting of a series of

familiar, recurring challenges that great leaders in an atavistic mould must be able to fight.

Perhaps, as the epic has it, good and evil really are two constant quantities in a hostile universe and "heroes" really are those who swash buckle through. Certainly, the power of epic thinking is strong: an unbroken line can be drawn from the heroes of Homer's *The Iliad* and *The Odyssey* through Dante Alighieri's journey in *The Divine Comedy* and the Adam of Milton's *Paradise Lost* to Tolkien's *The Lord of the Rings* and the subsequent and enormous canon of fantasy literature that thrives in our own day in books and films and video games, adventures that we begin to consume as children and the elementary laws of which we never quite relinquish. In J.K. Rowling's Harry Potter series and George R.R. Martin's *A Game of Thrones*, and in *Call of Duty*, *Gears of War* and *Battlefield*, the idea of life's unfolding as a series of hurdles and hazards of an epic nature continues to flourish. In all of these works is inculcated an archetypal sense of the mortal obstacles facing humankind and the repeating way of the world. Evil, lethal forces have, over the ages, different names and appearances, but they are otherwise unchanging and ever present. (In the physicists' construction of the universe, these forces would be called "conserved quantities"—elements that, according to the standard dictionary definition, "remain unchanged with time during the evolution of a dynamic system.")

For a while, the manifold wars and atrocities and genocides of the twentieth century appeared to have put an end to this fatalism. War-fighting simply seemed like a bad idea. Wars were never going to cease, they were never about to be "outlawed from the world," as U.S. general Douglas MacArthur would have had it (though, today, the extent of wars and violence can be statistically proven to have diminished, as evolutionary psychologist Steven Pinker did, in 2011, in his book

The Better Angels of Our Nature: Why Violence Has Declined), but there was at least the conviction that the forces behind them needed to be countenanced. It was necessary, for everybody's benefit, *not* to assume in mythic fashion that fighting wars was a permanent and unchangeable aspect of the human condition. After the bombing of Hiroshima and Nagasaki, it was obvious what the end result of unimpeded conflict would be and that "total"—that is, nuclear—war, needed to be prevented entirely, and lesser wars regretted and contained on the deplorable occasions when they proved necessary to fight.

But after a little more than fifty years, the terrible lessons of the last World War were forgotten, its horror shunted aside by the new imperatives of 9/11. Memory is a piece of Darwinian genius, a riddle of the human faculties that allows humankind, on the one hand, to survive through remembering and, on the other, the species to undermine itself through forgetting. Even in the face of all the mnemonics of documents and art, it seems that the memory of pain and misery that is inflicted through human conflict is kept alive for only as long as it takes for the dominion of the afflicted generation to be replaced by the next one as yet innocent of such terrible experience. Short decades after the Second World War ravaged Europe and cost her and other countries so much, the possibility of a nuclear catastrophe (or of biological and other threats) is less discussed though paradoxically more likely, and it is hard not to wonder whether societies have it in them to ever muster the will, let alone the means, to suppress war and avert its age-old cycle of violence and chancey repair. Perhaps the epic's primitive construction is the one that rings true, always, and the novel's more lofty, empathetic assumptions, invested as they are in the idea of humankind's progress toward a more just and peaceful society, are the illusory ones. Perhaps the war in Afghanistan really was about the fight against evil and the need to conquer it, and the wars stark truths were ones that needed to be faced: the Taliban are bad, Canadian soldiers are good and the security of the territory depends upon our accepting as much. Perhaps the war was never more complicated than that, and to look for some kind of advance in the way we undertake such causes truly is naive and foolish. Perhaps the true message of our times is that we'll be reading Homer's *The Iliad* or novels such as Joseph Heller's *Catch-22,* Charles Yale Harrison's *Generals Die in Bed,* Erich Maria Remarque's *All Quiet on the Western Front* and Jean-Jules Richard's *Neuf jours de haine* forever and come to regard these stories and their successors not as indictments but as *souvenirs* of war. Touched as we may be, these accounts will not change our behaviour one iota. Perhaps this will be our lot because the assumption of common humanity upon which the morality of novelistic stories is built—the idea that universal experience should even *matter* at all—is the lie. We have wars and heroes and see monsters at the margins of the territory because this epic construction is more accurate a reflection of the circumstances we know (and have survived) than is any abstract promise contained in the notion that we are, all of us, alike.

We can believe this, or we can believe in our capacity for agency.

Story provides the basis of a community—and its defence. Through stories we reflect the world back to ourselves and create a framework over which we erect a guiding system of morality and truths. That much is evident. To a much lesser extent do we see how different modes of storytelling play a critical role in conflicts between us. In the discombobulation of the present age, peoples and cultures and economies jostling for place as they compete for resources governments insist are scarce, battles are taking place not just on the ground but in story forms that embattled societies use to entrench their guarded positions. The most vital and consequential of these narrative contests is between the epic's and the novel's stances. Understanding how the frames of mind of the epic and the novel are fundamentally different allows us to recognize the immensity of the task of altering one point of view or the other so that negotiations, missions and grand plans—the attainment of peace, most of all—may be undertaken in good faith and with any hope of success or, should circumstances indicate otherwise, be postponed or not undertaken at all.

The novel is a humanist enterprise, which is to say that it puts the individual first even as it upholds the rights of the various communities that make up the greater society—women, or people of a certain colour or religious background, for instance. The novel is ill at ease with the epic's broad sweeps because, while it expects human beings to be able to profit from common standards, it does not forget that the totality of any community is made up of individuals whose rights and particular nature must be respected.

During the second half of the twentieth century—a period, in the West, of confidence, optimism and political outreach—the novel's more sophisticated point of view reigned. Its humanism was the bedrock of Pearsonian beliefs about peacekeeping, "soft power" and Canadian multiculturalism. The championing of liberal democratic values goes hand in hand with the burgeoning of the novel exactly because the latter is a narrative that, even when its characters are victims, imagines men and women as powerful actors. The argument of the preceding pages is not a rarefied one about narrative modes but an effort to demystify what we are talking about (and not) when we talk about war, with a view to bringing about a better future, sooner. In Canada, the country of novel thinking, there is no reason why the conviction that has been put to the task of restoring the country's armed forces should not be applied to providing them a more progressive shape, one that takes into account the new altered exigencies of the age and makes of the country an example not just to ourselves but also to others. A world with other than heroes and monsters is more complex, but the people who live in it have the chance of building bridges rather than chasms because of the stories they tell and thanks to the institutions that their narration fosters.

Theories that begin in the imagination need not stay there.

In the first decade of the twenty-first century, an epic point of view regarding the war in Afghanistan replaced the peacekeeping narrative. It extended beyond the floor of the House of Commons and politicians' occasional trips to Kandahar and the pronouncements of generals and the media's reporting on the war into the language used in sports and even the arts to support the work of nation-building that the Canadian Forces were doing in the far country but contributing to as significantly at home. The acclamation of the "warrior nation" bolstered the Conservative vision of the country with its orthodox patriotic demands, its simple mythology of winning and its reliance, for strength, upon the ethos and the vindication of Achilles' Shield.

But no nation's history is abstract, no nation's history exists outside of place, and if Canadians hold to a particular view of themselves even in the face of extraordinary political pressures it is because the expression of a country's character has deep roots. Canadians are inclined because of their history to act with soft power. They are inclined to see prosperity as a gift rather than as something to be hoarded, and to want to share their good fortune and to embark on war only solemnly and as a last resort when other means have credibly been exhausted. These tendencies and the myths that support them may take on a variety of guises, and—as they did for the first several years of the war in Afghanistan—may even recede for a time, but in their fundament they are demonstrably slower to change and harder to uproot than whatever are the tales swirling about their surface, morphing as the moment demands. In Canada, the predominant myth has always been one of caring and rescue. Its costume may be made up of a blue beret at one moment, or a green suit at another, but in each case the driving sentiment behind it has turned out to be, as has been true throughout the country's history, one of "making a difference"—of sharing the gift of Canadian good fortune and destiny with others.

For Canada is not an imperialistic power, as Harper finally chose to advertise in his address to Canadian troops fighting with NATO's Operation Unified Protector over Libya in spring 2011. In Canada, a particular set of topographical and historical conditions has fostered the onus that Canadians place upon the project of co-existence and the inquiry that we demand of ourselves when we ask what it means to be in someone else's situation. To see the challenge of it but also the good. What has resulted is a set of liberal democratic ideals of a very different kind of narrative, that of the novel. The widespread desire of citizens to share privileges developed in the context of an abundant and sparsely settled territory is the achievement of a poly-ethnic population that has managed its differences mostly without fighting. Canada's history of discussion, rather than subjugation; the extraordinary privilege of a winning draw in "Coupland's lottery"; and, after 1812, the rare situation of not having had to fight wars to defend the nation from invaders, has led to a particular sensibility guiding an army of essentially different character, one that does not seek to appropriate or secure property so much as to propagate values—"Canadian values"—conceived of in an abstract realm but made real by the nature of the land and its settlement.

The phenomenon is evident, at home, in the document and the practice of the country's Charter of Rights and Freedoms, and in the strain of multiculturalism that has thrived in Canada for half a century. Both are the principled expressions of a social contract, of a design for living that it has taken millennia for the peoples of the world to arrive at in barely more than his secluded corner of a troubled globe. These institutions, indeed *accomplishments*, of the Canadian nation-state say a lot more about the country's idiosyncratic nature than does a generic applauding of the military that does not recognize the particular character of the Canadian Forces. (All countries have armies, though how they are organized can say a lot). These institutions are all manifestations of a unique twenty-first-century blueprint for living derived from the unusual position of not so much having to, but *choosing* to work out agreements with the one set of peoples—the First Nations—that can stand by the idea of the land as an inheritance. (The First Nations, by and large, have mollified this stand in the spirit of Canada's legacy of co-operation and compromise. If this ceases to occur, if the Canadian Aboriginal peoples become rebellious, it will be because the government has taken an epic stand toward them—as, for instance, it was doing in early 2012 vis-à-vis those arguing against the Northern Gateway pipeline.)

However flawed, it is because of the Canadian recognition of the Aboriginal position that the country has developed, at its core, a multilateral inclination. It is one that can be attributed to the repeated historical experience of Canadians wanting to find their way in the new but also difficult land—circumstances that lead, time and again, to citizens needing to learn from those who have settled here before and asking not "How do I conquer" but "How do I *share* the territory?" "How do I learn to be in it?" This is as true for the new Canadian working at a Tim Hortons in Goose Bay, as a taxi driver in Inuvik or as a lawyer in Toronto or Vancouver, as it was in prior days for the French and English fur traders who absorbed lessons from the First Nations and Inuit, and the multitude of peoples who have arrived in the country in between. Canadian multiculturalism is different in kind from Europe's less tolerant version, which sees immigrants as guests who must learn the language and the manners of their former colonial masters for as long as they are allowed to stay (though it is less different from America's, where the newness, breadth and sheer power of the country provide its communities with a levelling array of aspirations). Canadian multiculturalism is different from Europe's or America's as only the Aboriginal peoples, in Canada, can claim to have been here "first," and old battles and the fur trade made them and the early settlers allies and necessary partners, rather than weaker occupiers to be budged in advance of the country's settlement. It is exactly the Aboriginal peoples that are, in a fundamental sense, the guarantors of Canada's multicultural society. Their presence is a gauntlet thrown down before the sort of proprietorial claims to a territory that, in Europe, make the absorption of new immigrants and their foreign ways a tense proposition and upon which, in America, the unfettered progress of the capitalist juggernaut depends. No matter how tarnished and ongoing the process of land claims negotiation has been, the fact of the settler peoples having chosen to reason with First Nations rather than simply conquer them is the historical fact that lies at the core of Canadian experience. Canadian multiculturalism conveys a message of hope and openness that says, Be here, share. Let's figure out how to live together in a way that respects the nature of our different communities while abiding by an agreed-upon set of principles, ones developed and made explicit in the country's Charter of Rights and Freedoms. The essential Canadian question, learned in its stories of pioneers and new immigrants and inculcated in the actual challenges of living in a country with a contrary climate and a multitude of peoples of different cultures and origins, is not "How do I make you behave like me?" but "How do we all get along?" "What should be the binding principles of our social contract—for today, and for a workable tomorrow?" It is a way of approaching the world that is innately at odds with the less tolerant, more proselytizing disposition of the monolithic society that finds its zenith, today, in the arrogant impatience of Big Oil and government to develop the Albertan tar sands now, and at any cost. The message of the Canadian Forces recruitment video is "I am ready to help you who are less fortunate because I would like you to know, for your children if not yourselves, good fortune such as I have experienced in this extraordinary and beautiful accident of a country that we are lucky enough to be able to live in."

It is as a result of these singular conditions that the country's democratic tendency is constantly being reasserted. Canadians are constantly having to address evolving democratic issues, regulated in the petri dish of a country that does not, *pace* Bercuson, resort to arms to make its points. The daily challenge of living in Canada is that it demands that citizens review, with each passing day, the basis of the social contract and the best form it can take. What constitutes a country or even a community? Are the rights of the individual and of the collective at odds? These qualities and historical events have defined the country as much as the Battle of Vimy Ridge and other myths of the new "warrior nation" have done.

As we conduct ourselves at home, so should we in foreign policy. The prior Canadian mythology of peacekeeping and empathetic thinking that the military lobby of the last decade has found so threatening to its constituency is the sum and effect not just of recent experience but of stories told and repeated for decades, if not centuries, within the boundaries of a specific territory. Their constant and unchanging nature, however, is not a given. They are the expression of the land, its evolving demographics and the accumulation of stories and their details. Over time, circumstances may alter these stories so that it is likely, for instance, that young and new Canadians coming of age or arriving after 9/11 will have different, less accommodating ideas about multiculturalism and a more single-minded attitude toward what should be our preferred undertakings in the realm of foreign policy. It may well be that, what with more Canadians being born into or acculturated by the country in its present, more bellicose frame of mind, that the more parochial, nineteenth-century version of the state coveted by the militarists—the Canada Harper said voters would not recognize—will come to be. If so, it will have done so legitimately—that is, because Canadians have voted its enactors in.

And yet there is, in the Canadian, always the slight but contravening shock that he has managed to make a home of the land at all. Understanding that others have done so "first," or may manage to do so better, is the realization that is the launch pad of the imaginative leap that Canadians make, a leap that reinforces an abiding respect for the capacities of others, and of the country's multicultural community as a whole. It is a realization that has made it impossible for the sentient Canadian not to feel himself part of a diverse and variegated team, one that renders it foolish not to want to pursue and to realize the potential and advantages that such heterogeneity offers. Understanding the singularity of this opportunity, and being able to act on such knowledge comfortably and without prejudice, is the powerful and empathetic assertion at the heart of Canadian democratic activity—one that not just the conflagration of the First World War brought to the fore.

In Jean-Jules Richard's 1948 novel, *Neuf jours de haine*, the bloody battles of the Second World War lead to a realization of the new country every bit as important as the effects of Vimy. The experience of the First World War, wrapped in its confused lexicon of valour, actually did little to break Canada's bonds of fealty to Britain, ties that had no patriotic resonance in Quebec and fell far short of vindicating the belief of Capt. Alex Kettersen and far too many of his compatriots that the "glorious death" of Canada's "brave crusaders" would forge "an indissoluble bond between the various parts of the Empire in years to come." It would take a later generation of soldiers and diplomats, one that included Lester B. Pearson, to graduate from another war fought by Canadians outside of the country, to begin politicking for a better world, and a freer country at home. These men shared, with the soldiers of Richard's C Company, an understanding of *le mal d'Europe*, "the sickness of Europe," and wanted their homeland to avoid it. They had a new kind of pride and tenacity, a new kind of vision.

In one of the later scenes in *Neuf jours de haine*, the soldiers rest during a lull in the fighting. One of the battalion's band of coast-to-coast Canadians is reading the army newsletter, *The Maple Leaf*. It includes a guide to the coming elections at home and, prompting the sort of debate that might have taken place around the DND's 2011 decision to reinstate "Royal" Navy and Air Force titles and insignias, a series of letters suggesting new emblems for the national ensign. "Some want to keep the Union Jack on the flag," says the soldier, reading. "If Parliament votes to keep it, that means the country will be stuck in its bastard state for another generation. The country will not mature, it will be neither North American nor Canadian if it needs the inspiration of a European symbol to distinguish itself. It will not be able to fly on its own wings. It will be infirm, deformed, embryonic, pathetic and incapable. It will continue to be governed by Whitehall." It falls upon Robert Nanger, a Quebecker who knows the Canadian arbour—as one who might have said, "Mon pays, ce n'est pas un pays, c'est la forêt"—to make a toast on Christmas Day, six bloody months after C Company has landed upon the Normandy shore. "To my country, Canada," says Nanger as he raises his glass.

> It's a fortunate thing to live in such a spacious land.
> We hope truly to be a part of the world one day. Today,
> we're just a far-flung corner of the British Empire. But
> soon we shall become more than a people. We'll not
> just be "Canadians," or British subjects, we'll be human
> beings—simply *human*, if that is the proper way to describe
> inhabitants of the world. Today we have the maple leaf for
> a symbol, but the maple leaf of official drawings is actually
> from the tree of the plains, a species of which the syrup
> is not even sweet. One day we hope to have a map of the
> world for a symbol.

This innately Canadian instinct, democratic and humanist in nature, is older than the history of its standing army, its legacy felt in the character of the military work the country has undertaken, no matter how contrived the presentation of the Forces' character and purpose may be at any particular moment. So, in one of the more enlightened passages of *The Unexpected War*, Stein and Lang write that

> when Canada commits to rescue failed and failing states,
> its political leaders are asking for an extraordinary act
> of imagination, one that asks Canadians to accept that
> they share a common fate, a destiny, with people who live
> halfway around the globe. Those in Britain who led the
> anti-slavery movement in the nineteenth century made
> this heroic leap, and saw their own humanity bound up

with the humanity of slaves. When Canadian soldiers go
to Kandahar—or to Darfur or to Haiti—Canadians must
be able to make this same leap. It has been a struggle of
centuries to stimulate this kind of imagination, and we
have failed more often than we have succeeded.

The "heroic leap" is equivalent to the "imaginative leap" that the
novelist and then the reader make, an equivalence that explains the
advancement of human rights occurring in tandem with the novel's
rise and flourishing. Novel thinking is inextricably bound up with the
politics of human rights—and vice versa.

The replacement of these admirable values by the packet of
rigid beliefs that is contained in the vessel of epic thinking has had
consequences for Canada both domestically and on the foreign
front. Internationally, the effects of the transformation of Canada's
abandonment of its Pearsonian-style of mediation and brokering
of (soft or hard) power will be felt for years to come. The failure of
Canada, in October 2010, to have won a seat on the UN's Security
Council for the first time in more than fifty years was an undeniable
embarrassment as the government had, after all, campaigned for
the position. It was an indication of the country's diminished profile
before the international community ("international," here, meaning
more than the United States or NATO) though, in conformance with
Conservative government behaviour, the international institution that
had denied Canada a place was demonized—in its entirety.

Once again, the epic view revealed itself to be the bulwark of
an insecure society engaged in a contest for advantage, hedging
against the rest of the world rather than contemplating bridges.
There is, from time to time, substance to such an attitude. It may be
true and warranted. And yet, even in wartime, the state of being to

which it is most suited, the epic view can fail a society. Its blanket characterization of one group as wholly good deprives a society of the potential benefits of doubt, inquiry and criticism. Its painting of a whole and little known group of people as the enemy, with a single undiscerning brush stroke, impedes a proper understanding of who within that group may be an ally, who not, and what are the phenomena that make a person either. Evil exists, but its conception is also much abused. A more assiduous assessment of whatever is the threat goes a long way, just as it does in the psychologically analyzed individual's life, to engendering an appropriate response to that fear and even annulling it—to recognizing its shape and causes and its real or fictional aspects. An enemy there may be, an inhuman wrong to undo, but it serves no one but fascists and warmongers (and the enemy itself) if the kinds of stories we tell push us on without knowing the object of our fear's true identity. If the enemy is a vague, ill-defined idea, then the threat of it will be harder to fight in the theatre of war and have unwelcome, likely bigoted, extensions at home, where the thuggish deportment of the society headily at war bullies without cause and undermines the values it purports to defend. The better we know the enemy's true nature, the more rationally and easily we are able to understand the essence of the conflict and to decide how to engage with it.

Sometimes the nature of a conflict situation is such that an enemy can legitimately be described as evil, with the consequence that a nation can embark on a "just" war and conduct itself in a manner that is unconstrained by the ordinary moral considerations of civil society. Justice may decree that an enemy's fate lies outside the law—that he is an "outlaw," as bin Laden was to the United States or Muammar Gaddafi to the people of Libya. (Adolf Hitler's bunker suicide saved the Allies from having to contend with the prospect of the German's "martyrdom" or any of the other arguments that were used, in 2011, to justify bin Laden's assassination and the swift, unceremonious disposal of the al-Qaeda leader's body, a black mark against the present day as there is no reason to expect that Hitler would not have been tried at Nuremberg as other Nazi war criminals were.) Bin Laden, said President George W. Bush, invoking the posters of the Wild West, was "Wanted, Dead or Alive" (though preferably dead), a rhetoric that President Obama adopted in May 2011 when the al-Qaeda leader was killed by U.S. Special Forces in his hideaway in Abbottabad, Pakistan. Yet it is questionable that, in the long run, this approach of vilification serves a liberal democracy well or its armed forces, strategically. Hence, at the end of 2010 — a tiring year in which the cost and "ambient violence" of the American troop surge was mounting — Brig.-Gen. Larry Nicholson, a U.S. Marine commander in Afghanistan's Helmand Province, remarked that "we've got to re-evaluate our definition of the word 'enemy.' Most people here identify themselves as 'Taliban.'" What Nicholson was saying is that the epic view's undiscriminating categorization of the enemy was useless. It was even *counter*-productive. Especially in these days of unconventional warfare fought by combatants mixed in with a general population, the imaginative leap of the novel's view makes it easier to recognize which of a society's traits are shared with the indeterminate mass of a mal-conceived enemy and which are not, so that a warring government is able to assess with greater authority the viability of the allegiances and promises it makes.

The permission for extraordinary measures that ten years of war in Afghanistan have provided has had serpentine effects. Beyond the battlefield, it has returned the practice of political assassinations to the United States and, in Canada, exacerbated the sense of unaccountability of police forces, compounded the already excessive withholding of information and secretive conduct of the Conservative government, and boosted politically expedient xenophobia, too. The Conservatives' technique of demagogic fear-mongering on vaguely racial grounds has been on display in the treatment of Omar Khadr; of the Canadian citizen Maher Arar, deported through a process of "extraordinary rendition" to Syria; of Abousfian Abdelrazik, the Canadian refused travel documents and left stranded in jail in Sudan in 2003 for six years before being put on anti-terrorist no-fly lists from which he was ultimately removed by UN (and not Canadian) action, and Harper's deliberately xenophobic invocation, in early 2012 of "foreign money" obstructing the development of a pipeline to export Albertan tar sands bitumen. But it was manifested most extremely after the seizure of two boats—the *Ocean Lady* in October 2009 and the *Sun Sea* in August 2010—both carrying Sri Lankan Tamil economic refugees to Canadian shores, the Harper government exploiting these events to raise the spectres of clandestine terrorists arriving amid illegal immigrants "jumping the queue." The *Sun Sea*, said Justice Minister Vic Toews, was a "test boat" trying Canada's porous borders, its arrival in B.C. waters "a situation being observed by others who may have similar intentions." Swiftly, the Preventing Human Smugglers from Abusing Canada's Immigration System Act was introduced, becoming a key plank in the party's 2011 election campaign for which Harper travelled to British Columbia and boarded the ships for photo-ops.

At home, the mobilization of the "warrior nation" had the ironic effect of suppressing admirable and inclusive values that used to be synonymous with the Canadian experience but that we now find ourselves applauding in countries other than our own. When, after the bombing and shooting massacre of seventy-nine victims perpetrated by a deranged Norwegian right-wing Christian extremist (who was branded a "terrorist" until the truth caught up with the news and it was learned he was not Muslim), the *Globe and Mail* columnist Doug Saunders wrote admiringly in July 2011 of Norwegian prime minister Lens Stoltenberg's steadfastness in the face of the grotesque criminal assault, and how he "responded not with anger and vengeance but with a call for more openness and more democracy." The paper's editorial team commiserated with Norwegians, pledging the country's moral support for a nation that had "played a role in ending or seeking to end bloody wars from Sri Lanka to Colombia, the Philippines, Cyprus, Sudan and the Balkans." Norway, it was decided, was a country that "in terms of per-capita foreign aid [is] at or near the top of the list of donor countries investing on the basis of ethical standards "intended to promote sustainable development [and] in particular to minimize the risk of complicity in serious human rights violations"—as Canada's own failed Bill C-300, lamented by the paper not one bit, would have had the country do.

In Canada (the old Norway), exactly this sort of strength, openness and recalcitrance from anger was not just frowned upon but excoriated during the decade of the Conservative project to fashion a more robust, militarized nation. "There is nothing like a war for breaking down class and other barriers and creating feelings of friendship and co-operation within a country because all of its inwardly directed aggression and resentment comes to be directed against an external enemy," writes Scottish Second World War army psychiatrist J.A.C. Brown in *Techniques of Persuasion: From Propaganda to Brainwashing* (1963). In Canada, as in any nation construing itself under siege, that external enemy has plenty of cousins at home. He is sometimes the equivocating Canadian, sometimes the Tamil or other migrant and sometimes the environmentalist. (When, in January 2012, Toronto Maple Leafs general manager Brian Burke complained about having to send down one of his enforcers, he blamed the NHL clampdown on violence that made him do it on "the Greenpeace folks.") In willful ignorance, we indulge in a fear of those who look like the enemy as we have imagined him to be so that we can decide, for home advantage, that a boat holds not the next decades of labourers and entrepreneurs (enterprising enough to have boarded the boat), but a payload of "terrorists."

It is the zeal for the military of politicians at all levels of government, alongside influential members of the media, a number of academics and the leaders of so-called think-tanks that has enforced this climate of fear—one that has dominated the discourse at the expense of the ordinary freedoms of the public. The militarized version of Canadian society this informal league prefers is nostalgic and fearful and hearkens, through a history that is predominantly Eurocentric and Christian, after a past it believes to be threatened by multiculturalism as it was conceived of in the Trudeau years; by immigration it imagines to be lax; and by tides of change against which it can defend itself only by shutting down borders. These are all the quintessential hallmarks of an epic frame of mind.

This was not at all the way in which, in prior decades, Chinese and Vietnamese boat people were received by a more tolerant Canada at a time when the destitution and fortitude of passengers stowed on board decrepit ships in deplorable conditions (for two and a half months, in the case of the *Sun Sea*) would have been emphasized, rather than portraying the human cargo of these vessels as terrorists and freeloaders. The number of refugee passengers on the two Tamil migrant ships totalled 566—a negligible fraction of the 35,000 to 120,000 illegal migrants that the Refugee Forum at the University of Ottawa estimated to be resident in Canada in 2010, the great majority of these having arrived at airports.

Clearly, the result of 9/11 and our participation in the war in

Afghanistan has been that the novel- and epic-narrating elements of
society have been in grave contention not just in Afghanistan but at
home, where the same dynamic of the demonization of a perceived
enemy has flourished. The G20 Summit that took place in Toronto
in June 2010 constituted the domestic flourishing of this demonizing
frame of mind; the state funeral of Jack Layton, attended by thousands,
its fascinating coda.

Threats to the security of the G20 political leaders gathered behind
a high chain-link fence in Toronto's downtown were used by the federal
government to turn, over the course of a couple of weeks, the largest
city in the country into a full-fledged police state. Anyone who was
in the urban core at that time was witness to motorcades of vans and
police cruisers and motorbikes that, careening through traffic lights,
were frequently thirty to forty vehicles long; to hundreds of police
officers clad in riot gear, some mounted on horses, some forming
phalanxes around public spaces; to metal barriers for the corralling
of demonstrators, the great majority of them ordinary civilians, into
delegated protest areas that severely curtailed their right of assembly.
Many protesters were subjected to beatings. Anyone who was not
on the streets but watching television or listening to the radio or
reading newspapers then would have been aware of the suspension
of civil liberties by laws designed for use in wartime (and that, it was
later revealed, may not even have been in effect though no police
officer or spokesperson in the police or government shared that news
until afterwards). Anyone thrown into jail at the whim of the overly
empowered police forces, such as protester Adam Nobody, maimed
and twice beaten, or who, as happened to the fifty-seven-year-old
Revenue Canada employee John Pruyn, had his prosthetic leg ripped
off by police as he was prostrate along the ground, learned about these
suspensions of civil liberties the hard way.

What was remarkable then—and in the autumn, when Toronto chief of police Bill Blair accused, prevaricated and successfully evaded the modicum of scrutiny to which the public was entitled—was the cowed and timid way in which civic leaders stepped out of the path of police forces and genuflected in timorous cahoots, as if the people whom the politicians themselves represented were suddenly the enemy (as they are wholly considered to be in police states). Blair's brusque, sweeping characterization of protesters as "anarchists" whose "criminality" needed to be restrained was cynical and dismissive and permitted an outright obstruction of justice that was abetted by many officers' removal of their identifying badges and the Police Services' *omerta*-like code of silence. Blair's was the conduct of a public official imagining himself beyond reproach. It was the behaviour of an officer who, the template having been provided by the federal Chief of Defence Staff, imagined that the police were "not the public service" and "not just another department." Their job, in a city seemingly under siege, was to control a bunch of "scumbags" who "detest our freedoms, detest our society and detest our liberties."

In the run-up to the G20 Summit, politicians at all levels—federal, provincial and municipal—showed themselves to be an altogether supine bunch, then mayor of Toronto David Miller most of all. Miller called Bill Blair's concerns "justified" and, afterwards, applauded the police chief and his forces for having done "a terrific job." The police work had become, in his estimation, "an impossible job," the mayor subsequently declaring—a most extraordinary thought in a functioning democracy—that "I don't think we should second guess our police." Said Miller, "They acted with professionalism and with respect for people's rights to lawfully demonstrate while trying to keep the peace." And then, as would be the case of the funeral for police sergeant Ryan Russell the following January, the mayor proceeded to

338 | CHAPTER FIVE

use an altogether military jargon, declaring that "people should stay calm and support efforts of Toronto Police including all their allies." Following the summit, the Toronto City Council endorsed Miller's message with a unanimous 36-0 vote commending the "outstanding" police actions. "I don't think there should be an inquiry or review. None whatsoever," said one councillor, Rob Ford, who would become the new mayor four months afterwards. "Our police force was more than polite, more than accommodating with the protesters." The officers, said another councillor, George Mammoliti, "run the risk of dying and we're on trial."

The language of the battlefield was all-pervasive and the forces of civilian oversight proved as toothless, in Ontario, as the Special Investigations Unit responsible for investigating police excesses had always been. The motto of the Police Servce in Toronto is "To Serve and Protect" but during the weekend of June 26-27, 2010, its creed was put in abeyance, the fenced-in leaders of the G20 being the only ones who were protected, and the Canadian "Harper Government" served most of all. At times, it was hard not to wonder if the whole grim circus had been envisioned by its Conservative organizers as a trial run for the sort of civil insurrection imagined by Jack Granatstein in *Whose War Is It? How Canada Can Survive in the Post 9/11 World*.

The inordinate sense of licence of the Toronto Police Service augmented in their number to some 11,000 by Ontario Provincial Police, RCMP and security firm reinforcements, was emboldened by "Support Our Troops" movements and several years of politicians' acclamation of men in uniform, phenomena that had their genesis in the World Trade Center ashes of 9/11. During the course of a long autumn, the bolstered police forces and their obstinate and contemptuous chief worked to obstruct any investigation, avoiding accountability being the name of the game. "Second-guessing" the police or the army is a part of that process of accountability, and vilifying those who are bold enough to do so—whether the focus of these activists' interest is the treatment of Afghan detainees, JTF2 excesses or police and RCMP brutality—diminishes Canadian democracy. Such consequences are an extension of the epic's cartoon frame of mind but also a way of thinking that has effects that are often far from comic. The call during a national television news program by Tom Flanagan, one of the architects of the Conservative revival in Canada, for the assassination of WikiLeaks founder Julian Assange was one of these instances. Here was an epic idea of the country and its enemies out of control. (Flanagan is also one of the country's prime authorities on Louis Riel. Perhaps John A. Macdonald's hanging of the Métis poet leader was the solution to dissent that was on the American-born University of Calgary historian's mind.) The old Canada had its military performance measured by the success of the peacekeeping operations in which it took part, and was awarded failing grades by the arbiters of the new "warrior nation." In the new epic paradigm, success was proving every bit as elusive though few were honestly gauging the measure of the missions anymore. Indeed, it was telling, in Canada, that gatekeepers of public opinion were steadily losing the dialectic capability to resist the new, overarching myth. When, in July 2011, CBC Radio's *Cross Country Checkup* asked the question "Canada's combat role ends in Afghanistan...was it worth it?" stand-in host Alison Smith had plenty of follow-up questions for callers trumpeting the war but none for any who opposed it. All she could do was listen and move on to the next caller. The more accurate phrasing of the program's leading question, demanding more than a "yes" or a "no," would have been, "Canada's combat role ends in Afghanistan...what are the ways in which it was worth it?" At least then, the rote patriotic monologue might have been superseded.

And yet the traits that have underpinned the Canadian proclivity for peace operations, and the country's support of the work that the United Nations does, were not stamped out in the twenty-first century's first decade. The death of Jack Layton in August 2011, commemorated with the state funeral that the Historica-Dominion Institute wished for John Babcock, provided in the sheer number of its mourners a riposte to the intimidating processions at police officers' funerals and a reminder that the civilian, too, may be "heroic." The attempt, in 2010, to win a Security Council seat by a political party whose leaders and supporters had for years been unrelenting in their disparagement of the international assembly may have been a cynical ploy, but it also suggested that the government had come at least three-quarters of the way round the circle. In a democracy, power often alters those who possess it. Campaigning in opposition is one state of affairs. Being responsible to the entirety of the electorate once a party is elected is another. The result of having power and not wanting to lose it is to push almost any party closer toward the consensual middle. In Canada, during the train of consecutive minority governments of the twenty-first century's first decade, that meant a return to the possibility of engaging with the UN again, if only for domestic appearance's sake.

In May 2000, before the events that changed our world forever, David Bercuson wrote in the *National Post* that "no healthy society can love war, and no real democracy can truly glorify it. But to ignore the hard reality—that war has been necessary for this nation to live, and that young Canadian lives were snuffed out to serve that necessity—is to deny who we are." This is true, to a point, though the contribution of blue-helmeted Canadian troops involved in more than half a century of peacekeeping missions deserve to be included on an equal footing.

If many Canadians have not strayed far from the reasons they had for supporting UN peacekeeping missions for so long, it is because a great number continue to want to "make a difference" beyond the borders of the country and not just to defend it. This desire is evident in the language that is used by many of the soldiers themselves, regardless of the motives of their superiors or the phraseology employed to send Canadian troops to war, keep them there and then, without a bona fide conclusion, bring them out of it. The Taliban has not been defeated in Afghanistan, but the defence of the country and the welfare of its citizens are no longer our business, no longer our watch. According to war's strange new twenty-first-century scenarios, in which exit dates are publicly announced, our (secondarily) stated aims—in Afghanistan, to provide a secure and equitable environment that Afghans can manage by themselves—recede into the fog. It is the lexicon of the mission that makes this ending possible. We are able to claim that no soldier has "died in vain" there because, even before the fortuitous timing of Osama bin Laden's having been killed by U.S. special operatives in the last months of the Forces' deployment, the battle was never actually for Afghanistan anyway. It was to show that Canadian soldiers can do the heavy lifting—and about this we have been told, repeatedly, we should be proud. The Forces have become the symbol of our "stepping up to the plate," of our "putting boots on the ground," and it is this bit of labour rather than the service to the Afghan people about which the administration briefly pretended to be concerned that pleases the DND and allows its leaders to conclude that the war has been successful, whatever the results on the ground or their likely permanence. We may not "cut and run," but we do cut and walk—first behind the wire and then out of the country.

And not without precedent: in his 2009 memoir, *Unembedded*, maverick Canadian foreign correspondent Scott Taylor, a veteran reporter of conflicts in Africa, the Balkans and the Gulf, writes that "the fact that we have been in Afghanistan now for seven years does not mean that our military fully understands either the conflict in which we are engaged or the people whom we are attempting to assist"—or that we ever really do finish the job. "The fact is," continues Taylor,

> that Canada has cut and run from every overseas deploy-
> ment it has undertaken since the Korean War. There are
> still UN peacekeepers in Cyprus, and NATO security forces
> in Bosnia and Kosovo—even though the Canadians have
> packed up their tents. Aussie soldiers are still deployed
> in East Timor, and Norwegians are patrolling Haiti—yet
> Canadians have long since walked away from those hot
> spots. In 1993 in Somalia, the U.S.-led coalition suffered
> some serious casualties at the hands of the warlords, and
> the entire Allied forces cut and ran—including Canada.

Military work, in today's world, has come down largely to a matter of shifts, and in Afghanistan, it can be argued, Canada's time card has been punched. This is as it may be. Why, today's burgeoning legion of critics of humanitarian interventions argues, should it be otherwise? There are simply too many causes for even the entirety of the Western powers to take up, too much work for it to be other than shared by arbitrary choices and a division of the labour between insufficient forces. It is hard, or shameful, to imagine a Canada persistently standing by as other less fortunate peoples suffer. It is simply not "the Canadian way." The national sense of obligation to a greater multilateral alliance—or at least the broad public consensus that, whatever the true motivations of the state, permits it—is repeatedly enacted, most recently in Libya (though not in Syria or Yemen). And yet there has been a simultaneous reluctance, in the more prosperous countries, to recreate institutions such as armies in ways that are more suited to an international order that has already arrived.

In Canada, it is this reluctance of the establishment to innovate that constitutes the real "lag." The failure to modify institutions in keeping with the Canadian desire to set an example and new standards on the international humanitarian stage is a failure of vision, a betrayal of an essential aspect of the national character that, beneath the surface changes of the last decade, remains unaltered. The change of mind of Pat Stogran, the lieutenant-colonel of the Princess Patricia's Canadian Light Infantry who had been among the very first Canadian troops in Afghanistan, illustrated this point of view clearly after the last troops had been withdrawn. Stogran's three-year term as ombudsman for Veterans Affairs Canada was not renewed after his public rebuke of the Harper government's tight-fisted 2010 package for the wounded—this entirely in keeping with the Conservatives' treatment of conspicuous dissenters in the civil service over the years. Stogran, in the words of one accomplished reporter on the Ottawa beat, "refused to be a lapdog and, complaining about how poorly veterans were being treated and how the government had broken the unspoken contract between them and the government, was allowed just one term. The Lt.-Col., retired, had always been outspoken. Said Stogran to the *Toronto Star*'s Mitch Potter, "I hated the word 'peacekeeper' when I got back from Bosnia, because it implied some sort of bloodless offering with no real danger." Stogran praised the performance of troops "that never lost a single tactical engagement" in Afghanistan, though less so the generals who "let down the troops with a flawed strategy" before pointing out that, "Instead of focusing on building up Kandahar, economically and diplomatically, we ended up just blindly going in and started whacking

Taliban, clawing over and killing a lot of Afghan civilians in the rush to get at the bad guys." The posturing of General Hillier, in particular, had done "more to disadvantage Canadian Forces in the longer term [than] anything else." When Stogran left Afghanistan, however, he found himself "with a new appreciation for our 'peacekeeping' legacy because what we were facing in Kandahar, I would submit, is not really all that different." The Canadians, Stogran concluded, "should have been in Afghanistan like a police force. In this new security environment we live in, if the future is about winning hearts and minds, Canada has the potential to be a superpower. As long as we don't believe in flexing our muscles to kill people."

When Bercuson says that the Canadian Forces "deliberately go into harm's way at the bidding of their community to kill or be killed," or Hillier that "we are the Canadian Forces and our job is to be able to kill people," they are stating the obvious. But they are also underscoring the critical difference in the culture of soldier and police officer that goes some way to explaining the practical limits upon the conflation of war-fighting and peace operations—and why, say, Clayton Matchee and other members of the disbanded Canadian Airborne Regiment behaved so badly in the 1993 Somalia Affair. Lieutenant-Colonel Stogran's remark that Canadian Forces should have been in Afghanistan to act "like a police force" rather than "flexing our muscles to kill people" is of the essence. The soldier and the police officer are two very different species, each following a different modus operandi. The point of a military is to defend national sovereignty. The military work that General Hillier described as "disciplined, managed violence" has, as its bottom line, the objective of obliterating the bodies that are the vessels of antagonistic feeling. As the only part of government, in David Bercuson's words, "sanctioned to use deadly force," the military depends upon the perpetration of murderous acts, ones that would be prohibited in civil society. It is this right to kill that constitutes the heroic weapon that provides an army its Achillean authority. Breaking the law is not only permitted but encouraged. ("The worst barbarity of war," writes Swedish feminist Ellen Karolina Sofia Key in *War, Peace and the Future* [English tr., 1916], "is that it forces men collectively to commit acts against which individually they would revolt with their whole being.") Hence, the unapologetic assassination of Osama bin Laden and rapid disposal of his body at sea (following religious practice, possibly, but political expedience, certainly), the more contentious assassination in Yemen of Anwar al-Awlaki, an American al-Qaeda operative, in October 2011, and the phenomenon of the Canadian military's most hallowed Special Forces unit, JTF2, being cloaked in secrecy explicitly because it operates above the law and outside of it.

These circumventions of ordinary civilian practices are not, at least in principle, permitted in the conduct of police officers. Policing exists, either within states or between them, to enforce social contracts and uphold the peace by means within the law. Where these limits are transgressed, mandatory investigations ensue. The training of police officers, for whom killing is an act that brings automatic investigation, is of an altogether different nature than that undergone by the soldier, who is trained to follow orders, to kill without regret and without explanation. (The order is the explanation.) The police officer has a much greater interaction with the public and killing, certainly, must be explained. "I was only taking orders" is not an acceptable defence of a police action gone wrong. Advocates of Canadian Forces, which, in their present configuration, undertake a whole gamut of jobs from extreme combat to peace operations, are opposed to the "blue beret" and the fact of peace-building, peace enforcement and peacekeeping, now "stabilization," being tantamount to a form of policing rather than military work applied to the global arena (as, in fact, the early UN action in Korea was described as being). The Canadian Disruptive Pattern (CadPat) of the "green suit" that Blatchford extols is the colour of the army and its mandate to kill. The light blue that the reporter's denigrates is the colour of UN peace operations, a job that she has repeatedly derided as one without teeth. The colour of the uniform is a symbol of the task at hand and the manner in which it is to be performed. Green is camouflage. Blue, light or dark, stands out and demands to be noticed, a symbol of the prospect of civil order and not strategic military subterfuge. In effect, all peace operations—and other missions such as the ISAF's in Afghanistan that are fought "under the authority of the UN Security Council"—could and probably should be fought with blue-helmets on. Were the soldiers' helmets blue, then the infrared-goggle-wearing, hyper-armed soldiers of the ISAF, each carrying gear of a value more than the ordinary Afghan would see in a lifetime, might actually be considered representatives of the "international community" rather than the nearly extraterrestrial figures of an invading army that they must seem to be to those who watch them pass by.

Proper historical comparison demands that we ask by what benchmarks it is being decided that UN campaigns have been fail- ures, but that ten years of war in Afghanistan have not been. The latter has entailed more loss of Canadian life than in fifty years of peacekeeping operations and will have cost, according to estimates of the government and the Rideau Institute, in the region of $18 billion to $29 billion by December 2011, the end of a year of high-profile Taliban assassinations, including Ahmed Wali Karzai, the president's brother and the governor of Kandahar; General Khan Mohammad Mujahid, the police chief of Kandahar; and Burhanuddin Rabbani, the ex-president of the country and chairman of the High Peace

Council. At best, the results are dubious but bode a worse future for the beleaguered country than the countries of the former Yugoslavia now know. The success of peace operations is measured, in the short term, by a cessation of killing and, in the long term, by the ability of democratic institutions to take hold and prevent a society slipping back into violence in the future. Today there is peace in the Balkans, Sierra Leone and Ivory Coast, to mention an important few of the fifteen countries in which, in May 2011, nearly 100,000 peacekeepers were serving, and there would likely be peace in the new state of South Sudan, too, were the UN able (as in any of these places) to muster a suitably formidable presence there.

Before a morphing geopolitical future, an agitated, warring West needs to reconsider its dubious record in Afghanistan and Iraq, but also the way in which it has passed judgment on the previous UN operations in which it took part. In the rapidly changing global context of today's world, the argument for humanitarian interventions and their imprimatur at the UN is twofold. The first is unchanged, the second not. The ability of wealthier nations to assist in the fortunes of those that are not brings with it a moral obligation to act, and we are fast reaching a moment in world affairs in which the sheer might of Western countries, and principally that of the United States, is no longer uncontested. Whether as NATO or as a smaller alliance such as the United States, Britain and Canada have been, after Afghanistan, tending towards, the Western powers are no longer able to act unilaterally without consequence. In the face of new imbalances, the West requires new friends—to be, as the popular adage would have it, "on the right side of history."

These are the strategic arguments for peace operations, should the moral onus be considered insufficient. The Achilles' Shield of American weaponry, and the economic supremacy behind it, has rivals—China and Russia, principally—and will have more. It is in Western nations' interest, as their economies falter and their armies are less overwhelming, to apply the greater ambition and vision of humanitarian work because the brute strength that provides the last moral argument behind the epic stance is quickly being eroded. All the more reason to address, now, the one charge against the viability of peace operations that had any substance: that Canada was not committing sufficient resources or "boots on the ground" to buttress its humanitarian worldview.

The criticism can be made concerning just about any member of the international community but is one in response to which this country can provide a pioneering example. For the truth of it is that this and any of the other routinely made charges that were levelled against the Canadian predilection for peace operations can be addressed through a single, radical measure, a forward-looking plan made up of three related components that, in their interrelations and their entirety, would constitute a uniquely Canadian way of preserving the humanitarian internationalist tendencies that are the true target of these critics' complaints. Finding a way to reinforce the proactive commitment of Canadian citizens to both their country and to the world would only benefit Canada and the humanitarian causes its citizens believe it is the country's obligation to further. This can be achieved through a simple adjustment to a few of our most important public institutions, a triad of measures that recognize and make the most of the constancy of the Canadian desire to "make a difference" and, while accepting the difference of the blue beret and green suit, create advantage out of their being cousin rather than rival ways of armies working.

The three measures would entail, first of all, the creation of a new regiment under the aegis of the DND that was dedicated specifically to the practice of peace operations rather than wars of existence.

The second would see the founding of a new college in which at least a minor degree in some aspect of peace operations was a necessary condition to graduate. The third would be the creation of a national community corps complementing the new regiment in its developmental activities in foreign territories but also at home. Taking these steps would allow the Canadian government and its military planners to depart from a rigid adherence to the old model of traditional wars and facilitate a new ethic of armed forces able to respond to the changing demands of world citizenship, ones that are only going to increase as relationships between countries in an ever contracting globe become more interdependent and intertwined.

The point of a separate Peace Operations (PO) Regiment would be to create a specialized Canadian military force acting as a third party and designed for the particular tasks and challenges of conflict resolution in global theatres in which Canadian interest, not *self-interest*, is the motivation. Some will argue that peace operations are but some of the many duties soldiers already perform so that such a dedicated regiment would be redundant, if not a duplication of scarce resources. But if JTF2 is able to exist and serve a specific purpose as a specialized unit (as did the Devil's Brigade before it), and if the Canadian Forces' Disaster Assistance Response Team (DART) can be created to function in the narrow circumstances of the immediate fallout of a natural calamity, then it follows that a regiment dedicated to the craft of peace operations and international policing with its own knowledge and modus operandi would have a legitimate raison d'être too. Certainly, there is a need for it, as any glance at a map or at the front section of a newspaper shows just how urgent and numerous are the opportunities for such a regiment's deployment.

The PO Regiment would, like the regular military, be fully equipped and fully trained and subject to the same rigorous standards of universal service. But its raison d'être would distinguish it. As an elite unit it would make a point of cultivating and relying upon the best intelligence, techniques of assessment, military strategies and physical resources in its endeavour to promote "peace, order and good government" in ways that do not escalate tense or abiding conflicts. The new regiment would serve as an example and as a challenge to other members of the "international community" to follow with similar commitments of their own. As the dedicated component of a global policing force that, as yet, only exists on a dubious, ad hoc and usually hastily assembled basis, the regiment would constitute a pioneering advance for humanitarian actions typically guided by wavering principles and limited, often to the point of futility, by the inadequate availability of soldiers.

Peacekeeping work is presently done by soldiers, though it does not follow that such work is best done by soldiers behaving as soldiers. Canada would still have forces wholly dedicated to its territorial and national security but, at the same time, have a separate regiment, with its own command, to commit to multilateral alliances or to execute interventions of its own. Such a regiment would offer a versatility of response to a government considering a mission in conflict zones and the terms on which it should engage. A dedicated PO Regiment would be in a better position to understand when a *mission* (not a war) might entail decades of work, and be able to prepare the Canadian government in its decision to justify and execute such an undertaking. It would help the population that is the client of the Forces' public service to distinguish between wars of existence, fought without illusion, authentic humanitarian interventions, likely of the RtoP sort, and other military ventures masquerading as humanitarian missions for political convenience. The existence of the regiment would militate against the convenient collection of these tasks under one armed forces umbrella that has benefitted, in the twenty-first century, the proponents of a combat-ready military imagining threats to national security at every turn and typically conceiving of only one possible response at the expense of any more forward-looking ideas about the Forces' best nature. The existence of the regiment would undermine the confusion of war-fighting and humanitarian operations that has allowed the pro-military lobby to argue that "when Canada does peacekeeping, it's really doing peacemaking or peace enforcement, both of which are just synonyms for war." It would make an appropriate nonsense of Canadians being told, on the one hand, that "peacekeeping is a job best done by soldiers" though, on the other, that soldiers "hate peacekeeping work." It would undo the duplicity of rhetoric, so useful to politicians in wartime, that was evident in the morphing narration of the Forces' deployment in Afghanistan—of an army routing "detestable scumbags," then "building girls' schools" and then, afterwards, promptly forgetting them.

Born in Canada, the PO Regiment would take advantage of the fact that there is hardly a part of the world that is not represented in the country's functioning multicultural society—a boon of languages, cultural sensibilities and knowledge to be reaped. It would corral the tremendous energy of Canadian youth that is already willfully directed toward humanitarian causes around the world. The fact of PO troops being trained, armed and ready, as other soldiers are, to shoot first (should doing so be mandated and required) would put an end to the caricature of blue-helmeted troops being ineffective and hamstrung or unable and even unwilling to shoot to kill. A significant budget would dispel the legitimate criticism that, for the better part of the last few decades, Canada was not actually allocating sufficient resources to put substance in the peacekeeping work that the militarists have been allowed to argue amounts to no more than a shallow myth. The creation of the regiment would make an institutional statement of the

Canadian affinity for others that has arisen out of the historical and topographical conditions that have given rise to the country's distinct nature. It would recognize Canadians' desire to "make a difference," as generations before them have done, and it would do so without leaving the business of serving in combat zones to soldiers drawn primarily from lower income classes. It would set an example for other nations, throwing down the gauntlet and challenging them to commit to their own component of a permanent, multilateral, interventionary force.

In the new century, strikingly without grand political visions, the sort of Pearsonian commitment that once inspired Canadians with some more sophisticated, ambitious and ultimately more selfless idea of the public good is rarely on display. However, it is simply untrue—or untrue in a sufficient number of cases—that Canadian soldiers "hate" peacekeeping work. Lt.-Col. Patrick Stogran is one case, Lt. Andrew Nuttall another, of soldiers striving to "make a difference," their aspirations entirely in line with the traditional "Canadian values" that the prime minister finally came around to vaunting in Libya. The creation of the PO Regiment would constitute the de facto intellectual acceptance by the government and people of Canada that, contra the caricature of peacekeeping work that has allowed the military lobby to ridicule the "blue-helmet," the craft of peace operations is neither dead nor moribund but an evolving craft and science just as conventional "war-fighting" is. No intelligent supporter of the multilateral peace operations that, prior to 2001, were typically (though not exclusively) conducted under the aegis of the United Nations believes that the rules of engagement should be identical in every case. And any supporter of such missions knows, in the wake of fifty years of difficult work, that just as the pattern of the previous war does not provide an unaltered template for the next, that peace operations must be versatile, reactive and build on experience.

To this end, it is only sensible that the regiment should be backed up by a parallel institution of higher learning in civil society. The second component of the three-part plan would entail the creation of a College of Peace Operations—not simply a military school, as the Royal Military College in Kingston is, nor an emasculated institute of peacekeeping studies such as the Pearson Centre for Peacekeeping is. (The Pearson Centre was situated in Cornwallis, Nova Scotia, on an abandoned Canadian Forces base before its headquarters was moved to Ottawa in 2006 and its Atlantic headquarters shut down in 2011. What remains of it is a pathetic shadow of the school it was intended to be.) Nor would it be a league of specialized departments of study such as the United Nations University is. It would be a college open to foreign and domestic students alike, to citizens planning a career in the military and others not, in which it would be possible to study Languages and Peace Operations, Engineering and Peace Operations, Economics and Peace Operations, Finance and Peace Operations and so on. The college would be free to soldiers who had served time with the PO Regiment or those committing to service in it. The constant influx and exodus of soldiers and students would ensure the currency of the institution and its curricula and the constant renewal of its founding ideas. The college would make a physical statement of the fact of peace operations being an evolving science by putting itself at the very centre of Canadian thought and bringing in the best and most experienced minds in the world to occupy and hold chairs—men and women such as former Supreme Court Justice and later UN Commissioner for Human Rights Louise Arbour, Lewis MacKenzie, American financier George Soros, but also, were he still alive, independent humanitarian operators such as the late Fred Cuny (who was assassinated in Bosnia for the restorative engineering work he was doing there as a private citizen) and intellectuals of the calibre of Samantha Power, David Rieff and Canada's David Malone, Stephen Staples—or Jack Granatstein (who is, after all, one of the first Canadian historians to chronicle and address Canadian peace operations, concertedly)—not to mention representatives of societies who have been on the receiving end of humanitarian interventions. For peacekeeping is not, as the Anglo-American axis has tended to view it, a rubric that can be imposed on a gamut of situations but one that must evolve with circumstance and be attentive to cultural specifics, a point of view that is learned in Canada's multicultural society easily.

The third, equally necessary component of the plan would be to institute a form of voluntary national service of one to two years that would serve to gather the energy of those who would like to "make a difference" though not to put on a uniform. Through a Canada Corps that, unlike the briefly operating program of this name that was started by the Canadian International Development Agency in 2004 (and disbanded in 2006), had a commitment that was both domestic and foreign, a person might serve in hospitals, in daycares, in libraries and social services or in the vast array of jobs that municipal, provincial and federal leaders are now keen to tell Canadians they can no longer afford. While a national volunteer program of this kind needs to be constructed in a manner that rewards interested participants without denigrating those who are not, such a measure would put credence in the notion embraced by liberal Canada that citizens are able to contribute to the betterment of society in myriad ways. The proactively supported program would serve as a concrete, practical measure that would alleviate many of the costs of the college and the regiment by providing services typically expected of Canada's three levels of government in other quarters.

The national volunteer, paid a modest but livable sum, might serve at home, or in other parts of Canada, helping to knit the fabric of the country as Katimavik, the pioneering program of this kind, has sought to do since its foundation in 1977. Or the person might serve with approved and vetted NGOs. The energy currently directed by young Canadians to NGOs or other organizations such as the Coady Institute in Antigonish, Nova Scotia, is a small measure of the outward-looking stance that Canadians take toward the rest of the world through a sense of greater social responsibility that is naturally forthcoming. But where, in the present moment, numerous young Canadians join NGOs or work hard at raising funds to contribute to them, and schools organize aid projects of their own as summer sojourns or as years abroad (and less reputable outfits take money to send students on dubious assistance projects), the existence of the PO Regiment, college and volunteer program would provide alternate, accredited and more trustworthy avenues for youth wanting to do such work. In this way, the triad of measures would provide a meaningful way forward to youth wanting to demonstrate a commitment to communities other than their own. It would allow a Canadian flag to be put to developments without their being seen as part of an aggressive, partisan campaign of occupation.

Those who did perform national service in the corps or in the regiment would be able to attend the college, receive capital credits toward the cost of their post-secondary education elsewhere or tax exemptions or grants toward other kinds of occupation should higher education not be the path selected. The service would teach that rights are inseparable from responsibilities and, through its conferring of benefits, that the Canadian ideal is one that must be proactively embraced if it is to be defended. Through its provision of human capital, the program would create the means for the Canadian ideal to be practised at home and abroad—for the country to "step up

356 | CHAPTER FIVE

to the plate" in a manner true to its character and that it was told by the critics of blue-beret work for decades it had not been doing. By providing all kinds of labour, national service would assuage the burden of programs such as daycare, the maintenance of cities and parks, libraries, waste services, hospitals and so on that Canadians have, by and large, come to expect, but also prove that selfless or "heroic" qualities are not solely the attribute of soldiers, police officers and other men and women in uniform.

Together, the college and regiment would foster the basis of an ongoing commitment to peace operations that would restore Canada's standing in the international community—that is to say, the community of nations beyond its allies in strategic partnerships. The combination of the regiment, dedicated university and national service corps would put credence in a country that can already claim a special relationship to the UN and to the development of its peace operations. It would put an end to the idea that the need for such forces, let alone the vision and aspiration behind them, is ended or not likely to recur. (The endlessly repeating cycle of war's boom and bust—of original insult, escalating injury and destruction before exhaustion sets in—tells us that.) It would allow a clear distinction to be made, in the public's mind but also in those of soldiers asked to make such sacrifices on society's behalf, between ventures that are about defence and security and never had anything to do with "building schools for girls," and others that are disinterested and "humanitarian" from the moment of their conception. It would restore Canada's reputation in a realm about which wealthy nations, in their present injured state, are skeptical. It would provide a beacon of hope to the multitude of peoples who desperately need such commitments from wealthier nations on a basis that at least appears to want to address and ultimately put an end to the arbitrary nature of today's humanitarian and RtoP missions. And it would do so with clarity. Through the distinction of forces at the disposal of the DND—one for defence and security, and another for humanitarian causes and peace operations, the difference between the deployment of soldiers in a "War on Terror," as was the case in Afghanistan, and the enforcement of a state's "Responsibility to Protect" its citizens, as occurred in Libya, would be simply and transparently made. No longer could it be said of a Canada committed to addressing conflict resolution in this way that the country was not "paying the bill" of proper international citizenship. And no longer would the clothing of a martial cause as a peace operation be quite so easy to manage.

Advocates of peace operations understand that wars are sometimes necessary and that the "peace" that is too often the political status quo (as was the case in Tunisia, Libya, Syria and Yemen before the uprisings of the Arab Spring) is the perversion and should not, in any way, be "kept." They know that "order" and "stability" are frequently political states that masquerade as a peace that may not, as we say of wars, be "just." They have learned, too, that the very efficiency of peace-building and peacemaking operations can also contribute to conflict. They know that most conflicts follow a particular pattern: that peace often has only superficial roots or may be built over social distortions that are so extreme that when finally they rupture, they can do so with a rapidity and an intensity that throws a stark, shocking light upon the suppressed disequilibrium of the previous years. This was the case in Eastern Europe when, in 1989, the fall of the Berlin Wall brought about an end to the Warsaw Pact; in the former Yugoslavia after the death of Josip Tito; in the Great Lakes of Africa region after the assassination of Rwandan president Juvénal Habyarimana;

and may yet prove to be the case with the Saharan Arab States. The RtoP doctrine that was invoked by the United States and the UN to put an end to the Gaddafi regime's suppression of the Libyan rebel uprising was possibly a watershed moment though also a face-saving opportunity that offered weary NATO governments dispirited by their campaigns in Iraq and Afghanistan the tonic of a short, easy war won from the air against something few thought the world would see much of again—a conventional uniformed army not mixed in with the civilian population and easily spotted against the white backdrop of the North African desert.

However, without the means or the will to address similar injustices—ones that include not only the murderous transgressions of dictatorships such as were extant, in 2012, in Syria and Yemen, but also, for instance, in the failure of the government of Myanmar to offer aid to its own citizens after the Cyclone Nargis in May 2008, the Somalian warlords' denial of famine in that country in 2011, or the brutalization of tribes overlooked by the leaders of the newly formed state of South Sudan—the decisions of greater powers to act can only be concluded to be inconsistent and arbitrary. Reasons for not intervening range from the legal and the logistical to the practical (the West is, in effect, *scared* to intervene in Syria) and sociological—as were tendered, for instance, by British historian and political journalist Timothy Garton Ash, who, repeating the Twittered sentiments of rebels in the initial weeks of the February 2011 Libyan uprising, argued that armed intervention by the West "would spoil the greatest pristine glory of these events, which is that they're all about brave men and women liberating themselves." But if an intervening force is sent in at the wrong time, it may hold in place an interim order that is as inherently unstable or corrupt as the society was previously, and do no good. If the intervening force is not sensitive to local conditions, to local history and culture or to the maligned constituency at that society's root, peace operations may effect little more than a brief cessation of hostilities before war becomes practical again and the age-old cycle of insult, escalating injury and ultimately carnage sets in: the peacemakers part, or are forced out, and the elastic situation resumes its only temporarily halted historical path. The advocates of the blue beret are aware that it is all too easy for a peacemaking, peace-building or peacekeeping force to engage and make treaties with parties that are able to speak its language, and that an unjust or volatile situation, a peace that is as superficial and distorted as the one that war eradicated, may again be the result.

In Afghanistan, the need for the ISAF to be able to speak to those who have the vocabulary to speak back to their tenuous authority has led to the perverse but historically familiar situation of the intervening power strengthening local warlords and entrenching the invaded society in its unstable state. The situation in today's Afghanistan is only slightly different from that which was played out in Sicily when, in 1943, Lt.-Gen. George Patton's invading U.S. 7th Army made allies of the Cosa Nostra, installing members in key positions because the army and the local mafia shared a language, forfeiting any chance of real local democracy and inadvertently installing a criminal organization that is still dominant. In Sicily, the alliances that the Americans made were designed to subvert first Mussolini and then the Russians; an open war and then a covert one were being fought. In Afghanistan, the Taliban is the foe, but the dynamic is the same. The alliances forged are aimed at peace, but the cementing of relations with a network of warlords with no franchise other than that established through force of arms is only going to lead to insurrection and a resumption of war when the intervening force leaves and the fragile democratic institutions it is holding in place can no longer be maintained.

The Taliban are Afghan, demonized under a collective heading for Western convenience, as American Brig.-Gen. Larry Nicholson effectively stated in Helmand Province in 2010. No matter how numerous and well trained the Afghan National Police are, Hamid Karzai or any president who follows will have no future unless he has an occupying force that is keeping him in power, as he does at the present time, or there is an intervening force in the country long enough for authentic democratic habits to have been instilled in the wider population. This is unlikely, not because democracy cannot be learned, but because the West does not have the commitment—or at least not the right kind. It routed the Taliban and, in time, found bin Laden, but the societal reconstruction and the winning of hearts and minds—the "building schools for girls"—was never about to be executed with the same conviction as combat was by the "warrior nation" of the campaign's first stage (even if an unambiguously declared "war on misogynists" might well have been more winning). The irony of the Canadian mission to Afghanistan is that even those who were confused about the reasons for it are justifiably as confused about the country leaving. Peace-building, and the reconciliation it demands, is difficult but far from impossible. It may take twenty, thirty, forty years or more, but it happens—the United States' present friendships with Japan, Vietnam and even with its own African and Native Americans all cases in point.

Demonizing a population enclosed within a particular territory or because of their beliefs or the costumes they choose to wear, or adulating "allies" without discretion because they are deemed to be friends, suits the proponents of the epic view and its simple construct of good and evil and heroes and villains but augments the possibility of war and the mounting sum of insults, injuries and deaths that are its first consequences. Proponents of novel rather than epic thinking understand this point better. They have in their arsenal a way of understanding the practicality and likelihood of empathy while, at the same time, being sensitive to its limits—to the sorry existence of outright hostility that, in cases to be gravely lamented, demands that wars be fought. They understand with whom it is possible to negotiate, and with whom such an effort would, indeed, be "in vain." They understand that if one party thinks the other is a "detestable scumbag," the Mother of All Evil or its Axis, negotiations in good faith are going to be a waste of time. They know that to create bridges and meaningful alliances, it is incumbent upon them to find and identify those who share their own internationalist, humanist ways of thinking. They know that if global conflict is no longer fought by two opposing armies on an open plain, then borders are, to that same degree, meaningless; that internationalism is the only way forward and that it will depend on like-minded democrats forging alliances in which old notions of national sovereignty take a back seat to a more globally embracing view of human progress.

In its understanding that we are all, in our essence, alike, the novel view attributes a greater respect to the enemy and the near certainty that he believes what he is doing to be right. This is not to say that the enemy *is* right, but that forgoing blanket conceptions of evil and conceding at least this bit of respect leads to a more realistic and ultimately more practical strategic assessment of the force that we should or should not be fighting. The respect of Greek heroes for their opponents was not a romantic notion wrapped up in the idea of a worthy fight but a matter of common sense: the enemy's ability was to be understood, not underestimated, patronized or ridiculed. By contrast, the epic's cartoon view of conflict as illustrated by the sort of windy bombast that made General Hillier popular may appear to be useful but it is folly in the long run as it was likely in the short term too. After ten years in Afghanistan, we may well have killed, maimed, handed over for imprisonment or temporarily disarmed a few of the "detestable murderers and scumbags," but there are few who believe that the Taliban, or some other al-Qaeda or Pakistan-based Islamist Afghan group, will not be back and ruling the country within a few years of ISAF's complete departure, when that finally takes place. This will be the West's fault because, having succumbed to epic temptation, it fought a war that should not have been entertained in the first place or that was fought for the wrong reasons, in either case making outrageous statements to gather public support for the mission, promising more than whatever was ever the actual intention. Or the war was simply fought badly because we were unable to take on the considerably more challenging task of the novel's humanitarian view. Had Canadians made more of a virtue of their innate humanism—of exactly the sort of alternative, imaginative thinking about difference, learned from the land, that a coalescing league of conservatives and militarists has been zealously scorning for a decade—then we just might have been able to make more inroads. Rather than alienate, the novel thinking that is the more enduring attribute of Canadians places a much greater emphasis on seeing and cultivating bonds between like-minded portions of populations that contain in their transnational and aggregate number the potential of a true, just peace.

ACKNOWLEDGEMENTS

Thanks are due, first of all, to Professor Paul M. Curtis of the Université de Moncton who took a big leap of faith when he invited me to deliver the 2010 Antonine Maillet-Northrop Frye lecture—an honour of a task that provided the genesis of this book, a long time coming—and to my publisher at Goose Lane Editions, Susanne Alexander, who knew better than I did that turning my short talk into a book was not going to be straightforward.

Several friends and colleagues read the manuscript at various stages of its evolution and gave advice that improved it. James Cudmore, the CBC's immensely able and talented national reporter in Ottawa who covered international politics and military affairs during much of Canada's war in Afghanistan, and the marvellous Janie Yoon both furnished invaluable criticisms delivered at opportune moments. Mark Luk and Matt Williams did me and the book many favours. My friends Doug Bell, Shelley Ambrose and my sister Emma Richler gave the manuscript encouraging early reads while historians Tim Cook, Margaret MacMillan and Desmond Morton provided later ones, generously offering comment despite important misgivings about a number of my arguments. Any remaining faults are, of course, entirely my own.

Many thanks are also due to John Cruickshank, the publisher of the *Toronto Star*, and Michael Cooke, its editor-in-chief, who made it possible for me to work in the newspaper's library, where Peggy Mackenzie and Astrid Lange assisted me without complaint despite having far more pressing duties. The Québec writers Louis Hamelin and Alain Farah, the former one of the province's best novelists and the latter a poet and professor in the Département de langue et littérature françaises of McGill University, guided me through the limited but rich field of French-Canadian war literature and toward Jean-Jules Richard's remarkable work. Scott and Krystyne Griffin, great patrons of Canadian literature in all its forms, offered very practical help.

At Goose Lane Editions, managing editor James Duplacey, creative director Julie Scriver, publishing assistant Angela Williams, design assistant Chris Tompkins and publicists Corey Redekop and Colleen Kitts comprised the marvelous team that, along with proofreader Dawn Loewen and editor Heather Sangster of Strong Finish, worked with me through many delays to make, of my many drafts, a book. And thanks, too, to Jack Rabinovitch, for his gift in memoriam of Nick Shinn's Richler font.

But no book would have happened at all—and never in quite so instructive or amusing a way—without the incredible love, good judgment and patience of my extraordinary wife, Sarah MacLachlan. *Merci à tous!*

NOTES

7   "Pro Patria" from *Civil Elegies* by Dennis Lee © 1972, reprinted
    with permission of House of Anansi Press, Toronto.

14 Excerpts from *The Custard Boys* by John A. Rae © 1960,
    reprinted by permission of Farrar, Strauss & Giroux.

18 Excerpts from *The Tin Flute* by Gabrielle Roy © 1945. Published
    by McClelland & Stewart. New Canadian Library Edition
    reprinted 2009. Used with permission of the publisher.

25 "i sing of Olaf glad and big" by E.E. Cummings © 1926, 1959,
    1991 by the Trustees for the E.E. Cummings Trust. © 1979 by
    George James Firmage, from *Complete Poems: 1904-1962* by
    E.E. Cummings, edited by George James Firmage. Used by
    permission of Liveright Publishing Corporation.

35 Excerpts from *The Iliad* by Homer, translated by Robert
    Fagles, translation copyright © 1990 by Robert Fagles. Used
    by permission of Viking Penguin, a division of Penguin
    Group (USA) Inc.

79 "Ypres: 1915" from *Selected Poems* by Alden Nowlan © 1969,
    reprinted with permission of House of Anansi Press, Toronto.

191 Excerpts from *The Great War in Modern Memory* by Paul Fussell
    © 1975, 2000, reprinted with permission of Oxford University
    Press Inc.

SOURCES

In the Raymond Carver story "What We Talk About When We Talk About Love" (Alfred A. Knopf, 1981), the cardiologist Mel says to his second wife, Teresa, and the story's unnamed narrator and his wife, Laura, "It ought to make us feel ashamed when we talk like we know what we're talking about when we talk about love." Despite painful lessons, and the likelihood that we should know better, it is clear that humans remain obstinately full of hope. Here, applied to that other human morass, is one of the several reasons I named this book the way I did. Hoping, one day, to be able to write with Carver's simplicity of style, is another.

What We Talk About When We Talk About War is a book about story and information and how it is used to convince a society to pursue a particular path, or not. I did not interview soldiers or travel to Afghanistan. Instead, I relied upon the barrage of information that comes any Canadian's way, principally from the media.

Of course, certain books were also essential. Paul Fussell's *The Great War and Modern Memory* (Oxford University Press, 1975) was, without a doubt, a huge inspiration in my writing this lesser book. Janice Gross Stein and Eugene Lang's *The Unexpected War: Canada in Kandahar* (Viking Canada, 2007) was necessary reading of enormous service, as was Michel Biron's *Histoire de la littérature québécoise* (Les Éditions du Boréal, 2007).

John Rae's novel *The Custard Boys* (Farrar, Strauss & Giroux, 1960) is hard to come by now, which is a pity, as it is the sort of short, atmospheric and elegantly written novel that most authors dream of being able to write. Jean-Jules Richard's novel of the Second World War, *Neuf jours de haine* (Éditions de l'arbre, 1948) is a fascinating companion to the American-born Montrealer Charles Yale Harrison's classic novel of the First World War CEF experience, *Generals Die in Bed* (1930, though most recently Annick Press, 2002). The fate of too many excellent novels either side of it, Richard's *Neuf jours de haine* does not yet exist in translation. Fortunately, the novels of the Israeli writer David Grossman do, including *To the End of the Land* (McClelland & Stewart, 2010), his most recent and, possibly, his finest.

The inclusion of a few lines from Homer's and E.E. Cummings's bodies of work needs no explication, though Canadian writers can always use a bit of a leg up, even when they are as outstanding as Alden Nowlan, one of the finest poets this country has ever produced. Nowlan's *Selected Poems* (House of Anansi, 1969) is an indispensable volume and I am truly sorry that I was not able to find some way to use the brilliant Ken Babstock's poem, "The Essentialist," in its entirety. Chris Hedges is a superb and enviably prolific polemicist. His *War is a Force That Gives Us Meaning* (Public Affairs, 2002) and *Death of the Liberal Class* (Vintage Canada, 2010) are mandatory reading for anyone distressed by the world's present slide into a bellicose state of being and the loss of direction of North American liberalism. The subject matter of Lt.-Col. Dave Grossman's *On Killing* (Little, Brown & Company, 1995) is grim, but its treatment is rigorous and fascinating.

The literature about the First World War is momentous and growing, and the English historian Niall Ferguson's *The Pity of War* (Allen Lane, 1998) is an excellent place to start. Tim Cook's comprehensive and eminently readable two-volume history, *At the Sharp End: Canadians Fighting the Great War, 1914-1916* and *Shock Troops: Canadians Fighting the*

Great War, 1917-1918 (Penguin Canada, 2007 and 2008), is essential reading
for Canadians wanting to know about their country's part, as is Desmond
Morton's *When Your Number's Up: The Canadian Soldier in the First World
War* (McClelland & Stewart, 1995). I have obvious quarrels with Jack
Granatstein's political views but his archival knowledge of Canadian
military history is formidable. The anthology he edited with Norman
Hillmer, *Battle Lines: Eyewitness Accounts from Canada's Military History*
(Thomas Allen, 2004), is illuminating and useful. *We Wasn't Pals: Canadian
Poetry and Prose of the First World War* (Exile Editions, 2001) is a much
slimmer but very memorable anthology, edited by Barry Callaghan with
Bruce Meyer. The latter author's book *Heroes: From Hercules to Superman*
(HarperCollins, 2008) is a survey of pleasing clarity about the idea of
the hero.

Canadian novels of the First World War are many, and a reader's tastes
can only be arbitrary. My favourites, I hope, are clear from the text. Andrew
Cohen's biography *Lester B. Pearson* (Penguin Group Canada, 2008) is a
very good example of short-form biography, though John E. English's more
comprehensive two-volume portrait is still the master text. The second,
The Worldly Years: Life of Lester B. Pearson 1949-1972 (Knopf Canada, 1992),
was particularly illuminating about the man who is deservedly regarded
by many as perhaps Canada's greatest international statesman. Scott
Taylor's *Unembedded: Two Decades of Maverick War Reporting* (Douglas
& McIntyre, 2009) and Paul Watson's *Where War Lives* (McClelland &
Stewart, 2007) both say a good deal about just how tormented the ride
of the committed front-line journalist can be and, as an antidote, Evelyn
Waugh's satirical novel *Scoop,* about an unsuspecting English journalist
made war correspondent in the fictional African country of Ishmaelia, is
still terrifically funny reading. I recommend the Penguin Classics (2000)
version, for the added treat of an introduction by the late Christopher
Hitchens, the friend who pointed out to me, on one of his several visits
to Canada, that the plaque at the University Club of Toronto unusually

remembers the Siberian Expeditionary Force in its commemoration of the "Members Of This Club Who Gave Their Lives In The War Of 1914-19."

Valerie Fortney's *Sunray: The Death and Life of Captain Nichola Goddard* (Key Porter, 2010), Liane Faulder's *The Long Way Home: Paul Franklin's Journey from Afghanistan* (Brindle & Glass, 2007) and Capt. Trevor Greene's autobiography, written with his wife Debbie Greene, *March Forth: The Inspiring True Story of a Canadian Soldier's Journey of Love, Hope and Survival* (HarperCollins, 2012) are a trio of marvelous, affecting books that impress upon the reader the remarkable and uniquely empathetic character and quality of our Armed Forces.

Margaret MacMillan's *The Uses and Abuses of History* (Viking Canada, 2008), written with her inimitable combination of warmth and authority, is a short and easily digested guide for first-timers, such as myself, needing a map before drawing their own conclusions from the past.

One of Canada's most engaged public intellectuals, Noah Richler is un-afraid of controversy, provocation or passionately speaking to the import-ant issues that define a country.

For many years a presenter and producer of radio programs, he has written and hosted documentaries for the BBC and CBC. He was the founding books editor of the *National Post* and is now a regular contributor of features and op-ed articles to the *Globe and Mail,* the *Toronto Star* and the *National Post* as well as *The Walrus, Maclean's* and the *NewStatesman.*

Richler's previous book, *This Is My Country, What's Yours? A Literary Atlas of Canada,* is a bold and impassioned portrait that considers the country through the work of its contemporary writers. Described as "lyrical, poetic and intelligent" by the *Literary Review of Canada*, "brilliant" and "erudite" by the *Winnipeg Free Press* and "sophisticated, funny, poignant and wise" by *The Globe and Mail, This Is My Country, What's Yours?* won the BC National Award for Canadian Non-fiction. The book also appeared on all of Canada's major Best Books lists and was named one of the Top Ten Canadian Books of the Decade by macleans.ca.

Noah Richler lives in Toronto and on the Digby Neck in Nova Scotia.